Et   s

R   s

CONTEMPORARY STUDIES IN SOCIAL AND
POLICY ISSUES IN EDUCATION:
The David C. Anchin Series
(formerly Social and Policy issues in Education:
The David C. Anchin Series)
Kathryn M. Borman, Series Editor

Assessment, Testing, and Evaluation in Teacher Education
edited by Suzanne W. Soled, 1995

Children Who Challenge the System
edited by Anne M. Bauer and Ellen M. Lynch, 1993

Comparative Higher Education: Knowledge, the University, and Development
by Philip G. Altbach, 1998

Critical Education for Work
edited by Richard D. Lakes, 1994

Early Childhood Education: Policy Issues for the 1990s
edited by Dolores Stegelin, 1992

Effective Schooling for Disadvantaged Students: School-based Strategies for Diverse Student Populations
edited by Howard Johnston and Kathryn M. Borman, 1992

Ethnic Diversity in Communities and Schools: Recognizing and Building on Strengths
by Kathryn M. Borman with M. Yvette Baber and Associates, 1998

Home Schooling: Political, Historical, and Pedagogical Perspectives
edited by Jan Van Galen and Mary Anne Pitman, 1991

Implementing Educational Reform: Sociological Perspectives on Educational Policy
edited by Kathryn M. Borman, Peter W. Cookson, Jr., Alan R. Sadovnik, and Joan Z. Spade, 1996

Informing Faculty Development for Teacher Educators
edited by Kenneth R. Howey and Nancy L. Zimpher, 1994

Investing in U.S. Schools: Directions for Educational Policy
edited by Bruce A. Jones and Kathryn M. Borman, 1994

Knowledge and Pedagogy: The Sociology of Basil Bernstein
edited by Alan R. Sadovnik, 1995

Metaphors, Maps, and Mirrors: Moral Education in Middle Schools
by Carol K. Ingall, 1997

Minority Education: Anthropological Perspectives
edited by Evelyn Jacob and Cathie Jordan, 1993

The Minority Voice in Educational Reform: An Analysis by Minority and Women College of Education Deans
edited by Louis A. Castenell and Jill M. Tarule, 1997

Pathways to Privatization in Education
by Joseph Murphy, Scott W. Gilmer, Richard Weise and Ann Page, 1998

Reinventing the University: A Radical Proposal for a Problem-Focused University
by Jan Sinnott and Lynn Johnson, 1996

Schoolteachers and Schooling: Ethoses in Conflict
by Eugene F. Provenzo, Jr., and Gary N. McCloskey, O.S.A., 1996

Social Reconstruction Through Education: The Philosophy, History, and Curricula of a Radical Ideal
edited by Michael E. James, 1995

Ethnic Diversity in Communities and Schools
Recognizing and Building on Strengths

by
Kathryn M. Borman
University of South Florida

with M. Yvette Baber & Associates

Ablex Publishing Corporation
Stamford, Connecticut
London, England

Printed in the United States of America

Library of Congress Cataloging-in-Publication Data

Borman, Kathryn M.
    Ethnic diversity in communities and schools : recognizing and building on strengths / by Kathryn M. Borman, with M. Yvette Baber & associates.
        p. cm. — (Contemporary studies in social and policy issues in education)
    Includes bibliographical references (p.   ) and indexes.
    ISBN 1-56750-386-1. — ISBN 1-56750-387-X (pbk.)
    1. Minorities—Education—United States. 2. Minority students—United States—Social conditions. 3. Community and school—United States. 4. Multicultural education—United States. I. Baber, M. Yvette. II. Title. III. Series.
    LC3731.B64   1998
    371.829'00973—dc21   98-5761
                                                              CIP

Ablex Publishing Corporation   Published in the U.K. and Europe by:
100 Prospect Street   JAI Press Ltd.
Stamford, CT 06901   38 Tavistock Street
                                      Covent Garden
                                      London WC2E 7PB
                                      England

This book is dedicated to William G. Katzenmeyer, director of The David C. Anchin Center at the University of South Florida, whose image of the banyan tree with its diverse, sustaining roots and uplifted branches inspires us all.

Contents

Acknowledgments

In preparing this volume, we have been fortunate to have worked with a number of people who immeasurably improved its contents. In fact, from its inception, the book has been referred to as the "buddy book"; it could have not been written without the contributions of the skilled ethnographers whose vignettes appear in these pages. Other members of the University of South Florida's David C. Anchin Center include Amy Fox, Kathleen E. Del Monte, Bill Goddard, Allyson Haag, Marcy Long, Doni Taube, Hina Patel, Caroline Peterson, Kirsten Pomerantz, Ellen Puccia, and Katie Velasquez, whose skills in tracking missing citations and constructing tables and figures are much appreciated. Barbara Schneider and an anonymous reviewer read the entire manuscript in its final stages and provided extremely helpful comments throughout. Johanna DeStefano used the book in manuscript form with her students enrolled in Linguistics in a Social Setting (Ed T&L 854) at Ohio State University in Spring, 1997. We thank both Professor DeStefano and her class for their help in focusing the volume. We are particularly grateful to the Director of the David C. Anchin Center, Bill Katzenmeyer, whose generous support during the summers of 1996 and 1997 allowed us to bring this project close to completion. At the University of Cincinnati, Dale Wilburn provided assistance in the early stages of preparing the manuscript.

Of course, the book would never have come together as it has without the contributions, acknowledged throughout, of the buddies—all of the researchers who have carried out extended studies of communities, families, and schools to which they have made long-term commitments. While acknowledging the contributions and support of all of these individuals, we hasten to take responsibility for all errors of commission and omission.

Preface

This book is premised on the belief that teaching, research, and development activities must be attuned to local student populations and their communities and schools. Research has consistently documented the failure of schools to reach students from linguistically and culturally diverse backgrounds. One reason suggested for this failure is teachers' lack of understanding and appreciation for students' home backgrounds. Most teachers are eager to become informed and supportive of their diverse students, but many have lacked the opportunity to develop the knowledge and skills appropriate to working with such students. This book urges teachers, their principals, and other school district staff members to improve practices to meet the needs of specific populations. Our intended audience also includes researchers and policy makers concerned with improving the education of culturally diverse students.

In this book, we hope, first, to examine how migration and settlement patterns have varied for these populations throughout U.S. history. Second, we document what researchers have learned about Latino, Native American, African American, urban Appalachian, and Asian American families, neighborhoods, and communities as these relate to children's learning through case studies (in the form of vignettes) conducted over time. Finally, we suggest how schools, communities, and universities can address the needs of culturally diverse students and their families.

The central theme or perspective taken in this volume emphasizes the importance for families and communities to seek a *sociocultural understanding* of children's relationships to schools and formal education. The analysis made throughout the book takes into account at least three important features that help to explain outcomes for children, namely: *structural barriers*, *cultural dissonance*, and *alienation* from academic learning in school. *Structural barriers* include the conditions imbedded in pervasive social and economic arrangements of society. As an example, immigration to and within the U.S. has followed traditional patterns; immigration has been motivated by political violence and economic scarcity, and it has escalated during times of severe oppression and terror in the nation of origin. These conditions result in structural barriers or constraints such as poverty and economic uncertainty for at least the first generation. *Cultural dissonance* refers to the strain between the core values and behaviors of individuals and institutions of one society—the U.S. in this case—and the values and behaviors of the newcomers. For example, Central American immigrants dream of returning to their countries, sending large sums of money to relatives who remain behind, and retaining their "core cultural values," a process Margaret Gibson and others have termed a strategy of "accommodation without assimilation." In the book's final chapter we examine patterns of cultural dissonance as aspects of *local* and *lateral* cultural ties. Local and lateral ties represent ways of conceptualizing strengths unique to specific groups and must be considered in creating effective pedagogical strategies.

Finally, *attachment* and its converse *alienation* from school result in large part from the "fit" between students' perceptions of their strengths, talents, and aspirations and the construction of the school curriculum. While a proliferation of courses, especially at the secondary level, is not a policy recommendation that we would suggest, it is clear that school learning must be framed to take into account the values, memories, narratives, and systems of meaning of those attending U.S. schools (Heath & McLaughlin, 1993).

Our interest is in examining how various school, family, and community conditions influence instruction and learning. While literacy learning by students in grades kindergarten through 12 is frequently used in the volume to illustrate important issues faced by students and teachers, this volume is not narrowly focused on literacy learning and teaching. Rather, we view literacy skills along with skills in math, science, the arts, music, and social studies as critical for all students to acquire throughout their careers in school. Literacy skills are, however, foundational to the acquisition of virtually all other capacities in our society and, therefore, take on considerable importance in the child's educational career.

Educators are moving toward a model of literacy as reasoning within multiple discourses, characterized by the integration of ways of thinking, talking, interacting, and valuing as well as reading and writing in a particular social setting. This conception centers on the idea that children learn culturally appropriate ways of using language and constructing meaning from texts in their early years at home. Culturally relevant teaching values students' linguistic and cultural diversity and highlights the knowledge that students bring to schools from their communities. This approach, however, does not ignore the importance of students achieving to high standards that govern what they should know and be able to do at various points in their school careers. The contributors to this book believe that it is possible to take both aspects—cultural relevance and academic excellence—into account in the day-to-day teaching and learning that occurs in U.S. schools.

A NOTE ON TERMINOLOGY

We are in an era that invites our reconsideration of terms such as "race" and "ethnicity" as well as specific referents to particular groups. In this volume we generally use ethnicity rather than race to refer to the diverse populations considered throughout. In the volume we use other terms interchangeably, notably "Black" and "African American" and "Hispanic" and "Latino." In some regions of the U.S. one term is preferred over another. For example, "Chicana" and "Chicano" refer to individuals whose heritage is Mexican American.

The issue of "race" as opposed to "ethnicity" and vice versa is a non-issue to anthropologists who view race as a concept that unites rather than separates members of the human family. Ethnicity, on the other hand, is useful in providing a convenient means for distinguishing among the different sets of habits, customs, values, and behavior which, when woven together, constitute the fabric of a particular group. It is in this sense that we use the term "ethnicity" or "ethnic group" in the current volume.

1

Families and Schools:
Contexts for Student Learning

With M. Yvette Baber and the assistance of Linda Evans

At the current century's fast approaching close, nearly one-third of the nation's school-aged children will claim diverse linguistic and cultural backgrounds. By the year 2010, African Americans and Latinos will account for 33 percent of the child population. When combined with the numbers of children from other diverse backgrounds and language groups, these children will be the majority, mainstream population attending our public schools.

In more than 30 of the nation's largest school districts, Anglo students are in the minority. In the Dade County (Miami) Public Schools—the nation's third largest district—85 percent of all enrolled students speak Spanish as their first language. Chicago—the fourth largest—has experienced a rapid rise in students of Mexican American heritage. The number of limited-English-proficient (LEP) students in public schools in California alone increased by more than 6 percent (from 1,079,000 in 1992 to 1,152,000 in 1993). Such students now constitute 22.2 percent of the 5,195,777 students enrolled in public schools in California. With these changes in our demographic makeup, the face of America's schools will be transformed forever (Barr & Parrett, 1995; U.S. Department of Commerce, 1992).

In the past, schools have dealt with the variability among students with two major strategies: the use of tracking and ability grouping, and the segregation of "different" students into special classes, for example, special education or bilingual education. The diversity in the student population has become so marked that such solutions today are no longer sufficient. They were, of couse, neither just nor adequate. In response to these challenges, practitioners, researchers, and curriculum developers have been hard at work changing the organization of schools and classrooms and introducing new methods of teaching. Our overall goal in this volume is to encourage the reader to examine, understand, and seek to alter the contexts important for students' growth, development, learning, and success. Our hope is that such efforts will take into account the diverse strengths that students bring from families and communities to the school. Our ultimate objective is to encourage the reader to create school programs, curriculum, and outside-school experiences that lead to success for culturally diverse students in school and in their communities and families.

The first topic we address in this chapter is literacy skills required for success in adulthood. What U.S. society expects competent adults to know and be able to do sets the stage for children's subsequent learning. We then move to a discussion of determinants of children's access to learning in school, using literacy as an example. The third major topic covered in Chapter 1 touches on second language acquisition. We then consider the social and ecological framework we have adopted for understanding the multiple contexts and influences on children's learning before moving to an analysis of tensions that persist between families and schools. These tensions are particularly problematic for diverse students and their families.

WHAT SOCIETY EXPECTS FROM SCHOOLS AND STUDENTS

In current school policy frameworks, all students are increasingly expected to achieve in school in line with standards governing the acquisition of skills and competencies in a variety of subject matter areas at various points in student careers. Establishing voluntary opportunity to learn standards is part of the Goals 2000: Educate America Act, passed by the U.S. Congress in 1991. On a voluntary basis, states are expected to develop comprehensive state-wide improvement plans containing strategies for meeting the National Education Goals.

One set of National (and, increasingly, state and local) Goals ensures that all students receive fair opportunity to learn the knowledge and skills described in state curriculum content standards and state student performance standards. Among the factors included in each state's plans for its schools are quality and availability of curriculum; capability of teachers to provide high quality instruction for meeting students' diverse learning needs; and access to professional development for teachers. Some have criticized these opportunities to learn standards for not taking into account subtle social factors such as student readiness for learning, proficiency in English, and other characteristics of students that have an impact on learning (Braddock & Williams, 1996; Cohen, 1996).

The National Literacy Act, also passed by Congress in 1991, authorized the creation of a National Institute of Literacy to strengthen and support a host of programs through state literacy agencies, including family literacy training in connection with Even Start programs and workplace literacy training. Finally, the National Education Goal for adult literacy requires that "by the year 2000, every adult American will be literate and possess the knowledge and skills necessary to compete in a global economy and exercise the rights and responsibilities of citizenship" (Campbell et al., 1992). Clearly, it is one thing to legislate goals such as the ones just described. It is quite another to realize them for all schools and students.

LITERACY SKILLS REQUIRED FOR SUCCESS IN ADULTHOOD

In addition to programs to support research and training on literacy acquisition, the U.S. Congress in 1988 called upon the U.S. Department of Education to carry out a survey of the literacy skills used in daily life by American adults. The result was the Educational Testing Service (ETS) 1992 study and subsequent report documenting results of the most comprehensive profile of English literacy skills of the U.S. adult population ever assembled.

The National Adult Literacy Survey (NALS), carried out with a nationally representative sample of 13,600 American adults aged 18–64, relied upon face-to-face data collection strategies to ensure the validity of the results. Survey researchers gathered information on both demographic issues and literacy skills, acknowledging that such factors as country of birth, length of residency in the United States, current proficiency in English and other languages as well as self perception of language proficiency influence the acquisition of literacy skills. This approach broke new ground by taking into account the kinds of everyday skills adults need to have to be productive citizens and workers. ETS developed 165 different tasks to measure literacy proficiency in alternative ways. These tasks included locating facts in a newspaper article, doing arithmetic problems, and carrying out simulations of everyday tasks and chores such as paying household bills. The objective was to assess a full range of literacy behaviors.

Increasingly, social and behavioral scientists are in accord on a simple fact of life: material wealth shapes opportunities and possibilities throughout our lives. Even if money can't buy happiness, it *does* promote access to what has come to be called social capital (Coleman, 1988). Social capital includes webs of social relationships and social ties which are the result of access to both formal and informal educational opportunities. Some researchers have attempted to conceptualize social capital with respect to the resources children have available to them at home. While not perfectly correlated with socioeconomic status (SES), there is a relationship among family material resources, parental education and parental occupation (the major components of socioeconomic status) and such important home environment variables as playing games with educational content and taking children on outings to museums, concerts, and plays—all of which provide children with important experiences that support their school learning activities.

Other dimensions at play in the distribution of social capital in the household are less well associated with SES. Although poorer households generally are single-parent (and most frequently female-headed), not all children who grow up in single parent homes are from economically disadvantaged circumstances since 50 percent or more of *all* marriages end in divorce. We now know, for example, from analyses of another large scale national survey, similar in name to the NALS—The National Education Longitudinal Study or NELS, an ongoing national study of individuals who were in eighth grade in 1988, the first year of this longitudinal survey—that aspirations to attend college and subsequent actual plans to do so are most powerfully affected by SES as opposed to race, gender, ethnicity or other factors.

ETS researchers in carrying out analyses of NALS data found that the strongest relationship existed between one's location in the literacy distribution and whether or not the individual in question lived in poverty. Tasks, as mentioned previously, covered a wide range of literacy skills including *prose literacy*, the capacity to use connected discourse such as material encountered in newspapers and books; *document literacy*, the ability to use information in non-prose formats such as graphs, charts, maps and advertisements; and, finally, *quantitative literacy*, the capacity to both process print and solve problems in basic arithmetic. Skills in each of these areas were subsequently rank-ordered and assessed for each individual respondent according to criteria as outlined in Table 1.1, illustrating dimensions of literacy scales with representative tasks. Table 1.1, The Literacy Scales and Sample Tasks, shows skills commensurate with each of the five levels developed by the ETS researchers. For example, the lowest level (Level 1) of prose literacy involves the ability to locate a *single* piece of information in a short news article while the highest level (Level 5) encompasses the skill to interpret information from a lengthy news article.

Results reported from analyses of the NALS data such as those seen in Figure 1.1, linking difficulty levels of literacy tasks with percentages of individuals living in poverty, make clear the point that economically disadvantaged individuals— those living in poverty—are also those with the lowest levels of performance on the three types of literacy tasks—prose, document, and quantitative—included in the NALS. As shown in Figure 1.1, there is, in fact, a direct, linear relationship between level of performance and poverty status with no more than 6 percent of the most economically impoverished individuals performing at the highest possible level (Level 5) on any of the three dimensions of the literacy task battery. The largest percentage of this group performed at the lowest, least competent (Level 1) level in each of the three categories of literacy tasks.

In a similar vein, as shown in Figure 1.2, when study participants between the ages of 25 and 64 who were members of the civilian labor force were asked whether they were currently enrolled in any type of school program, results show a strongly

TABLE 1.1. The Literacy Scales and Sample Tasks

	Prose	Document	Quantitative
	to understand and use information in texts such as news articles, stories, and poems	*to locate and use information in materials such as forms, maps, schedules, and tables*	*to apply arithmetic operations using numbers found in printed materials*
Level			
1	locate a single piece of information in a short news article	enter signature on a form	total an entry on a deposit slip
2	locate two pieces of information in a news article	locate information on eligibility for employee benefits in a table	calculate postage and fees for a mailing
3	write a letter explaining billing error	determine which bus to take using a schedule	calculate discount from a bill paid early
4	contrast views expressed in two editorials	identify export patterns across years using information in a table	calculate annual benefits using information in a pamphlet
5	interpret information from a lengthy news article	summarize information in a table from a school survey	determine the cost of carpeting for a room using a diagram

Source: National Adult Literacy Survey (1992).

positive relationship between location in the distribution of literacy skill levels as assessed by the NALS and enrollment in school. At a time when adults increasingly acquire more training to advance in careers or simply to gain increased pleasure in life through continuing education and other types of formal and informal instructional experiences, these results are particularly notable. Indeed, chances are far better (three to one) that those *most* proficient in literacy skills (at Level 5) will be engaged in some form of education.

Further, as shown in Table 1.2, those with the highest levels of literacy skill in the area of prose literacy also tend to hold jobs as professionals, managers, and technicians—occupations that typically provide the best salaries and benefits. As shown, fully 70 percent of those performing at Level 5 on the NALS hold jobs in these categories.

Although the debate about literacy skill requirements for jobs in the 21st century continues, what seems to be clear is that, as jobs requiring lower skill levels disappear, they are replaced by jobs with tasks demanding greater skills according to analyses performed using NALS data. Thus, skill requirements for all types of occupations will have increased by the year 2005 in all three aspects of literacy with skills in the quantitative dimension most profoundly accelerating as requirements for high growth and all growth occupations. Clearly, literacy and other skills will continue to be in demand in the 21st century workplace.

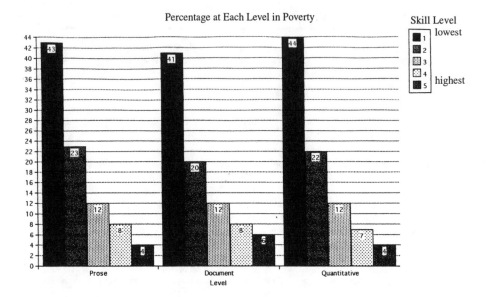

FIGURE 1.1.   Percentage of adults in each literacy level who were in poverty.

Note: Adults in poverty are those who are either poor or near poor.
Source: National Adult Literacy Survey (1992).

As the NALS makes clear, the U.S. economy *currently* demands higher levels of skill for satisfactory job performance across *all* occupations. As a result, those who lag behind in skill development suffer unequal employment and income outcomes. Skill differences are attributable to educational opportunities denied, conditions of poverty and ethnic group membership as a recent, comprehensive analysis of NALS data shows (Raudenbush & Kasim, 1998). This analysis, for

TABLE 1.2.   Percentages of Adults in Each Literacy Level on the Prose Scale Who Were in Selected Occupations

	Level 1	Level 2	Level 3	Level 4	Level 5
Professionals, managers, & technicians	5	12	23	46	70
Sales, clerical	15	28	34	30	20
Craft, service	43	36	27	17	8
Laborer, assembler, fishing, & farming	37	24	16	7	2

Source: National Adult Literacy Survey (1992).

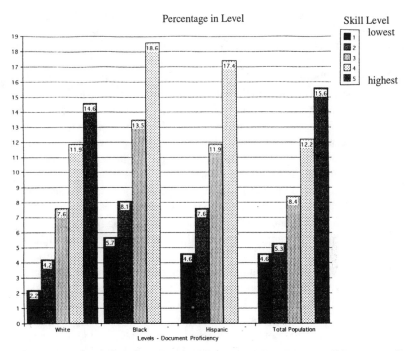

FIGURE 1.2. Percentage of 25–64 year old civilian labor force participants enrolled in school by proficiency level & race/ethnicity.
Source: National Adult Literacy Survey (1992).

example, reveals an enormous earnings gap between African American and Anglo males within the same occupations. The authors of this study conclude:

> There are clearly important differences in cognitive skills among persons sharing the same educational backgrounds, and these differences are linked to prospects for employment and earnings. This finding lends urgency to the task of improving the quality of schooling and of non-school educative environments, especially for Hispanic American and African American youth (Raudenbush and Kasim, 1998, p. 65).

Large numbers of those coming to our shores in recent years, with the exception of Hispanics as a group, are reasonably well educated. For example, 45 percent of the non-native born Asian group arrives in the United States with a college degree or better compared to only 8 percent of Hispanics.

When taken together with the other NALS results reported in this section of the chapter, we see that literacy issues facing the United States today are far from simple to address. One thing, however, is very clear: literacy skills are developed early on in children's lives and receive an important boost during children's school careers.

ACCESS TO SKILL LEARNING IN SCHOOL

Skills emerge and are developed early in children's educational experience and are also nurtured in households before children's formal schooling begins. The ground-breaking study of Shirley Brice Heath (1983) documenting the contrasting literacy learning experiences in households of a single community has forever altered the way we think about resources that reside in culturally diverse settings. What this research demonstrated was that, while black children in a southern Piedmont area community were frequently exposed to such activities as list making, their white Appalachian counterparts were most often engaged in literacy tasks such as letter writing to distant kin. These differences in everyday tasks and chores orient children to learning in school in distinct ways, demonstrating the strength and persistence of early patterns of acquiring and using information.

Programs such as Head Start in preschool settings have included an emphasis on literacy learning through self directed play and learning center activities since the earliest implementation of these programs in the late 1960s. Research has supported the claim that learning literacy-related skills in Head Start programs places students at a distinct advantage in their later school experiences (Teale, 1982, 1986). Nonetheless, in the development of Head Start curricula, an emphasis on strengths developed in the home and community that Heath's study implicitly argues to be effective has not been consistent. This emphasis would strengthen the well established positive effects of Head Start by requiring that teachers and curriculum makers in early childhood education be invested in understanding and utilizing dimensions of the local ethnic cultures in devising curricular content. Because early childhood education as a field has been keenly sensitive to cross-cultural variations in the home environment, there is increasing evidence of such culturally-sensitive approaches (see, e.g., Tobin, Wu, & Davidson, 1989).

In the elementary grades, literacy learning begins to assume important gatekeeping functions, screening less economically and socially advantaged children from easy access to avenues of traditional academic success. Placement in less able reading groups in elementary school, some argue, foreshadows placement in general education or vocational tracks in junior high and high school. Such grouping practices result in fewer years of school completed. In fact, school dropout rates are highest for students enrolled in general education tracks with 40 percent or more of such students withdrawing from school before twelfth grade (Maloney & Borman, 1987; Natriello, McDill, & Pallas, 1990).

There is little question that middle and secondary school students in lower tracks who are not traditionally "school-literate" face discrimination in a number of areas including counseling practices, school record keeping, and classroom instruction. Students in low ability classrooms, as a consequence, have poorer quality curricula and lowered teacher expectations for their success (Gamoran, Nystrand, Berends, & LePore, 1995; Oakes, 1985). In their examination of 92 middle school class-rooms, Gamoran and his colleagues analyzed seven indicators of instructional discourse as these varied across eighth and ninth grade honors, regular and remedial English literature classes. Not surprisingly, achievement gaps between honors and regular classes and between low ability and regular classes were not large over the course of a single year; they were, nonetheless, statistically significant in the expected direction. The researchers' analyses revealed that one aspect of instructional discourse—coherence—the extent to which teachers asked students to write, discuss, and relate previously encountered material to current instruction—was particularly effective in promoting achievement across *all* types of classes. This finding is important because it suggests an *institutional* strategy—building upon students' strengths—in this case, their prior learning. We favor arrangements in school that allow teachers to coordinate teaching and learning activities across subject matter areas, ability levels, and grade levels, a topic we explore in Chapter 8.

Also of importance in the Gamoran study were findings regarding authentic questions—questions that relate to students' interests, sentiments, and moods. Such questions and subsequent discussion in the context of honors English classes focused on the subject matter at hand rather than upon unrelated matters. In remedial English classes, class discussion was concerned with a wide variety of topics such as students' feelings about taking a test that day rather than being concerned with substantive "ideas and issues found in literary texts" (Gamoran, 1995). The consequences for students in remedial English classes are clear: their literacy skills, skills that the NALS demonstrates to be critical for later successful adult outcomes, may be slighted or neglected altogether.

Segregation into ability groups or curricular tracking arrangements places students in relatively stable peer groups that vary—one from the other—in their academic skills. As a direct result, students in the same grade cohort within a given school hold quite different strengths in academic performance and attitudes toward and expectations about future schooling outcomes depending on whether their placement has been in honors, academic, general education, or vocational courses. In a local sample of urban Appalachian working class students, researchers at the University of Cincinnati noted that placement in the academic track for girls resulted in higher levels of performance as well as association with middle class peers from outside their blue collar and poor neighborhood (Borman, Mueninghoff, & Piazza, 1983). In contrast, boys in the higher tracks exhibited the same patterns of cutting class, absenteeism and erratic performance as their male peers in the lower tracks. Thus, peer and gender influences as well as cumulative socioeconomic disadvantage reflected in low levels of cross-generation mobility contribute to success or failure in school (Obermiller & Philliber, 1987). The national data on school dropouts suggest that school policies to reduce both school and class size, to eliminate remedial classes, and to sharply improve instruction through teacher collaboration foster a set of circumstances that will inhibit the dropout process (Wehlage, 1987). One such strategy is bilingual education, particularly when it is combined with a challenging academic program that recognizes the process of second language acquisition.

SECOND LANGUAGE ACQUISITION

According to 1990 census figures, approximately 9.9 million of the estimated 45 million school-age children in the United States live in homes in which languages other than English are spoken, up from 8.1 million in 1980. Of these 9.9 million students, nearly 6 million are from Spanish-speaking homes. Language-minority school-age children live in every state; the numbers range from approximately 2.5 million in California to 9,000 in Vermont. Of the states with numbers between these extremes, Texas has approximately 1.4 million, New York has 972,000, and five other states—presented here in rank order from largest to smallest numbers—have at least a quarter-million language-minority students: Florida, Illinois, New Jersey, Arizona, and Pennsylvania (Waggoner, 1994). Hearing languages other than English spoken between parent and child and in other family groups in public places is commonplace in the 1990s.

These children enter schools in the United States with a need to continue their cognitive development, learn a new language, and acquire a new culture. Many factors influence how successful students will be in acquiring the skills needed for high achievement in school: these can be grouped into personal, linguistic, and situational factors.

Personal Factors

Second language acquisition is, not surprisingly, affected by characteristics of the learners who are acquiring the language. Personal characteristics cover a spectrum including intelligence, aptitude for language learning, attitudes toward the target language and speakers of that language, age, and socioeconomic status.

Attitude also has received emphasis in the study of second-language acquisition. Although attitude is regarded primarily as the student's attitude toward learning a second language, this can be influenced by the attitudes of parents, teachers, peers, and the community. In fact, studies have shown that others' attitudes can have a profound negative or positive influence on a student's achievement in a second language (Feenstra, 1969; Gardner, 1968; Gardner & Lambert, 1972).

Another aspect of attitude that has been considered in the literature involves the reasons why the learner is learning a second language. Gardner and Lambert, who have conducted considerable research in attitudinal orientations in second language acquisition, coined the phrases *integrative orientation* and *instrumental orientation* (Gardner & Lambert, 1972). Students with an integrative orientation learn the language largely because they wish to join the language group's cultural and social activities, find their roots, or form friendships. Students with an instrumental orientation learn the language for utilitarian reasons such as finding a job, passing examinations, or furthering career prospects.

Linguistic and Situational Factors

Two types of linguistic factors may influence the process of learning a second language: differences between the students' native language (L1) and second language (L2), and characteristics of the L2 itself (Izzo, 1980). The operative word is "may": although L1 seems to have some influence on L2, it can vary from student to student and situation to situation.

Learning situations have a variety of effects on acquisition of a second language. Situational factors such as length of time spent in language study, as well as differences in social and cultural settings for language learning, have been shown to influence the acquisition process. Studies have shown very clearly that for majority language students (English-speaking) in French immersion programs in Canada, the greater the time spent in French, the greater the fluency in the French language (Genesee, 1978; Halpern, 1976). Some studies, however, point to the importance of the manner of using the target language; learners who used the target language as the medium of instruction rather than only as a focus of study became more proficient in a shorter time (Genesee, 1978; Tucker, 1977).

The relative status of the majority and minority language groups can affect the acquisition of the second language. If the minority language group identifies readily with the majority language group (English speakers), then the language-minority student will learn English more easily. This may be due to attitude, contact with members of the target group, or availability of input in the target language from sources such as television and reading materials (Schumann, 1976).

Another factor considered by Schumann was the length of time the language-learning group plans to stay in the target language area. If the group is composed of refugees who cannot return to their homeland, they will be more likely to seek acceptance in the majority culture through language learning and assimilation. If a group is more mobile and perceives (realistically or not) that they may return to their homeland in a short time, they will be less inclined to invest the time and energy in learning more than the basics of the L2 needed for survival.

Continuum of Language Development Programs for English-Language Learners

Taken together, personal, linguistic, and situational factors combine to partially answer the question commonly asked by schools that educate language-minority students: How long will it take students to acquire the level of English proficiency needed to achieve academically on a par with native English-speaking students? As shown by the many aspects of language learning discussed previously, acquiring a second language is a complex process. Studies on length of time have reached similar conclusions: The greater the development of the students' native language skills, the greater the ease and the greater the achievement in learning and using the second language in an academic setting (Collier, 1992; Cummins, 1980; Ramirez, 1992). Furthermore, research has shown that a firm foundation in the native language promotes greater long-term success in English literacy and mathematics skills (Cummins, 1980; Hakuta, 1986; Ramirez, 1992). If children lack that foundation, they may make great gains in basic English skills in the short term, but will begin to struggle as the language becomes more conceptually dense and complex (Cummins, 1980).

Public school instruction for language-minority students spans the spectrum from maintenance bilingual programs to no special instructional program outside the mainstream curriculum. These variations are in large part attributable to political factors. Some locales in the United States hold firmly to tenets supporting "English only" curriculum despite the evidence on how children acquire language skills. This is often a reflection of local attitudes toward non-native populations who may reside in the community, a point we will take up in Chapter 3 and throughout the vignettes in Chapters 4 through 7. Other locales simply have few or no speakers of languages other than English, although such areas in the United States are increasingly rare. *Our position in this volume is that, given the range or continuum of approaches to second language learning, schools should adopt an approach that will best address the needs and abilities of their students while aiming at access to academic learning and challenging curriculum for all.*

Bilingualism and Literacy Development in the Schools

If we recognize literacy as essential to educational success, we must look at the diversity in the schools and develop ways to provide the greatest opportunities for acquiring literacy skills. Research over the past 50 years has told educators a great deal about how to teach reading and writing, the basic components of literacy, and how students learn to receive and communicate information through the written word. Similarly, researchers have learned much about bilingualism in the past 30 years. Nonetheless, a relatively small amount of this literature is concerned with the overlay of literacy on bilingualism, particularly in regard to students in schools who are learning to read in a nonnative language. As we work toward creating classrooms in which all students can achieve their full potential, we must explore, analyze, and attempt to reconcile what is currently known about learning to read, write, and speak a second language in an academic setting, as well as what is involved for students in learning new concepts in a language in which they are not fluent—formidable tasks indeed.

We know little about the experiences of young children acquiring English language and literacy skills solely in English with little or no native-language literacy support. What we might conjecture is that children in these circumstances may become alienated from family members who are not acquiring English language skills and cultural knowledge and understanding. Vignettes later in the book in Chapters 4, 5, 6, and 7 including, for example, "Isolation from High

Achieving Peers," the story of two refugees from Hong Kong, Dan and Mei and their family, provide case examples of such individuals.

We will now turn to an examination of *contextual factors* that have importance in children's acquisition of academic skills and learning. These are exceedingly important for us to understand because in so doing we can alter, rearrange, add or eliminate factors, actions impossible to consider in the case of individual factors such as age and SES. In the remainder of this chapter, we first consider the structural context for children's development using a social context or ecological model. This model is useful because it captures the *structural* elements constituting children's social, economic, and political environments and strongly influencing children's *attachment* or *alienation* from school. We learn from three of the forthcoming vignettes, "Community Resources Enhance Children's Literacy Learning," "Community Terror Creates Attachment to School," and "From Mountain to Metropolis," that strong local community ties promote *either* attachment *or* alienation among various ethnic groups—Mexican American, Puerto Rican and urban Appalachian in these examples.

We then examine two extremely important and often conflicting social spheres, namely the school and the family. In Chapter 2 we go on to analyze Ogbu's model for understanding children's sociocultural worlds. Both the structural, ecological model developed by Bronfenbrenner and described next and the sociocultural model developed by Ogbu and others (and described in Chapter 2) form the framework adopted in this volume for understanding children's school experience.

NESTED CONTEXTS FOR LEARNING

According to Bronfenbrenner's (1979, 1986, 1989) social-ecological model, individual development is located within a set of contexts forming the social, cultural and economic web encompassing the individual. Indeed, individuals are predisposed to interact—humans are socially oriented from birth. It is difficult to imagine development divorced from social relationships. As shown in Figure 1.4, Bronfenbrenner's conceptualization of an ecological model for individual development is a useful rubric for understanding the linkages among children's experiences in the variety of situations they regularly and routinely inhabit. The model includes the concepts of the macro-, exo-, and microsystems seen as overlapping contexts for children's learning and development. The individual's developmental trajectory is seen as composed of three aspects (as depicted at the bottom of the figure): individual history, biology (the chronosystem), and the characteristics of the life span or life course taken by the individual over time. Finally, the mesosystem is the system of norms, values and beliefs—the cultural influences which cut across institutions and influence the developing individual throughout life.

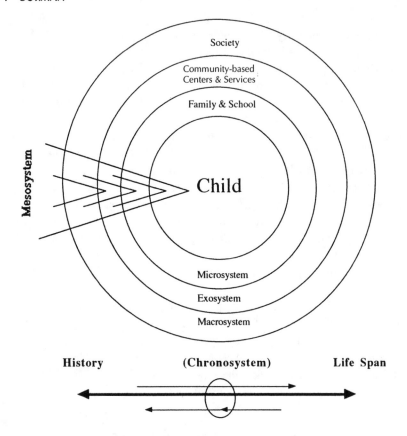

FIGURE 1.4.   A sociological-ecological framework for development.
Source: Garcia et al. (1995, p. 109).

The Macrosystem

In Bronfenbrenner's scheme, the macrosystem is the outermost core of political, economic, and social systems. The macrosystem includes the belief system undergirding the social organization of the school and the content of the curriculum. How students are organized or tracked for instruction from the earliest grades largely determines the contents of the curriculum to which they will be exposed as well as a number of outcomes as mentioned earlier in this chapter. Sometimes the systems of values and beliefs held by parents, particularly those from enclaved, predominantly ethnic and low income inner-city communities, differ from predominant societal beliefs. For example, although urban Appalachian children come from families where academic learning is prized, compared to this kind of knowledge, reliance on "common sense" and the desire to enjoy life may be even more highly valued in the community setting (Borman, Mueninghoff, & Piazza, 1988). African American parents in similar enclaves desire that their children succeed in life by acquiring academic knowledge but also hold the expectation that family members in extended kin networks can count on each other through life for material and emotional support (Ogbu, 1986; Stack, 1974).

The macrosystem's constellation of values and beliefs at the community level is grounded in the social, political, and economic history of the community. Although some political leaders have spoken about "family values" as though all families hold to a single, monolithic value code, families in the United States are actually quite diverse in their backgrounds and histories. As we will see in Chapters 2, 3, 4, 5, 6, and 7, new immigrant groups as well as more settled entrenched, "caste-like" groups have distinctive perceptions of what kinds of school learning frameworks and processes are critical for children's development. These perceptions are often culturally dissonant from those informing school-based practices.

Development with respect to children's talents and skills is viewed differently by different groups. In contrast to Anglo-American and Mexican-American parents who value problem-solving skills, verbal abilities, and creative talents, parents of first and second grade students who had recently emigrated from Cambodia, Mexico, the Philippines, and Vietnam prized *both* these "cognitive" skills and "non-cognitive" characteristics such as motivation, social skills including the ability to get along with others and practical school skills (Okagi & Sternberg, 1993).

Despite the presence of language development programs in many schools, these and other institutions often construct enormous barriers to the success of immigrants and other minorities. Families in turn must discover how best to create paths for their children. Among the Punjabi American families she studied, Margaret Gibson found that parents urged their children to use a strategy in school based on the principles of accommodation and acculturation without assimilation. *Accommodation* refers to the latitude or space given to the institutions and practices of the new society. *Acculturation* refers to the process of culture change and adaptation that results when two (or more) cultures make contact. Gibson points out that "acculturation may be an additive process or one in which old and new traits are blended" (Gibson, 1993). Acculturation, unlike *assimilation*, does not lead to the cultural absorption of immigrant peoples by the dominant society along with loss of immigrant peoples' identities. Gibson found that Punjabi parents chose to minimize problems faced in school and the community by themselves and their children. For example, Punjabi children, particularly in the high school Gibson studied, are told they stink, accused of being illegals and are physically abused by majority white students who regularly and routinely "spit at them, refused to sit by them in class or on buses, crowded in front of them in line, stuck them with pins, threw food at them and worse" (Gibson, 1993). Gibson notes:

In one way or another Punjabi students are told that India and Indian culture are inferior to Western and American ways. They are criticized for their hairstyle, their diet, and their dress. They are faulted because they place family ahead of individual interests, defer to the authority of elders, accept arranged marriages, and believe in group decision making. They are condemned most especially for not joining in majority-dominated school activities and for resisting as best they can the forces for cultural assimilation. While teachers commend Indian students for their diligence in the classroom they are perplexed by their parents' reluctance to attend school functions. Some Punjabi parents had never visited the high school, and most came only if a school official called specifically to request a meeting about their child. Teachers seemed to assume that for children to excel academically their parents had to participate directly in school affairs. Few seemed conscious that the Punjabi model of non-intervention worked equally well, perhaps better, at least in the Punjabi context. Punjabi parents urge their children to achieve in school which most do. They also expect that in conforming to the school's and teacher's demands, their children should "turn the other cheek," once, twice, but the third time defend yourself. (Gibson, 1993)

The Punjabis display a particularly flexible, rational and pragmatic approach to issues of extreme sensitivity for any racial or ethnic group. In part, Gibson attributes Punjabi accommodation strategies to the varied political experiences Punjabi settlers have had in several nations. Indeed, Punjabi parents saw that, compared to either Canada or Britain, Punjabis in the United States received much better treatment and had much better prospects for their children's achievement. In Canada, deep hatred of the Punjabis is rooted in resentment over their economic success. In England, because they were once British colonial subjects as citizens of India, Punjabis faced severe prejudice owing to the feelings of superiority held by a people (the English) who had formerly had near absolute colonial power over them.

In her concluding discussion, Gibson urges that, for us to understand variation in the school performance of different groups of minority children (not just Punjabi Americans), we must take into account at least the following factors: (a) the social structure of U.S. society (Bronfenbrenner's macrosystem), (b) the cultural (including the political) background of the minority group, (c) the minority group's perception of its own historical context, and (d) the group's relationship to the dominant group. To understand how to orchestrate the school experience of various groups it is also important to be aware of the cognitive and social cognitive patterns of learning and teaching that can best inspire the achievement in school of particular groups. This is exceedingly difficult since there are clearly individual differences within each group. We will, nonetheless, remain concerned with group experiences in this volume. These are manifested in the histories of the groups considered here and constitute the sociocultural milieu—the topic pursued in Chapter 2.

This book is principally organized to explain influences on children's learning in the family, community, and school and among children's peers. Bronfenbrenner's conceptions of the exosystem and microsystem describe the crucibles of relationships in which children's learning is forged. We turn to these next.

The Exosystem

The exosystem, applied to an analysis of the relationship between communities and schools, encompasses such issues as how school district mandates present an agenda to teachers (and subsequently to students) through textbooks, the formal curriculum, and the social organization of schools (Borman & Spring, 1984). Moreover, the manner in which the school's instructional curriculum is organized carries with it assumptions about how children learn and what kinds of learning are prized. Marketplace English, for example, is valued as cultural capital in the school (Lareau, 1989).

The Microsystem

Schools are far from neutral places. Both semanticists and semioticians find schools advocating a particular system of signifiers, symbols, and signs full of meanings (English, 1988). Such meanings, according to neo-Marxists, correspond to those held by the larger society such as taken-for-granted and, therefore, hidden economic messages (Bowles & Gintis, 1976). Part of the "hiddenness" of such messages is grounded in the simple routine of school life: schedules, permission slips, clock watching, assignments and grades, tracking and the like. The day-to-dayness of schools constitutes the microsystem. Because messages are implicit in the way schools are run, they are sometimes referred to as the "hidden curriculum" or "structured silence" (Aronowitz & Giroux, 1985).

Much of the "structured silence" is unintended by administrators, teachers or students. Rather, structured silence exists because school routines are rarely questioned; they are enforced and minded to. That they "match" the larger social and working conditions of contemporary work life is taken for granted. Most U.S. citizens, for example, view themselves as members of the vast "middle class" (*New York Times*, January 9, 1992). This is the taken-for-granted reality and schools attempt to prepare students to live in it. Virtually every report on effective schools has indicated that the significant involvement of the family is absolutely essential for children's success. Yet in no school is less parental involvement typically in evidence than in those schools which serve economically disadvantaged, minority students.

Schools clearly differentiate among their clientele using ethnicity as a marker. According to NELS Second Follow-up Parent Survey data (1992), while less than 19 percent of white parents and an even smaller percentage (17%) of Asian parents reported being contacted by school personnel concerning their child's negative behavior in school, 30 percent of Black, 19 percent of Hispanic, and 28 percent of American Indian parents included in the survey were contacted for this reason. Similarly, while 58 percent of white parents received requests to volunteer at their child's school, only 25 percent of Black, 38 percent of Hispanic, 47 percent of Asian and 42 percent of American Indian parents received similar requests.

The levels and quality of interactions between families and the school have undergone a great deal of research in the past quarter-century. Although cooperation is the goal, many schools have found it difficult to reach out to and engage all parents. When educators sought reasons to explain these difficulties, some of them turned again to deficit explanations and placed the responsibility on the family rather than on systemic influences. Harry (1992) and Harry, Allen, and McLaughlin (1995) examined the participation of Puerto Rican and African American parents in special education and found that the professionals' deficit view shaped their interactions with parents. Their explanations, and the intervention models that grew from them, had an "inside-out" focus that emphasized school-based programs in which teachers could engage parents in on-site activities as opposed to in their homes or neighborhoods. Many of these programs failed to reach the parents who most needed to be involved; taught skills that parents may not have wanted to learn; and implied that school success was only for those children whose parents were willing to conform to the established norms of the school (Connors & Epstein, 1994; Flaxman & Inger, 1992). While large-scale family policy to encourage parental involvement is not feasible, reforms in school policy at the school level that structure participation by parents *are* possible. Promising avenues of intervention in school to prevent student failure and to involve parents are inherent in policies such as school choice and school governance (Education Studies Group, 1991; Borman & Pink, 1994; Timm & Borman, 1997).

PARENTS AND TEACHERS

When interactions between teachers and parents become heated, difficult or unre- solved, the school demonstrates its power by summoning experts in the form of counselors, psychologists or administrators. Nearly 50 years ago, Becker described the balance of forces in Chicago's inner-city schools in terms that, unfortunately, still characterize many such schools in the late 1990s. Teachers and administrators in Becker's study created a unified front for mutual protection against interference by parents: "Teachers made an implicit bargain with their superiors that they would support the organization as long as the organization served to protect them from critics" (Lightfoot, 1978).

Fortunately, school reform efforts, notably in Chicago over the last 10 years, have been aimed at involving parents in meaningful ways on local school advisory boards that have considerable say in school governance issues such as hiring and firing administrators and allocating resources at the building level (Hess, 1994, 1993). At the same time as such efforts are progressing in many places, evidence surfaces from time to time that reinforces the image of schools as well defended fortresses much as Willard Waller described them in the 1930s. In the spring of

1996, *The New York Times* (May 14 and 15, 1996) exposed a wide-ranging set of examples of political patronage such as the appointment of school board members' relatives to the school principalship. Even more damning was the evidence mustered in this report that such patronage resulted in chaotic and low performing schools, many of them attended by children from low income and ethnic minority households in New York City.

Although we are characterizing contact between teachers and parents as frequently strained, some evidence exists that portrays the complexities of parent involvement as shaped by SES with respect to both the resources parents have at their disposal and the kinds of involvement teachers in turn request from parents. Annette Lareau (1989) argues that at least some teachers work diligently to develop strategies for increasing parent involvement. Lareau's case studies examined parent involvement in two northern California elementary schools, one working class and the other upper middle class, both predominantly Anglo.

While all of the parents in each of the schools included in Lareau's studies valued the educational success of their first and second grade children and while teachers used virtually identical strategies to engage parent involvement, there were enormous differences between the two sets of parents.

Upper middle-class parents, particularly those whose offspring are low achievers, try to take a leadership role in their children's schooling. They do not depend on the school for authorization, nor do they automatically defer to a teacher's professional expertise. As a result, the purpose and meaning of parents' activities differ. There are much tighter linkages between upper-middle-class parents and the school than between working class parents and the school because upper-middle-class parents closely supervise and frequently intervene in their children's schooling (Lareau, 1989, p. 9).

The upper-middle-class parents in Lareau's research lobbied aggressively for the removal of teachers they viewed as incompetent; structured family outings that strengthened children's grasp of specific school subject matter; and interacted regularly with large numbers of their children's classmates' parents and their own well educated relatives about school-related issues. These strategies all contributed to assuring the "acceptability" of their children by the teacher.

In contrast, working-class parents, lacking the skills and confidence to assist their children in school, left children to their own devices and rarely challenged such decisions as retaining children in a grade for an additional year. Rather ironically, working class parents were far more respectful of teachers' authority and professional expertise than upper-middle-class parents. Lareau's findings are particularly important in highlighting the influence on children's school achievement of family-based cultural capital including resources such as a well developed academic vocabulary and a circle of well educated friends and relatives.

STRUCTURAL AND CULTURAL DISCONTINUITIES AMONG
SCHOOL, FAMILY AND COMMUNITY

Discontinuities between the institutions of school and the family are produced both by their structural properties and by their cultural purposes. By "structural properties" we mean the way schools are organized to educate a large number of students, while families are set up to informally nurture a small number of children. In our society, schools have very different cultural purposes than families. All children must reckon with these discontinuities as they move from home to school (Lightfoot, 1978). An understanding of the dissonance between families and schools is that such dissonance has little to do with deficiencies in the cultural capital which children bring to school and much to do with the limited number of intersections between the worlds constructed in schools and those constructed in families and among culturally diverse youths. Because the overlap between school and family is often small, the young often have only a limited attachment to school. Generally sets of push-and-pull factors contribute to an individual's success or failure within the system. If schools are to become attractive sites for culturally diverse students, school policy that creates environments supporting affirmation and activity must take into account individuals' values, memories, narratives, and systems of meaning (Heath & McLaughlin, 1993).

Two national studies illustrate the importance of social structure in affecting human lives in urban, suburban, and rural places. In the first study, Crane (1991) used the percentage of workers in a neighborhood who held professional and managerial jobs as an index of neighborhood quality. He determined, in a sample of 92,512 adolescents, that the neighborhood effect is extremely large for both blacks and whites in urban ghettos. In all cases, adolescent pregnancy and school leaving increased dramatically at the same point in the distribution: in neighborhoods where only 4 percent of the workers held high-status jobs.

The second example is drawn from an analysis of High School and Beyond, a national longitudinal survey initiated in 1980 with high school sophomores. Researchers followed this cohort through five waves of data collection. The students who eventually left school before completing twelfth grade differed in a number of ways from those who remained. The dropouts had lower test scores, did less homework, came from homes with weaker educational support, had poorer school performance, exhibited more behavior problems in school, were more alienated from school life, and had more friends who were themselves alienated from school (Eckstrom, Goertz, & Rock, 1989).

Social structures—including indices of neighborhood unemployment and cohort dropout patterns—that encompass human lives, neighborhoods, families, and peer groups are relentless in their effects. This book stresses the importance of understanding these structures, their effects, and the ways in which children must cross borders and boundaries in their attempts to attain high academic standards and create meaningful lives.

There is some evidence that schools may be simply responding to what they accurately determine to be parents' desires. As mentioned earlier in this chapter, Okagi and Sternberg (1993) found that parents of first and second graders had different desires for their children's learning in school. While Cambodian, Mexican, Filipino, and Vietnamese parents valued both cognitive and noncognitive skills, Anglo-American and Mexican American parents valued only cognitive problem-solving, verbal, and creative skills associated with academic learning. Perhaps even more importantly, the new immigrants rated conforming behaviors in their children as more important than autonomous behaviors; the reverse was true among American-born parents who favored autonomy and independence from authority over conformity.

FAMILIES' VIEWS OF THE SCHOOL

The view that education is a means of mobility is widely held in many ethnic minority communities and clearly documented in the literature on family life and school achievement. Thirty years ago, Hylan Lewis reported that "the added value placed on education of black children as a means of escaping low status and achieving high status is a myth-like cultural theme" (Lewis, 1967). Ogbu (1974), in a study of African American urban neighborhoods, found distinct norms and values regarding achievement and the utility of schooling as a vehicle for success. Suarez-Orozco (1987) argues that, for Central American children and their families who have escaped war-ravaged conditions and settled as refugees in inner-city neighborhoods, the school presents tremendous opportunities in comparison to the situation left behind. Many stay in school and display extremely high levels of achievement motivation. Few develop oppositional behaviors toward school. However, high parental aspirations, when countered by the real social and economic limitations on children's opportunities, may well motivate children's oppositional behavior in other cases.

How can economically stretched, ethnic minority families keep their faith in education in the face of the overwhelming evidence that it does not provide mobility for their children? Many economically disadvantaged parents, no matter what their ethnic background, feel that they can do little but turn their children over to the school, the institution that arbitrates success and mobility, and hope for the best (Lareau, 1989). Such parents "lose control of their child's daily life, as someone else becomes the expert and judge of their child's abilities, and as they are perceived as interlopers, unwelcome intruders" (Lightfoot, 1978). Thus parents come to see themselves as powerless to help their child succeed in school.

FAMILY INFLUENCES ON ACHIEVEMENT

The dramatic effect of family participation on school achievement is well documented. Virtually all of the relevant studies show that there is a strong "curriculum of the home," manifested in conversations, daily routines, attention to school matters, concern for the children's progress, and recreational and leisure activities, which can enhance or impede school performance (DiPrete, 1981; Graue et al., 1983; Gray, 1984; Walberg, 1984a, 1984b). In a summary of the effects of parental involvement on children's achievement, it was determined that the creation of a positive learning environment at home, including the encouragement of positive attitudes toward education and high expectations of children's success enhanced children's school achievement and attachment. Middle-class family practices, however, may be idiosyncratic to that group because of the close congruence of values and goals between such homes and mainstream educational institutions. The practices in low income and minority households that encourage school success have been less well documented.

Clark (1983, 1992) suggests that these norms and values may be transmitted by families in ways that mediate negative environmental effects. Clark found that the families of high-achieving low-income African American students possessed a strong intellectual ethos which raised learning and schooling to a high level of consciousness in the household. In Chapter 7 we examine the vignette "Achievement Across the Generations" that shows how a family in St. Petersburg has instilled the notion of "Gotta do better" in successive generations. In Clark's research, this intellectual ethos is characterized as a strong moral code and standard in the household; both sacred and secular moral codes are highly developed in high-achieving students. Family norms, rules, and expectations take the form of achievement demands that are discussed, linked to specific outcomes, and generally understood by the child. Parents' dispositions toward acquiring knowledge are characterized by the willingness to place the child's growth and development ahead of their own. In turn, the notion that parents were making a sacrifice for the child's education is a strong theme recognized by children. Children are favorably disposed to school learning by the parents' responsibility for helping them develop general knowledge as well as special literacy skills, by their encouragement of the pursuit of knowledge, and by their belief that children would participate in some form of secondary and postsecondary training.

High-achieving children's families often have a process of deliberate pedagogy in the home. Children are routinely rehearsed by their parents on how to handle teacher–pupil relationships; homework and study were regular, almost ritualized, activities; and home lessons were taught as the opportunity arose in daily life. An implicit pedagogy also pervades the homes of high-achieving students; this consists of games and recreational activities that related to improved school performance, including recreational reading and discussion about activities such as viewing television shows together.

The potential mediating role of parents' beliefs and perceptions in their involvement in their children's learning may be extremely important. The separate influences of school and home on children's motivation and learning have been studied thoroughly, but the mutual influence of these overlapping spheres calls for our attention. One of the few exceptions to this situation is the work done by Annette Lareau and her colleagues mentioned previously in this chapter. Her findings confirm what we have pointed out thus far in our discussion: there are considerable differences across families varying by SES and ethnicity in what Lareau and Shumar (1996) refer to as social resources or social capital that parents bring to their interactions with their children's schools. Among both African American and white working class and low income parents, these researchers found that many believed: (a) that school personnel were the authorities regarding their children's education and that their role as parents was properly limited to making sure children were on time for school, dressed appropriately and the like; (b) that less contact with school authorities was best, particularly if families were at odds with service providers in other spheres; (c) that information on school events and issues was adequately provided by children. This last assumption was at least partially grounded in parents' quite different conceptions (as compared to those held by teachers) of such terms as "helpful," "supportive," "concerned," and "informed." In short, these parents remained outside the loop because they lacked both social power and adequately "dense" social networks of well informed adults to help ensure their children's success in school.

BARRIERS TO COLLABORATION BETWEEN FAMILY AND SCHOOL

Since the turn of the century, schools have used social science data to simplify and categorize a complex set of variables that interact to influence learning by children sent to their care. Literature on the successful school performance of poor and minority youths, however, suggests that social background data can be used best by a teacher to "elaborate and expand her repertoire of behaviors toward a single child" (Hale-Benson, 1982).

Most economically stretched, ethnic minority parents possess the values of achievement that support school success. Many of these parents, however, lack the skills necessary to operationalize their aspirations for their children. Numerous experimental programs have been launched to assist parents in helping their children succeed in school, and their success has been credible. These programs, however, generally are designed to encourage parents to accept the school's practices and to work with their children, largely outside the school in the context of homework, to advance school goals that parents may not comprehend. These efforts, unfortunately, show relatively little evidence of mutuality or collaboration (Epstein, 1994; Topping, 1986).

Structural impediments to collaboration between the school and poor and minority families are many and formidable. The estrangement of the economically distressed from the school grows more profound with each passing year of poverty and economic hardship. In our view, as we will stress in this book's concluding chapter, policy at the local school level should emphasize a systematic and particu-larized agenda for reinforcing productive family achievement values and norms with children. School-level policies should also focus on practices used by schools in sustaining meaningful participation by parents. A third dimension is the role of community-based organizations in providing programs and services that frequently function as a safety net for children. The fourth component is the systematic reform of teachers' education through careful and sustained transformation of the ex-pressed curriculum, teachers' education, and classroom pedagogy. This is an ambitious agenda but, in our view, absolutely essential in creating the kinds of reforms necessary to address the central issue of concern in this book: the successful learning and skill development of all children, particularly those who have been traditionally disenfranchised by the schools.

OUR ORIENTATION AND THE ORGANIZATION
OF THIS VOLUME

In the past, children from neighborhood communities were received by the schools without much thought about the social and demographic character of these com-munities. The role of schools as institutions in the early years of the 20th century was to "Americanize" the children of immigrant and poorer groups. When Bor-man's mother was in kindergarten at Harvey Rice School on Buckeye Road in Cleveland in the late 1920s, she was sent home by her teacher with a stern message to her mother (Borman's grandmother) that she was not to attend school until she spoke English rather than her native Hungarian. In 1948 when Borman began elementary school with the same kindergarten teacher in the same school, any traces of Hungarian, Italian, Polish, and Slav cultures had been swept from the corridors, even though ethnic bakeries, butcher shops, churches and social clubs were still a strong presence on Buckeye Road. Today many fourth generation Hungarians and other ethnics are eager to learn about their cultures, wishing they had acquired their kin's native language as children.

Baber's maternal grandparents were both professionals (doctor and teacher) who had achieved middle-class status in the pre-integration Midwest (1920s–1940s). They worked hard to make sure that their children and grandchildren acquired the language and social skills of white American society, replacing black dialect with standard English pronunciation in every conversation. Black culture was supple-mented with exposure to "classical" music, dance, and literature in an effort to encourage us to be "as good as white people" in order to compete successfully in American society. Assimilation was the goal for my (Baber's) grandparents and parents, and we were not allowed to even consider that we were in a "castelike" position or deficient in any way. This legacy of strength and positive identity that emanated from the black community is often ignored by today's teachers, who view many African American students as deficient.

Nonetheless, many teachers and administrators desire to understand their students' homes and communities because they know how important these institutions are in shaping children's lives. Unless teachers grasp the powerful influence that family, culture, and social institutions have on the students they teach, they will remain frustrated in the classroom. However, many immigrant and refugee parents today worry that schools are "Americanizing" their children in objectionable ways. For example, a Cambodian American political refugee and parent of four children told Borman that he resented his children's teachers' belief that the family's routine practice of pressing coins to their child's chest when the child was ill constituted a form of "child abuse."

Borman's first teaching job was in San Francisco's Inner Mission in 1963. The middle school at which she taught was attended by children from low income Mexican American, Chinese, Appalachian, White Russian, African American, and Central American families. Nothing in her preparation at an academically excellent, but isolated, Midwestern university could have prepared her for the ethnic stream that surrounded Borman at Everett Junior High. She was not a very successful teacher at Everett simply because she could not decipher the significance of students' differences. She did not understand those differences, and did not know either students' neighborhood communities or their political histories as racial and ethnic entities. As a result, Borman's teaching and her students' learning were extremely haphazard processes. She also recalls that the best teacher in the school taught science, was Mexican American and was highly regarded by students and faculty.

Although it is difficult to examine all ethnic groups that have emerged in the United States during the last two decades, it is possible to focus on major groups including Asian Americans, Appalachians, African Americans, American Indians, and Latinos. It is, however, nearly impossible to discuss all aspects of ethnicity that are related to children's school learning. For example, such features as language structure or social organization among Cambodian immigrants, while exceedingly significant for the teachers of Cambodian American children, are beyond the scope of this volume.

Chapter 1 has examined what society sees as expectations for student outcomes, skills required for adulthood, as well as family, community and school as contexts for learning; Chapter 2 considers community diversity by examining how institutions in different neighborhood communities work to buffer and to link families with schools; Chapter 3 focuses on the large scale demographic shifts that occurred in the 1980s with the migration of large numbers of individuals from Asia, Central and South America. In particular, the social and political meaning of their experiences is considered; Chapters 4, 5, 6, and 7 contain 11 vignettes as vehicles for connecting macro-level, political, economic and social conditions with micro-level processes, particularly interactions in families. These vignettes, as summarized in Figure 1.4, are drawn from the field work of several anthropologists and ethnographers whose work has involved them over a period of time with particular ethnic and racial groups.

The first four vignettes offer insight into the varieties of experience characterizing the Latino community. The first vignette, "Community Resources Enhance Children's Learning" by Concha Delgado-Gaitan focuses on very young Mexican American children and their families in Carpinteria, California, and demonstrates the strength of local community ties in fashioning networks of parent volunteers working with teachers to promote children's early learning.

Although it, too, contextualizes school experience in the community, the second vignette, "Community Terror Creates Attachment to School" by Pamela Quiroz, shows how young Puerto Rican gang members and homeless students in Chicago form strong attachments to school as a safe haven. Unfortunately, school learning is sacrificed in the process. "Young Children's School Success and Failure" examines lives of Honduran refugee children in "Lakeland," Wisconsin, showing how school personnel are likely to develop stereotypic images of their ethnic students based on little to no first hand knowledge. The concluding vignette in this section, "The Power of Ritual and Language" is the carefully observed celebration of a young Cuban American woman's Quinceañera that highlights cross generational differences in language use and attachment to school.

In "Isolation from High Achieving Peers" Li-Rong Lilly Cheng traces the difficult passage of a refugee family from Hong Kong whose daughter, Mei, becomes estranged as she identifies ever more closely with her Latino classmates. In "The Importance of Diagnosis," the same author illustrates problems faced by the Hmong-American parents of a young boy, Washington, whose reading difficulties have been misdiagnosed, undermining his self confidence in accomplishing classroom lessons. Finally, in "The Construction of Identity in Schools," the second "Lakeland," Wisconsin vignette, the young Hmong girl, Mai, finds herself negotiating both the world of her elementary school where she is considered "shy" and that of her family where she is considered appropriately deferent.

The next section begins with the vignette by Abbie Willetto and Margaret LeCompte entitled "What if I Forget How to Talk Navajo?" and encompasses stories of two children from the same family in Arizona. In "From Mountain to Metropolis" Kathryn Borman attempts to cover several aspects of the lives of urban Appalachian children, their teachers, families and advocates to demonstrate a highly successful model for creating neighborhood based opportunities and services.

"Achievement across the Generations" by Evelyn Phillips aims at portraying the cross-generational patterns of success in school of her own family in St. Petersburg, Florida. The final vignette by Michele Foster, "Good Teaching Makes a Difference," demonstrates how African American children in Boston profit at levels as diverse as the community college and the elementary grades from teaching that promotes student learning.

These vignettes taken together make the case for respecting the power of history, experience and core cultural values. Those who work with or seek to understand racial and ethnic groups: must (a) develop a *sociocultural understanding* of families and communities; (b) take into account at least three important features that help to explain outcomes for children, namely: *structural barriers, cultural dissonance,* and *alienation* from academic learning in school; and finally, (c) seek to understand specific patterns of *local and lateral cultural ties* that characterize the experience of various groups as a way of conceptualizing strengths unique to specific groups.

Finally the concluding chapter, Chapter 8, examines approaches to teaching and learning in schools where teachers, administrators, students and parents alike are

Vignette	Title	Author	Location	Grade Level	Family Ethnicity
#1	"Community Resources Enhance Children's Learning: Mexican Children in Carpinteria, California"	Concha Delgado-Gaitan	Carpenteria, CA	Pre-K - 6	Mexican-American
#2	"Community Terror Creates Attachment to School: Puerto Rican High School Students in Chicago"	Pamela Quiroz	Chicago, IL	High school	Puerto Rican-American
#3	"Young Children and the Construction of School Success and Failure: A Honduran Refugee Student in 'Lakeland', Wisconsin"	Marianne Bloch, Jay Hammond Cradle, Carolyn Dean, Miryam Espinosa-Dulanto, B. Robert Tabachnick	Lakeland, WI	Elementary school	Honduran-American
#4	"The Power of Ritual and Language: Maria Teresa Takes Her Place in Tampa's Cuban Community"	Jim King, Mary Alice Barksdale-Ladd, Richard Alvarez	Tampa, FL	High school	Cuban-American
#5	"Isolation from High Achieving Peers: The Story of Dan & Mei, Refugees in Los Angeles"	Li-Rong Lilly Cheng	Los Angeles, CA	Middle school and high school	Chinese-American
#6	"The Story of Washington, A Hmong Child"	Li-Rong Lilly Cheng	Los Angeles, CA	Elementary school	Hmong-American
#7	"The Construction of Identity in Schools: The Role of Gender and Ethnicity"	Carolyn Dean	Lakeland, WI	Elementary school	Hmong-American
#8	"'Mom, What if I Forget How to Talk Navajo': Collisions of Culture in the Public Schools"	Abbie Willetto, Margaret LeCompte	Castle Rock and Stone Creek, AZ	Elementary school and high school	Native American
#9	"From Mountain to Metropolis: Urban Appalachian Children and Youth"	Kathryn Borman	Cincinnati, OH	High school	Urban Appalachian
#10	"Achievement Across the Generations: Negotiating a Better Education for Three African-American Children in St. Petersburg, Florida"	Evelyn Phillips	St. Petersburg, FL	Elementary school, middle school, high school	African-American
#11	"Good Teaching Makes a Difference: African-American Students at Regents Community College and in an Elementary School in Boston"	Michele Foster	Boston, MA	Elementary school, community college	African-American

FIGURE 1.5. Vignettes—Defining characteristics.

committed to social justice and respect for diversity. We take into account programs and strategies such as Success for All, the Center for Research on the Education of Students Placed at Risk (CRESPAR Program) that enhance children's skill learning while taking into account the strengths they bring to the classroom.

2

Diverse Communities, Different Realities

With the assistance of M. Yvette Baber

During the 1980s and into the 1990s, schools and communities were swept up by large scale demographic shifts. Numbers of immigrants and political refugees from Central and South America, Mexico and Indo-China including Cambodia, the Philippines, and Laos settled in the United States. In addition, cities became increasingly poor and non-Anglo as earlier patterns of middle class city-to-suburban migration intensified.

In turn, schools attended by non-traditional populations of U.S. school children were buffeted by the immediate need to serve these populations and by ongoing pressure from business and government to become more "effective," efficient and accountable. At the current moment, first and second-generation immigrant children constitute the fastest growing segment of the U.S. population under the age of 15 (National Research Council, 1995). Second language learning and the acquisition of literacy and other skills are and will remain powerful and important issues in our schools, families and communities for some time to come.

In line with our over-arching conception of the importance of a sociocultural understanding of children's worlds, we turn in this chapter to a consideration of the social structural forces of current immigration and settlement patterns. Thus, the chapter is organized to examine the nature of the "new" immigration of Hispanic and Asian peoples as well as the experiences of other nonwhite and white historically colonized peoples— namely American Indians, Appalachians, and African Americans. In addition, demographic changes occurring during the 1980s and 1990s are considered, particularly as these changes have significance for children's learning in virtually every U.S. city, town and hamlet with few exceptions. Not many places in the United States are like the state of Pennsylvania. Approximately 80 percent of the population currently residing in that state was born there. In contrast, during the same period—the 1990s—only 15 percent of Florida residents were born in that state, now the nation's fourth most populous. Arizona, New Mexico, New York, Texas, and California experienced developments similar to Florida's. These demographic facts not only suggest that flows of people differentially seek new residences, but also that different places are enriched by new talent and ideas (as well as issues and problems), while other places languish and perhaps suffer from a myopic, inward gaze. Most importantly, from the perspective of this volume, waves of external (and internal) migration present the single most important set of structural changes affecting school-aged populations today. These demographic shifts can be seen as a set of impacts at the macro-systemic level that reverberate throughout all levels in the system.

The political and social developments accompanying these demographic shifts are far-reaching. Children's individual identities and, consequently, children's school identities are shaped in a number of contexts including homes, schools, and communities as we argued in Chapter 1. An important aspect of individual identity is derived from dimensions of the racial and ethnic group with which an individual consciously and unconsciously identifies. We saw, for example, in our discussion of bilingual education in Chapter 1 that identification with a particular language group affects language acquisition. Group identity in turn is closely tied to the ebb and flow of political and social power, real and perceived, held by group members. Policies and other political practices allocate, channel, increase, decrease and cut off resources to specific communities and the individuals who reside in them. Literacy and language acquisition are important resources in a society such as ours that requires a mastery of "Standard" English for individual social and economic success.

In this chapter we present an analysis of the large-scale societal forces shaping children's learning followed by an examination of the migration experience. These processes give rise to the creation of local ties or, conversely, the strengthening of lateral ties. This analysis focuses on the outermost layer of the *macrosystem*, to use Bronfenbrenner's terminology as discussed in the previous chapter. Chapter 3 considers the history, political struggle and the demographic and social outcomes for select groups in United States society, those traditionally disenfranchised by our system who constitute the inner layers of the macrosystem as well as the *mesosystem*. These aspects of a group's experience have critical importance for children's success in school. In Chapters 4, 5, 6, and 7, through a series of vignettes, we examine dilemmas facing children in the schools, especially as these dilemmas affect learning in classrooms serving new immigrants and others who have not fared well in our nation's institutions.

THE SIGNIFICANCE OF CHANGING U.S. DEMOGRAPHICS
FOR CHILDREN'S LEARNING

Forces Affecting Children's Learning

During its history, the United States has been the recipient of large numbers of families who have been compelled by economic difficulties, political and religious persecution or seizure against their will to leave their native lands (Takaki, 1993). The most recent arrivals, the new immigrants, have faced many of the same barriers to successful settlement as earlier peoples. Yet some immigrant minorities historically have done very well in school and move relatively easily into the labor market, particularly when second language learning is not an issue and native cultural values are isomorphic with those in U.S. society (Ogbu, 1993; Perlmann, 1988).

Nonetheless, today's multicultural U.S. society is far more difficult to characterize with respect to its relationship to school achievement and to its association with cultural values, practices and predispositions. John Ogbu's careful, detailed and systematic analysis of the linkages between school achievement and minority group status is far too complex to consider in depth here (see Ogbu, 1982, 1987, 1993a). However, it is important to understand aspects of his formulations if we are to grasp the significance of why this volume is devoted to building bridges between schools and diverse communities.

First, Ogbu contends that a set of "complex and interlocking forces" affect both the social behavior and academic performance of minority children. His understanding is similar to that of Bronfenbrenner, whose ecological model is outlined in Chapter 1 of this volume, in that the "forces" affecting children emanate from the wider society, the school and the classroom as well as from minority communities themselves. We discuss Ogbu's theoretical perspective here because of the salience it has to the group histories and experiences described in this chapter, especially as these have meaning for children's lives.

Second, Ogbu argues that minority communities vary both with respect to their distinctive features and their experiences in U.S. society. Thus, minorities vary on several dimensions (or as Ogbu terms them—distinctive features) including cultural differences, social or collective identity, a "folk theory of making it" and survival strategies. Distinctive features include both those primary cultural differences that existed prior to immigration and secondary cultural differences, those features that arise after the minority group comes into contact with U.S. society. In some respects, these secondary cultural differences have the most profound impact on children's school success. For those groups whose experience after contact and settlement are, from the minority group's perspective, socially negative, politically repressive or economically exploitative, it becomes necessary for those group members to develop a new sense of their identity in opposition to that held of them by the prevailing or dominant group. This process has quite clear and discouraging implications for the educational outcomes of children from such minority communities.

Third, as a result of the complex forces and corresponding distinctive features which characterize different minority groups, it is possible to discuss different types of minorities. This aspect of Ogbu's theoretical reasoning is probably also his most controversial. Ogbu argues that, in order for us to fully understand the forces emanating from minority communities themselves, it is important to spell out very clearly and with reference to particular groups exactly how different types of minority status (as defined by the group's distinctive features) have implications for schooling.

Specifically, Ogbu identifies three types of minorities: *autonomous minorities*, *immigrant minorities*, and *castelike* or *involuntary minorities*. In the case of U.S. society, autonomous minorities are those who constitute a minority group or community only in a numerical sense. While some traces of prejudice or discrimination may linger in the larger society, such groups are not socially, politically and economically subordinated. Ogbu illustrates this type by referring to religious minorities, Jews and Mormons. However, older ethnic groups who still maintain ethnic communities could also be included. Such communities are still present in Chicago and other large cities where distinct ethnic cultural boundaries have served to create communities within the sprawl of the city.

Next, Ogbu distinguishes immigrant minorities whose journey to the United States was undertaken voluntarily. Such groups include several recently arrived Asian peoples, particularly Chinese, Filipino, and Japanese settlers. The Punjabi Indians mentioned in Chapter 1 constitute another example of such individuals who, as Ogbu puts it, may "experience difficulties due to language and cultural differences" but who "do not experience lingering, disproportionate school failure" (Ogbu, 1987).

Finally, castelike or involuntary minorities are those who were either brought into the United States involuntarily as slaves or those who were incorporated through economic, social and political exploitation. It is this dimension of Ogbu's explanatory framework that draws the most fire. Many argue that Ogbu's representation of groups such as African Americans, American Indians and Appalachians unfairly labels and stereotypes group members, thereby increasing their difficulty in breaking free from the constraints of such a depiction. Ogbu's defense is that his classification system should be employed as a heuristic device; it is not his intent to stereotype individuals. Further, while Ogbu characterizes group members of the three different minority community types according to a set of distinctive features as we have seen, it is also true that there are, in addition, individual and subgroup differences.

Our position here is that Ogbu's explanatory framework is highly useful in characterizing how a group's history and experience in U.S. society interacts with that group's distinctive features to create a way of understanding the school experience of a particular community's children. In a very practical way, Ogbu's framework helps to set limits on which group's experiences should be considered in a volume such as this, meant to be an overview of the subject. Therefore, we use Ogbu's typology to help identify those groups whose distinctive features have often been transformed by this society's institutions into deficits with corresponding negative effects on the minority communities in question. However, we wish to be clear that, far from considering various groups as exhibiting deficits as a result of their social and historical contexts, we view communities as exhibiting unique strengths. These strengths can only be identified by understanding the political, social, and economic circumstances surrounding each group's odyssey. In agreement with Douglas Foley (1990), we argue throughout the volume and most graphically with the case material presented in Chapters 4, 5, 6, and 7 that "a complex interactional process among ethnic groups and societal institutions results in the construction of ethnic cultural identities" (Foley, 1990). With that point made, we next turn to the important demographic shifts that have moved populations into and around the United States.

WHY PEOPLE MIGRATE AND HOW THEY ESTABLISH SOCIAL CONTEXTS

First, it is important to consider why people migrate and what happens after they do. So-called "standard" explanations for why people leave one place for another have emphasized the importance of sets of economic "push-pull" factors that serve to propel individuals from their homelands to different shores. As an example, the usual (and to some extent likely) explanation for the large scale internal migration from the farms and coal fields of Appalachia to the cities and towns of the Midwest is the expansion of manufacturing in the North alongside the contraction of mining and farming enterprises in the Appalachian region during the years following World War II.

However, Portes and Bach also see migration as part of a broad, large-scale global historical trend:

> The varying historical origins of population movements—from outright coercion through deliberate inducements to the current "spontaneous" outflows from Third World countries—can be more properly attributed to the gradual incorporation of peripheral areas into the world economy, the diffusion of expectations from the centers and the resulting internal dislocations in these subordinate societies. (Portes & Bach, 1985)

We can best understand population shifts, according to Portes and Bach, by seeing migratory passages as firmly grounded in world-system or global economic trends. Moreover, "centers" such as the United States in general and particular regions of the country at specific times serve as targets for migration. Those who migrate internally leave "peripheral areas" such as the long journey northward taken by

African Americans throughout our nation's history from before the Civil War, but with increased intensity from the 1860s onward. Their destination was the tier of northern cities with booming economies and jobs. Peripheral areas include rural Thailand during the 1980s. The destinations in the United States for Thai people, however, were more varied than in the case of the Great Migration from South to North principally because the Thai immigration was "engineered" by religious organizations, agencies and offices of the U.S. government and targeted particular cities and towns.

Not all migrants, however, come as immigrants seeking a larger share of the world economy's pie. Some are political refugees, such as those who left Laos during the late 1970s and throughout the 1980s. Others may be highly successful entrepreneurs from nations such as the Philippines who desire to raise their children in a society (the United States) that they believe has more egalitarian ideals than those commonly held in their homeland. A good example of the latter case is a very successful couple who own a thriving Midwestern manufacturing plant specializing in making filters from hemp and other natural fibers. Although they take their children to the Philippines every summer for a month and have enrolled them in Saturday classes to learn Chinese—the father's native language and the language, the family believes, of commerce for the twenty-first century—they have no desire to rear their children in the Philippines. This is because they believe their children might grow dependent on household servants and acquire values and expectations that they do not desire their children to hold. The couple's business would be an even more lucrative venture in their homeland, underscoring the depth of their philosophical commitment as parents.

Once immigrants settle in the United States, a particular exosystem, milieu or social context becomes established. Social context in part refers to the web of social, economic and other relationships created by interaction among the newly settled migrants who typically create "colonies"—neighborhoods in which they settle. The social context or exosystem is also influenced by interaction with the majority society. Oftentimes, migrants do not receive a warm welcome from native-born employers. One strategy used under such conditions is to work in firms owned by relatives and others who have well-established businesses. A notable example of such arrangements is in Miami where "Little Havana" is home to several generations of immigrants from Cuba.

The Midwestern filter plant mentioned previously employs five newly arrived members of the area's Asian community. Although the owners are Filipino-Americans, the workers are more recently arrived Cambodians whose regularly spoken language, French, is heard most of the time on the shop floor. In Garden City, Kansas, the meat packing plant—where approximately 5,000 Asians and Mexicans are employed—hires very recently arrived immigrants who in turn recruit Asian and Mexican-American workers from economically hard-hit areas such as Fresno, California. These recruiters are trusted by individuals willing to come to a part of the United States they have never seen on the basis of assurances of work and a contract offered by their countryman, a virtual stranger.

There is considerable variation among social contexts that the new immigrants inhabit. Some such as Little Havana in Miami become so comfortable that people do not use these communities as "launching pads" into the larger society but instead remain as residents in these port-of-entry neighborhoods. Others, such as members of a Cambodian community near Cincinnati, rely on members of other Asian groups for employment. Still others such as the Laotian and Mexican immigrants in Garden City, Kansas are recruited from their original settlements close to their port-of-entry communities (Fresno, California; border town in Texas) by trusted strangers who are their countrymen. Finally, many refugees are placed, as the southwestern Ohio Laotians were, by the federal government's Refugee Resettlement Program or by church and synagogue groups "sponsoring" refugees seeking religious asylum such as Soviet Jews in the early 1980s.

The social contexts that different groups establish are maintained in large part because the people who inhabit them enjoy interacting with others who relish the same foods, practice similar religions, share the same histories and together seek a sense of community. For example, Japanese and Chinese immigrants to New York, San Francisco, and other large cities rely on the proximity of other immigrants to establish and maintain important folk institutions that ensure the group's economic well-being. The Chinese rotating credit association that loans money to Chinese immigrants depends on the face-to-face familiarity of association members to create strong, trusting relationships in the community (Takaki, 1989).

Tightly bounded communities are also maintained because the larger society is uncomfortable with or threatened by differences. Much of the hostility such social and ethnic groups experience is grounded in resistance to contact between the children of majority and minority groups as we saw in the Punjabi case in Chapter 1 reported by Gibson (1993). In Garden City, Kansas, the population in the early 1990s is 20 percent foreign-born (compared with 7.2 percent nationally) and 40 percent non-white. Ethnic antagonisms have largely remained masked since white residents and their migrant neighbors live, work and play in worlds that barely intersect. Most new settlers live in a neighborhood of trailers in the community of East Garden, Kansas outside Garden City. The only time that trouble seemed imminent was when schooling became an issue:

In 1987, several years after East Garden Village opened, a new elementary school was built nearby. Victor Ornelas Elementary was known "with a lot of animosity as that school for those kids," said Ms. Thompson, a teacher there. When the school district proposed busing some white children there, parents rebelled. It was as close as Garden City has come to a public confrontation over the town's changing population. Now, the 6-year old school, spacious and modern, has a devoted staff that prides itself on adapting to an America that defies the Norman Rockwell image of their childhood. A kindergarten teacher joked recently about preparing a bulletin board of student self-portraits, where crayon-drawn faces were decorated with colored yarn for hair. "It's not like the old days," said the teacher, Linda Walker. "I didn't need much yellow yarn, as you can see." (*New York Times*, October 18, 1993)

Teachers at Victor Ornelas School, all of whom are native-born, take considerable pride in their students' achievements and enjoy teaching them in a school that remains separate from Garden City's white majority. These conditions in the long run work against the provision of a rich educational experience that benefits all children; however, there is probably considerable value of such arrangements to most immigrant children in the short run. For one thing, these children are able to establish and maintain a strong positive sense of who they are. Nonetheless, and particularly under conditions of economic privation, such arrangements can be highly detrimental to the social and economic well being of all concerned because "difference" in this society almost always is equated with "deficit" by majority group members. The important dimension in our consideration of newcomers' social contexts is the nature of social ties that are created in the process of becoming established. These webs of relationships can be local, lateral, or both local and lateral. As we will see in Chapter 8, these arrangements can serve as the "handle" for creating school-linked programs. We turn next to a consideration of trends accompanying the large scale demographic shifts of the last 30 or so years.

DEMOGRAPHIC PATTERNS

It is important to recognize that particularly brutal social facts characterize the lives of U.S. children in today's society. An increasing share of children live with their mothers in father-absent families. Reconstituted or blended families consisting of one biological parent and a step parent are also on the rise. These family structural arrangements have an impact on skills important for school learning including, for example, identifying colors and recognizing the letters of the alphabet, rudimentary skills in the hierarchy of school learning. Very young children from families with a single parent or other relatives as principal caretakers perform less well on measures of such skills than children with both biological parents present or with one biological and one step parent in the home.

American children today are nearly twice as likely as the elderly to be poor, and child poverty rates have increased over the past 15 years. In 1992 the poverty rate among children was 22 percent, a rate of economic deprivation higher than in any year since the 1982 economic recession. As shown in Figure 2.1, more than 40 percent of all black and American Indian children live in very poor conditions with total family incomes below 50 percent of the poverty line. Figure 2.1 also shows the tremendous disparities both within and among all groups in the United States. All groups have families who live fairly comfortable middle class lives, but all have numbers of families who are not doing well. The implications of child poverty,

Under 18 years: Related children in families below poverty level

Year	Total	Number	Percent
ALL RACES			
1995.........	69,425	13,999	20.2
1994.........	68,819	14,610	21.2
1993	68,040	14,961	22.0
1992.........	67,256	14,521	21.6
1990.........	63,908	12,715	19.9
1988.........	62,906	11,935	19.0
1986.........	62,009	12,257	19.8
1983.........	61,578	13,427	21.8
1982.........	61,565	13,139	21.3
1980.........	62,168	11,114	17.9
WHITE			
1995.........	54,532	8,474	15.5
1994.........	54,221	8,826	16.3
1993	53,614	9,123	17.0
1992	53,110	8,752	16.5
1991	51,627	8,316	16.1
1990.........	51,028	7,696	15.1
1988.........	50,590	7,095	14.0
1986.........	50,356	7,714	15.3
1983	50,183	8,534	17.0
1982.........	50,305	8,282	16.5
1980.........	51,002	6,817	13.4
BLACK			
1995.........	11,198	4,644	41.5
1994.........	11,044	4,787	43.3
1993	10,969	5,030	45.9
1992	10,823	5,015	46.3
1991.........	10,178	4,637	45.6
1990.........	9,980	4,412	44.2
1988.........	9,681	4,148	42.8
1986.........	9,467	4,037	42.7
1984.........	9,356	4,320	46.2
1983	9,245	4,273	46.2
1982.........	9,269	4,388	47.3
1980.........	9,287	3,906	42.1

Under 18 years: Related children in families below poverty level

Year	Total	Number	Percent
HISPANIC ORIGIN			
1995.........	10,011	3,938	39.3
1994.........	9,621	3,956	41.1
1993	9,188	3,666	39.9
1992.........	8,829	3,440	39.0
1991.........	7,473	2,977	39.8
1990.........	7,300	2,750	37.7
1988.........	6,908	2,576	37.3
1986.........	6,511	2,413	37.1
1984.........	5,982	2,317	38.7
1983	5,977	2,251	37.7
1982.........	5,436	2,117	38.9
1980.........	5,211	1,718	33.0
ASIAN AND PACIFIC ISLANDER			
1995.........	2,858	532	18.6
1994.........	1,719	308	17.9
1993	2,029	358	17.6
1992	2,199	352	16.0
1991.........	2,036	348	17.1
1990.........	2,098	356	17.0
1988.........	1,949	458	23.5

FIGURE 2.1.   Poverty status for children under 18, by age, race, and hispanic origin: 1980 to 1995.

Source: U.S. Bureau of the Census, U.S. Department of Commerce.

Note: Numbers in thousands.

especially long-term or chronic poverty, are clear. Poor children are more likely than non-poor children to be in ill health, to perform less well in school (i.e., have higher dropout rates), and to be economically disadvantaged as adults (Children's Defense Fund, 1991).

Declining marriage rates and increasing unmarried childbearing have eroded additional socioeconomic gains among certain economically disadvantaged ethnic minorities. For example, roughly two-thirds of African American children are born outside of marriage (The National Center for Health Statistics, 1996). These children face an extraordinarily high probability of poverty. The situation for Puerto Rican children parallels that of blacks. The percentage of families and of individuals in poverty rose for all groups except African Americans between 1979 and 1989, after falling for all groups except Hispanics during the 1970s. The poverty rate for children increased in the 1980s for *all groups*. The better news is that, for all groups, neighborhood and family living arrangement patterns demonstrate a predominance of married-couple families. Such family structural arrangements ranged from 50 percent among black families to 66 percent for American Indian families, 70 percent among Latino groups; and 80 percent for both Asians and whites.

In order to understand changes in the lives of young adults between 1980 and 1990, it is essential to note the dramatic population changes in race and ethnic composition. Young Americans became much more ethnically and racially diverse throughout the period of the 1980s. In 1980, 77 percent of persons aged 18—24 were white. This percentage declined to 71 percent in 1990. The largest share of the growth in minorities was accounted for by the rapid growth of the Latino and Asian groups. By 1990, the number of young adults who were Latino was approaching that of blacks, and the number of Latinos in the United States population can be expected to exceed blacks by early in the twenty-first century. Since many Latinos settle in larger cities and towns while others are engaged in agricultural work, many as seasonal workers, we can expect that schools in such areas can expect to see growth in this population.

While the overall Asian population size remains small, their proportion in the population of young adults more than doubled over the 1980s. However, significant proportions of the most rapidly growing minorities—Asians and Latinos—are foreign born, and this percentage has increased over time. By 1990, 70 percent of Asian and 42 percent of Latino young adults were foreign born.

Clearly, then, an important and immediately visible trend in the past two decades has been the increasing overall racial and ethnic diversity of the nation's population. America's so-called minority populations—defined to include blacks, American Indians, Asians, and Latinos—have grown much more rapidly than the population as a whole. This growth reflects younger age structures and higher fertility rates and, most strikingly, the increased immigration of Asians and of Latinos (Harrison & Bennett, 1995). Whereas whites constituted approximately 90 percent of the United States population in 1960, by 1990 they were slightly less than 75 percent. This trend will continue into the twenty-first century with the Census Bureau projecting figures of 60 percent by 2030 and 53 percent by 2050. Currently, in six of the nation's 10 largest cities whites are in the minority.

As mentioned previously, some groups, notably Asians and American Indians, have increased over the last four decades. American Indians, overwhelmed by policies of genocide, came close to being obliterated in the late 19th century, while persons of Hispanic origin were not documented in the census until 1980.

Immigration

Immigration after the 1956 Immigration Act nearly doubled the Asian population in each decade since 1960, and grew to 7.3 million (nearly 3% of the population) in 1990. The Latino population grew by nearly 50 percent or more in every decade since 1980. Latinos numbered 22.4 million (9%) of the population in 1990. The American Indian population reversed a downward trend to grow by 5 percent in the 1960s and 1970s, and by 38 percent between 1980 and 1990. The combined Latino, Asian, and American Indian population is now larger than the black population, and by 2010, Latinos are expected to be the largest minority group.

The 1980s saw a tremendous flow of migrants from Asia, Latin America and the Caribbean. During this period 8.6 million individuals settled in the United States (*U.S. News and World Report*, October 4, 1993, pp. 47–54). The foreign-born population enumerated in the 1990 census is the most diverse in our history, and yet one out of every five immigrants comes from only one country, Mexico. Table 2.1 shows Mexico as the leading country of origin for immigrants in both 1980 and 1990; the proportion of the total foreign-born who are from Mexico increased from 16 percent to nearly 22 percent over the decade. As also shown in Table 2.1, the Philippines ranked second, moving from seventh in 1980 (4.5% of total population in 1990).

There is considerable variability across the United States with respect to patterns of ethnic enrollment in the schools as a consequence of migration and settlement patterns. It is estimated, for example, that California is host to the largest number of Spanish-speaking individuals with seven million such residents. Indeed, more than 12 million of the estimated 15 million Spanish-speakers in the Unites States reside in the states of California, Texas, Arizona, New Mexico, and Colorado (U.S. Bureau of the Census, 1984).

These states together with the tier of southern and eastern states form a "necklace" of states with near "majority minority" populations. These states vary in their percentages of minority enrollments from 25 percent to more than 35 percent of the total number of students enrolled in public schools. By 2047 demographers indicate that ours will be a population characterized by its diversity—the Anglo population will be in the minority. Construing these shifts as strictly a coastal issue or an urban problem ignores important current demographic trends. States such as Washington, Minnesota, and Wisconsin were the recipients of large numbers of Indo-Chinese immigrants such as the Hmong.

Regional and Urban Concentration

The new diversity is concentrated in specific regions and areas of the country, reflecting both the enduring legacy of each group's history in the United States and the location of ports of entry for recent immigrant groups. More than one half of all blacks still live in the South. Asians, American Indians, and Latinos are concentrated in the West—the most racially and ethnically diverse of the regions.

The South's substantial Hispanic population (8%) is barely visible outside Texas, Florida, and the District of Columbia. There are only a few states where the major groups are all represented in large numbers: California, Texas, Florida (Miami),

TABLE 2.1.   Top 20 Countries of Birth Among the Foreign-Born, and Selected
Demographic Characteristics: 1990

Rank in 1990	Country[b]	Rank in 1980	Number (1,000s)	% Dist.	Median Age	Ratio Males to Females	% Naturalized	% Immigrated Since 1985
1	Mexico	1	4,297	21.8%	29	123	23%	30
2	Philippines	7	882	4.5	38	77	54	26
3	Canada	3	755	3.8	53	71	53	11
4	Cuba	6	713	3.7	49	94	53	7
5	Germany	2	633	3.6	53	53	74	6
6	United Kingdom	5	583	3.2	49	71	49	14
7	Italy	4	583	3.0	59	98	75	3
8	Korea	10	575	2.9	34	79	38	34
9	Vietnam	12	552	2.8	30	113	44	25
10	China	11	524	2.7	45	99	42	32
11	India	16	446	2.3	36	114	35	32
12	El Salvador	28	446	2.3	29	109	14	34
13	Poland	8	378	1.9	58	88	61	20
14	Jamaica	18	344	1.7	35	83	39	24
15	Dominican Republic	19	341	1.7	33	86	25	32
16	USSR	9	332	1.7	55	82	59	30
17	Japan	13	279	1.4	37	61	27	45
18	Colombia	23	277	1.4	35	85	29	28
19	Taiwan	33	244	1.2	33	87	40	33
20	Guatemala	39	228	1.2	30	104	19	39
All Other			6,160	31.2	38	98	42	26
Total			19,724	100%	37	96	40%	25%

Source: 1990 Census of Population, Public Use Microdata Sample.
Note: Native-born: median age 33; ratio males to females 95.
[a]All data refer to 1990, except rank in 1980.
[b]Germany includes East and West Germany, United Kingdom includes all constituent units, USSR includes all areas of what was the former USSR, China includes Hong Kong but not Taiwan.

New York (New York City), New Jersey, and Illinois (Chicago). Nearly three-quarters of immigrants are clustered in six states, with California the leading destination. One-third of the nation's foreign-born populations lived in California in 1990, with 14 percent residing in New York and 5 percent each in Florida and Texas.

Only 47 of the 3,141 counties in the United States have more than twice the 8 percent average national proportion of foreign-born residents. The county with the highest proportion is Dade County (Miami), Florida at 45 percent. These figures, of course, have implications for the schools in these areas. For example, in the Dade

County schools, the nation's third largest system, 85 percent of the students speak a language other than English as their native tongue. Among the top 20 metropolitan areas of intended residence given by immigrants entering the United States, eight were in California. Major destinations in that state were the Los Angeles and San Francisco Bay areas. Other targets included Miami (the fifth ranked residence for those admitted in 1992) and Houston (the seventh ranked). More than three-fourths of all Latinos and more than 70 percent of all Asians resided in these "new diversity" states at the time of the 1990 census. Nearly one-fifth of Asians live in the greater Los Angeles area. Half of resident Puerto Rican and Cuban populations lived in either New York or Miami. Almost 75 percent of all Mexicans resided in California or Texas. Among American Indians, nearly one-half resided in non-metropolitan areas in 1980 and 1990. Thirty-seven percent lived on reservations and other areas set aside for American Indian and Alaska Native populations.

More than two million children and teenagers were born outside the United States, according to analyses of 1990 census data. California and New York lead the country with one in nine youngsters and youths living in California, and one in 14 in New York. In addition, immigrant parents may also have children born to them in the United States. These are native-born children, but they are, of course, the consequence of international migration. One of every seven school aged children speaks a language other than English at home. Along the Southwest border including the states of California, Arizona, New Mexico, and Texas and also in New York, one fourth or more of the school-age population can speak a language other than English. Among immigrants aged 25–64, 80 percent reported that a language other than or in addition to English was spoken in the home. Spanish, reported by nearly half (47%), was the language most frequently cited.

Internal Migration Patterns

Once they have arrived in the United States, immigrants to our shores do not necessarily stay in the port of entry cities and communities where they first set foot. Rather, many groups begin a process of staged migration that may take them many miles from their original destinations. Blacks, Asians, and Latinos are all likely to move to the growth areas where there are large populations with similar backgrounds including, in many instances, close family friends and kin.

American Indians and Asians were more likely than whites and blacks to move, both within and across state lines. Latinos were the group most likely to have moved within states and the least likely to have moved between states. This behavior suggests that Latinos in general have less access to national labor markets and networks, reducing, in effect, their opportunities for economic mobility. A notable exception are Cuban Americans residing in Miami who have been exceedingly successful in establishing themselves. The same generalization applies to American Indians whose attachment to place through networks of local ties is marked. With few exceptions, the interstate moves of each group resulted in net movement from the Northeast, the Midwest, and the South Central regions, and net immigration into Florida, the other South Atlantic states, and the West, including California.

Approximately 80 percent of the net internal migration of whites and Latinos and 86 percent of that for blacks was concentrated in the South Atlantic region, particularly Florida. In fact, three of every four Latinos that the South Atlantic gained went to Florida. Among Latinos, two thirds of that group who moved to Florida came from the Northeast, and another sixth from Texas and California. One of Florida's major cities, Tampa, the location of Chapter 4's vignette, "The Power of Ritual and Language," ranks as one of the most important cities in the United States for second wave migration. Asian net immigration into Florida and the South Atlantic was substantial, but the primary destination in seven of ten cases was California. A larger share of Asians are foreign-born (66%) than is the case among Hispanics. There is also a greater degree of heterogeneity with respect to nation of origin. Further, the Asian population in the United States tends to be concentrated in or near traditional ports of entry. In 1990, over half of all Asians in the United States resided in Los Angeles, San Francisco, or New York.

Migrant youths, whose families follow the growing seasons across the country present a set of educational issues uniquely their own in such states as Texas, California, Florida, and Michigan. These students come mostly from large, intact families whose members place substantial value on educational achievement. Yet they often confront obstacles that place achievement goals beyond their reach. In addition to the barriers imposed by mobility and poverty, migrant students report obstacles related to parental discomfort with an academic school culture that places little value on their role as partners in their children's education. It is important to explore the context of family life as it relates to aspects of resiliency and vulnerability, which may contribute to migrant students' academic achievement.

Metropolitan areas affected by immigrant-dominated population changes have acquired substantially larger minority population profiles than those metro areas (such as Tampa) whose gains stem from internal migration. Eight of the ten highest immigration-dominated metropolitan areas have white percentages well below the white national average, including two where whites are no longer the majority population—Los Angeles and Miami. Highly concentrated in a few metropolitan areas, recent immigration has consolidated that concentration. Currently 4.8 million immigrants live in the Los Angeles Metropolitan Area; 2.8 million in New York; and 1.1 million reside in Miami (Frey, 1995).

By the late 1970s, the South-to-North internal migration pattern for African Americans had reversed itself. The South and California became primary destinations during that period and subsequently. Black migration during the 1980s shifted to the growing South Atlantic region including the states of Alabama, Maryland, Florida, Virginia, North Carolina, and Georgia. The largest urban concentration of black populations remains centered in New York and Chicago; however both cities are losing this population through out-migration.

TABLE 2.2.   Rates of High School Completion for Individuals Under 24 Years of Age, 1940, 1960, and 1990

Ethnic group	1940	1960	1990
White	One in Four	One-half	Four-fifths
Black	One in Ten	3 in 10 (1970)	Six in Ten
American Indian	[No Data]	One in Three	Two-thirds
Hispanic	[No Data]	One in Three	One half

Source: U.S. Department of Commerce, Census (1990).

Patterns of residential segregation persist throughout the United States, isolating ethnic minorities, particularly African Americans who were the most segregated group in both 1980 and 1990. Latinos ranked second, while Asians were more highly segregated than American Indians. Patterns of racial segregation either remained stable or declined modestly for blacks during the period from 1980–1990. Changes in residential segregation during the decade were relatively small and evolutionary. Since 1940, there has been a dramatic, but unheralded, reduction of racial and ethnic differentials in high school completion as noted in Table 2.2. All groups have dramatically increased their high school graduation rates since 1940.

Response of Receiving Communities

Many people in the communities receiving immigrants during the most recent influx of newcomers to our shores were often less than warm in their reception of the new residents. For example, the 1993 Empire State Survey, a poll conducted by survey researchers using a random digit telephone dialing technique, yielded a number of negative findings. More than 60 percent of those surveyed believed that the influx of 854,000 immigrants to New York City in the 1980s was too great, and a similar percentage believed the city was a worse place to live because of this influx. Interestingly, more than half those surveyed believed that the United States was no longer a "melting pot" and that current immigrants were likely to retain their national identities. It is not clear that those responding saw the retention of national identities as a positive good, however. In fact, while 85 percent believed that migration had benefitted U.S. society in the past, only 41 percent believed that current migration was a national good (*New York Times*, October 18, 1993, p. A12).

At the time this poll was conducted, New York City was still reeling from the bombing of the World Trade Center some six months earlier, and the nation as a whole was suffering the lowest point in its overall sense of social well being in two decades. Despite the prevailing negative stereotypes held of new immigrants by many U.S. residents, the *U.S. News* (October 4, 1993) study showed a profile of reasonably well educated, self-supporting people whose forms of livelihood did not represent jobs wrested from American workers and whose political views bore a striking similarity to those held by American-born citizens.

As noted earlier in this chapter, by far the largest group of immigrants during the 1980s came from Mexico. These individuals numbered 2.1 million, averaged less than a ninth grade education and earned an average $18,233 per year, although only 2 percent received welfare payments. The second largest immigrant population is the Filipino settlers who, on average, are college graduates earning $17,645 a year. Many Filipino women pursue careers as nurses or in other professional positions in the field of medicine. Puerto Rican migrants, numbering 400,000, constitute the third largest group. Unlike most other immigrants in the 1980s, Puerto Ricans targeted the nation's East Coast rather than California, Texas, or Florida.

In addition to the new immigrants, other groups including African-Americans, Native Americans and urban Appalachians continue to fare less well in schools than their Anglo counterparts. As mentioned earlier, these groups have been characterized as victims of forces of colonization and exploitation relatively early in U.S. history (Ogbu, 1974). However, in recent years these groups have successfully mobilized community resources through advocacy and political lobbying, building strong local ties while often maintaining strong lateral ties, a point we return to in Chapter 8. Adhering to a strict characterization of one or another of these groups as a "caste-like" minority is no longer an altogether accurate or useful characterization.

In the next part of this chapter and in Chapter 4, we will discuss socio-historical and political circumstances attending patterns of settlement for the groups considered here. We do this separately for each group because we hold to the belief that a more critical understanding of current conditions is bound to an analysis of history, community, and social relations (Walsh, 1991). While we focus on commonalities of experience throughout this book, we also acknowledge the importance of understanding the unique significance in children's school success of growing up Hmong, Puerto Rican, or African-American, particularly, though not exclusively, when Marketplace English is not always resident in such families. The remainder of this chapter, then, considers patterns of settling in and gaining political power as immigrants establish themselves in the United States.

PATTERNS OF SETTLING IN OF THE "NEW" IMMIGRANTS

More than 50 years ago, a sociological study of immigrant youth, *Italian or American? The Second Generation in Conflict* (Childe, 1943) sought to analyze the socialization processes involving one ethnic group's Americanization. The pressures leading to compliance with ethnic group values and behaviors and those pushing young Italian Americans to embrace an identity as "Americans" were the focus of the book. During the 1920s, post-World War I xenophobia restricted the great tides of immigration that had flowed from Central Europe to U.S. shores from

1865 onward. As a consequence, the number of newcomers declined rapidly and the subsequent emergence of new immigrant communities, still vigorous in the post-World War II era, went largely unnoticed.

The United States has again become a country of immigration. In 1990, the foreign-born population reached 19.8 million, or 7.9 percent of the total. Although still a far cry from the situation 70 years earlier when immigrants accounted for 14 percent of the American population, the impact of contemporary immigration is both significant and growing. Numerous publications have called attention to this revival and sought its causes, first, in a growing, "restructured," global American economy and, second, in the liberalized provisions of the 1965 Immigration Act, legislation designed to expand the U.S. economy in the context of the Vietnam War. This legislation abolished the restriction on immigration that had virtually confined the flow of new immigrants to northern Europe.

A common exercise is to compare this "new" immigration with the "old" inflow at the turn of the twentieth century. Similarities include the overwhelming urban destination of most newcomers, their concentration in a few port cities, and their willingness to accept the lowest-paid jobs. Differences are more frequently stressed, however, for the "old" immigration was overwhelmingly European and white, while the present inflow is, to a large extent, non-white and comes from countries of the Third World. After two-and-a-half decades of accelerated immigration, the "new" second generation is expected to grow rapidly and to surpass its former peak of roughly 28 million (in 1940) sometime during the 1990s. Part of this growth is due to the relative youth of the new immigration, which has brought the median age of the foreign-born population down from 52 in 1970 to 37 in 1990. Mexicans, Salvadorans, Haitians, and Vietnamese, four of the fastest growing immigrant minorities, are also the youngest, with median ages of about 30. Up to 70 percent of these groups is formed by immigrants aged 15 to 44 (U.S. Bureau of the Census, 1993).

These groups, as well as other Latin American and Asian immigrants, have high levels of fertility, which is the second reason for the rapid growth of this "new" second generation of immigrant-born children. Compared to the birthrate of 1.7 children per lifetime among white native-born women, those of Mexican-American women average 2.9 and of Vietnamese women, 3.4. In the late eighties, native-born women averaged 67.2 live births per 1,000 while the foreign-born averaged 96. Mexican, Filipino, Korean, and Indian women surpassed this figure, exceeding 110 per 1,000 (U.S. Bureau of the Census, 1991).

The condition of this rapidly growing segment of the population, its economic future, and social adaptation is not analogous to the experiences of the prior peak second generation who grew up in the period between the two World Wars. Over 85 percent of their immigrant parents were Europeans, and they came of age at a time when the American economy looked very different than it does today. At present, 67 percent of the foreign-born come from Latin America and Asia and close to half (48.8%) are classified as non-white (U.S. Bureau of the Census, 1993;

Rumbaut, 1994). Moreover, they are coming at a time of rapid change in the American economy, when an increasing polarization of the labor market has reduced opportunities for sustained occupational advancement across generations (Harrison & Bluestone, 1988; Sassen, 1991).

Segmented Assimilation

The leading sociologist of immigration in the United States today, Alejandro Portes, has identified an emerging paradox in the study of today's second generation of immigrants—the peculiar forms that assimilation has taken for some of its members. Segmented assimilation refers to the alternative paths taken by second generation immigrant children. Acculturation to American outlooks and norms does not represent, as in the past, the first step toward social and economic mobility, but may lead in the exact opposite direction. This was illustrated in the course of Portes' fieldwork by the experiences of second-generation Haitian, Nicaraguan, and Mexican children. Their parents, almost without exception, try to instill in them a sense of national pride, high aspiration, and the value of education. However, the immigrants' low-incomes force them to live in or near the inner-city. In school, immigrant children clash with a very different peer outlook. They are often derided for their foreignness, their docility to school authorities, and their aspirations (Matute-Bianchi, 1986; Portes, 1994; Rumbaut, 1990).

A common message received by second generation children is the devaluation of education as a vehicle for the economic advancement of minorities, a message that directly contradicts immigrant parents' expectations. As immigrant families attempt to rein in their children's consumption patterns, while simultaneously encouraging them to succeed in school, the message that these youth receive from school peers is frequently the opposite (Portes and Zhou, 1993). As a result, in anthropologist Matute-Bianchi's (1986) words, many "learn not to learn."

Portes' evidence indicates that this path of downward assimilation is common but by no means universal. Other children of immigrants, mostly those attending mixed suburban schools but including some in the inner-city, manage to follow the traditional pattern of acculturation to middle-class mainstream norms and to integrate them successfully with their parents' aspirations. Still others—exemplified by Cuban-American children attending private schools in Miami—experience a process of bicultural adaptation where the immigrant community's language, values, and goals play a dominant role (Portes and Schauffler, 1994).

Portes (1994) argues that each immigrant and refugee group forms "highly dense communities" in locales where they settle. Thus, Haitians and Cubans in Miami, and Mexicans and Vietnamese in southern California each formed their own institutional fabrics to support their economic development as well as other dimensions of their lives such as their children's educational experiences. However, because of the more favorable treatment they received as immigrants and refugees (including the granting of citizenship after one year's residency), their greater stability and longevity, the Cuban community in Miami was able to create "a network of parochial and private schools . . . [which insulate] Cuban American children from contact with downtrodden groups as well as from outside discrimination" (Portes, 1994). In addition, these schools were staffed by teachers who are bilingual, share a common heritage with their students, and reinforce parental values in addition to keeping children isolated from peers who might ridicule them. Unfortunately, the less materially provisioned Haitians in the same city struggle in schools where they are often mocked for their language patterns and folkways. Similarly, Mexican immigrants in southern California, although benefitting from longer residence in the United States than their "new immigrant" counterparts, continue to hold jobs as menial workers, principally in agricultural jobs and also to have less well developed institutional structures than the recently arrived nearby Asian populations. This latter group follows traditions that include creating strong individual enterprenuerial business pursuits in combination with internal regulation of these pursuits imposed by boards of directors similar to the *tongs* that regulated trade in the first Chinatown of San Francisco in the 19th century. We will return to these themes in this and the following chapter and in the course of laying out the stories told in Chapters 4 and 5.

Gaining Political Power

In his moving account of young Central American refugees in southern California high schools, Marcelo Suarez-Orozco (1989) describes the perceptions held by many U.S. citizens of virtually all ethnic groups. Although Suarez-Orozco is referring to Hispanic groups, many of his observations apply to a broad range of concerns related to minority status and adaptation in a plural society. A fundamental problem facing all non-Anglo groups is the tendency of Anglo teachers, politicians and other powerful figures to minimize differences *among* various ethnic groups that may be present in their classroom. To counter this position, Suarez-Orozco argues:

> Mexican-Americans, Mejicanos, Puerto Rican Americans, Cuban Americans, Americans of South American origin and the more recent arrivals from Central America are *distinct populations, each facing different realities, each with its own subtle set of interpersonal concerns, world view and adaptation.* (Suarez-Orozco, 1989, p. 157, emphasis added)

We agree with Portes, Suarez-Orozco, Ronald Takaki, Paul Robeson, Jr. and others who argue that the melting pot ideology stressing the homogeneity and lack of difference among people serves largely to disenfranchise non-Anglo groups. Urging cultural uniformity and the need for the conservative restoration of European classical contexts (Bloom, 1990) legitimates traditional patriarchal ideals. Such conservative strategies undermine the growing awareness among different ethnic and racial groups (and among women) that their empowerment hinges on their ability to create personal identities and cultural niches where they may sense their strengths and create their own possible futures. At the same time that many Anglo citizens discount cultural differences, they focus on both ethnic and class differences almost exclusively when making critical political and educational decisions. Unfortunately, we might add, little systematic research has been done on the extent to which gender—a third factor—affects decision making.

Voting patterns in many cities where there are large populations of poor and minority groups illustrate the tendency of middle class Anglo voters to support candidates who resemble themselves. This pattern illustrates what Meier and Stewart and others have termed the "group competition" view or "power thesis" of groups in society. According to this view, "groups compete with each other for tangible benefits in the political process," creating inter-group rivalries and conflict (Meier & Stewart, 1991). Meier and Stewart explain in the case of Hispanic Americans:

> The power thesis is directly applicable to achieve political representation. In 1985 the Latino median family income was only 20% of the Anglo median family income; Latino graduation rates were only 63% of Anglo rates. If social class differences are a reason why Anglos might react negatively to Hispanics, then Hispanics who have made it in Anglo society would be perceived as less of a threat. (Meier & Stewart, 1991, p. 9)

There is evidence in voting patterns to suggest that the power thesis operated in a number of city council and school board elections throughout the country in the 1980s. For example, in Crystal City, Texas, Mexican-American candidates eventually were elected to fill all the seats on that town's city council and school board in the 1970s. However, it was not until Anglos were confronted by threats from unrepresented Mexican-American voters that this occurred. Crystal City has a large working class population of both groups. In the Crystal City case, according to Meier and Stewart:

> . . . the tactics of the Anglo population, when confronted with a working class Mexican-American political revolt, are revealing. Rather than continue to run Anglo candidates, they ran Mexican-American candidates with business ties and higher levels of education. Anglo support went overwhelmingly for middle class Hispanic candidates rather than those perceived as lower class. (Meier & Stewart, 1991, p. 10)

The same logic that explains the success of middle class Mexican-Americans in achieving political power in Crystal City also supports the notion that Anglo voters are more likely to support middle class Hispanics than black candidates with working class roots if presented with this choice. Social class linked to ethnicity conveys a powerful political message in U.S. society.

Election to city councils and school boards, then, is affected by minority group status, level of education (as a marker for social class), the proportion of other minority groups in the population as well as whether or not the minority group represented by the candidate in question has previously achieved representation in other political institutions. In other words, although we as a society may ignore social class, ethnic differences, and relative political power in our polite conversation, in the voting booth these become key factors in determining our behavior.

This chapter has offered the view that, in recent years, the demographic profile of the nation has undergone major changes as a result of changing patterns of family structural arrangements, alterations in the economic fortunes of the population, and most profoundly as a consequence of immigration. Far from seeing this latter shift through a single lens of something termed the "immigration experience," we argue that patterns of arrival and settlement are highly varied—some seeking political refuge, others economic opportunity. It is critical for educators to understand the particular exosystem or milieu that is established by recent arrivees in specific locales throughout the U.S.

3

Multiple Realities: A Brief Socio-historical Overview

In this chapter we present an overview of "different realities" confronting both new immigrants and other groups that, according to Ogbu's scheme, might be considered older "caste-like" minorities. According to our understanding of these groups—Appalachians and blacks, in particular—their geographic mobility, collective organizational strength at both local community and national levels, and their strong sense of the importance of their collective lived histories points to both their strength and resiliency despite the oftentimes quite blatant measures taken to politically and economically disenfranchise group members.

The accounts that follow are hardly definitive of the often harrowing and always complex experiences undergone by these populations. All non-Anglo groups have experienced a number of issues stemming from "primary cultural differences" from the majority Anglo population that were present before they came into contact (Ogbu, 1987; Suarez-Orozco, 1989). These issues make it possible to begin to formulate some general applications to learning and schooling. However, our focus here is upon the unique sagas characterizing these groups' lived realities. Thus, the reader will quickly realize that the following accounts are not constructed in parallel fashion. Rather, the historical portrait of American Indians emphasizes the genocide waged against these indigenous peoples from early in the nation's settlement and development by whites.

As another example, the picture of the urban Appalachian experience is caught up with an account of this group's settlement in cities such as Cincinnati, Columbus, Cleveland, Chicago, and Detroit following the out-migration from what we now refer to as the Appalachian Region following the post-World War II coal mining bust. What has been attempted in each case is to draw upon the relevant social, economic, and historical details that seem to encapsulate each particular group's experience. We will go on in the next four chapters to provide vignettes focused on stories drawn from the lives of students whose identities are tied to the histories we outline next.

LATINOS IN THE UNITED STATES

While Latinos in 1987 were the nation's second largest minority group constituting approximately 8 percent of the total population, by the year 2047 they will be the largest U.S. minority. This is largely due to both higher fertility rates (60% higher than for non-Latino groups) and continued migration. Current population estimates for persons of "Spanish origin" residing in the United States exclude "the millions of Latinos who have crossed the southern border without legal documentation" (Suarez-Orozco, 1989). Throughout their history, all Latinos, with the arguable exception of Cuban-Americans, have been incorporated into U.S. politics following military conflict and have then subsequently voluntarily immigrated to the United States.

Mexican Americans

Mexican Americans constitute the largest subgroup of Latinos, some 60 percent of the total according to 1980 census figures. Incorporated into the United States first by conquest and subsequently through immigration, this group has also had the longest period of residency (Meier & Stewart, 1991). Texas, Arizona, New Mexico, Colorado, and California were annexed from Mexico following the Mexican-American War and the Treaty of Guadalupe Hidalgo in 1848 and residents were granted U.S. citizenship. Although agricultural needs, particularly in such labor-intensive crops as cotton, grapes, lemons, and other fruits, avocados, lettuce, and other vegetables spurred large numbers to migrate from Mexico from the late nineteenth century on, not all live in rural areas today. Approximately 80 percent of Mexican Americans reside in large cities, particularly in Texas and California and also Chicago.

Both legal and illegal immigration from Mexico to the United States continues today primarily because wages in the United States are as much as seven times greater than in Mexico (Estrada et al., 1988). Many communities such as Carpinteria, near Santa Barbara, California, have experienced development from an exclusively crops-producing region in the 1890s to widespread suburbanization in the mid-1920s, continuing suburban development in the 1980s, and diversified economic growth with continued reliance upon agriculture in more recent decades.

Delgado-Gaitan's (1990) profile of employment in Carpinteria shows that, among that city's Mexican American residents, employment as laborers, and as agriculture and service industry workers predominates. Successive waves of immigrants built upon the earliest experiences in communities like Carpinteria to create opportunities for their children, grandchildren, and great-grandchildren.

Puerto Ricans

Like Mexican Americans, Puerto Rican Americans, the second largest group of Latinos in the United States, have settled in the States largely through initial incorporation (following the Spanish-American War) and more recently through immigration. Currently, approximately 14 percent of Latino residents in the United States are Puerto Rican. Puerto Rico is a U.S. territory, politically organized as a self-governing commonwealth, a status it has had since 1952 (Meier & Stewart, 1991). Although Puerto Ricans are technically citizens of the United States, those who reside on the island do not have voting rights in U.S. presidential elections and are represented in Congress by one non-voting member in the House of Representatives.

Unlike Cuban Americans, Puerto Ricans maintain a fluid relationship with their island homeland. As a result, Puerto Ricans households are overwhelmingly Spanish speaking. Many U.S. residents return to the island when the economy turns up and return to the States when it declines (Bean & Tienda, 1987; Meier & Stewart, 1991).

In her account of the "struggle for voice" by Puerto Rican Americans, Catherine Walsh shows how U.S. policies have been aimed at destroying national solidarity and creating "the patriotism of the colonial" (Walsh, 1991). Walsh describes the disengagement from self, social world and culture that Puerto Rican American school children constantly confront in classrooms where reference is made disparagingly to their "poor study habits, low attendance, depressed home life and lack of motivation" (Walsh, 1991). One consequence, as Meier and Stewart's (1991) analysis of Puerto Rican political engagement shows, is that despite their settlement in "electorally strategic major cities" in the United States such as Boston, New York, and Chicago, Puerto Ricans' political development has been slight. Meier and Stewart argue that there are reasons for this dilemma:

1. Migration between the United States and Puerto Rico is fluid. Puerto Ricans come to the mainland when the economy on the island declines, but return when the "home" economy improves. As a consequence, island politics take on greater meaning in general than do politics stateside.
2. Cities serving as sites for Puerto Rican migration have well organized local political machines. The inclusion of Puerto Ricans in city government structures both alienates Anglo ethnics and has historically been unnecessary in order for machine politicians to maintain control in New York, Chicago, and Boston—major sites of Puerto Rican settlement in the United States.

3. The Office of Commonwealth, first developed by Puerto Ricans in New York
    and later in other cities served both to aid newcomers and later to buffer them
    from social, political and economic threats. The unfortunate outcome is that
    Puerto Ricans were prevented from developing political solutions to their
    problems through participation in political institutions such as city government
    and the school board.

Cubans

Unlike Mexicans and Puerto Ricans, Cuban Americans, who constitute approximately 6 percent of the United States' Latino population, initially came to the United
States following a major political upheaval in their government. The establishment
of Fidel Castro's political power in 1959 ended the regime of Batista and established
an economic policy hostile to middle and upper-middle class Cubans. In the 1950s
these individuals began to arrive in the United States and continued to come and
bring their financial assets with them until the Bay of Pigs debacle in 1960.

Actually, the political climate of this period in the United States suggested that
what is today regarded by some as a rather bizarre attempt to secure the Cuban
homeland was, in 1960, not unreasonable given earlier U.S. efforts in Guatemala
in 1954 to overthrow a left-wing government in that country. First and foremost,
both Republican and Democrat presidential candidates in 1960 had pledged support
to assist U.S.-based Cuban efforts. In addition, a strong political organizational
structure among Cuban refugees was firmly and actively dedicated to the removal
of Castro. Following the Bay of Pigs, Cuban immigrants focused their political
efforts on winning increased influence locally. Their efforts were facilitated by the
favorable status they enjoyed in the United States in comparison to other Latino
groups that led to higher naturalization rates than most other immigrant groups
(Meier & Stewart, 1991). Meier and Stewart illustrate the political gains made by
Cuban Americans with the case of Miami city politics. By 1967, only seven years
following the attempted island coup, two Cuban American candidates ran (though
unsuccessfully) for city council. In 1973 the first Cuban American was elected,
followed by a second successful candidate in 1979; by 1985 not only did Cuban
Americans constitute a majority of Miami's city council, they also held positions
as mayor and city manager of the city.

Interestingly, unlike Mexican Americans in particular, Cuban Americans have
not been actively engaged in pressing for representation in formal educational
structures such as the school board or the administrative ranks of the public schools.
This is somewhat surprising, perhaps, since relatively fewer Cuban Americans,
compared to Mexican Americans as a group, consider English their first language.
However, at least four sociocultural distinctions explain Cuban Americans' disinterest in public schools: (a) the economic resources upper middle class Cuban
Americans brought with them initially, (b) the large investment made by the U.S.
government to settle Cuban immigrants, (c) the generous policies established by

the government to provide citizenship in a year's time following Cuban settlement, and (d) the strong commitment to Catholic schools that the earliest immigrants brought with them. In this connection, Meier and Stewart point out that 36 percent of these refugees had completed high school or some college compared to only 4 percent of the resident Cuban population at the time of pre-Mariel immigration. (See pp. 114–115.)

Central Americans

Immigration from the war-torn countries of El Salvador and Guatemala escalated during the 1980s as atrocities and terror increased in both countries. Most of the immigration from these countries was by way of Mexico and southern California. Approximately 67,000 Salvadoreans legally immigrated to the United States between 1971 and 1985; while both illegal and legal immigration from Guatemala also accelerated during this period. It is estimated that approximately 200,000 Guatemalans have taken up residency in the United States since the 1950s (Suarez-Orozco, 1989).

In both cases immigration has followed traditional patterns; it has been motivated by political violence and economic scarcity and it has escalated during times of particularly severe oppression and terror. Suarez-Orozco, whose psycho-social study of young men who had fled intolerable conditions of political repression, torture and hidden murders, summarized his informants' accounts of their struggles as follows:

> Without exception, the informants reported having left Central America, El Salvador, Nicaragua, Guatemala- *por la situación.* They used these simple words to refer to a nightmarish world of war, disappearances, systematic torture, random killings, bodies in the streets with political messages carved in the flesh, kidnapping, forced recruitment into wars foreign to their hearts, and economical scarcity. Political terror has again become the idiom for social consensus in Central American history. The numbers of politically motivated killings appear meaningless when checked against the desperate faces of the survivors. (Suarez-Orozco, 1989, p. 51)

Estimates of the numbers slaughtered in these countries range as high as 100,000 in 1984 and have continued until just recently to mount.

As agricultural economies with past histories of earlier Spanish colonial rule and later dependency upon the United States for aid, conditions in both El Salvador and Guatemala can be viewed as a classic struggle between the haves and have nots. Peasants in these predominantly rural countries, suffering near destitution (the average income for all Salvadoreans in 1984 was approximately $680 U.S. dollars), were organized by activist Roman Catholic priests in the 1970s. The vivid images of the brutal murders of four Maryknoll Sister missionaries in the 1980s arrested the attention of many U.S. citizens who, for the first time, recognized the brutality of the massive genocide occurring in Central America (Suarez-Orozco, 1980).

As was true for many earlier immigrants and, to some extent, for Cuban Americans, many Central American immigrants dream of returning to their countries, send large sums of money to relatives who remain behind, and retain their "core cultural values," a process Margaret Gibson and others have termed a strategy of "accommodation without assimilation." Similarly, parents value education and perceive opportunities for their children in the United States. This is in marked contrast to their native countries where "survival and success were strictly limited to prior wealth or *por apellido* (because of your last name) and to networks of relations with people in good positions" (Suarez-Orozco, 1989). Hard work, individual effort and persistence alone are believed by many to assure success in the United States. In Suarez-Orozco's conversations with the young men, they point to examples in the media such as the case of Vietnamese girl who had arrived in the United States as a refugee 10 years before graduating from West Point. Like Cuban Americans, Central American immigrants have adopted a rather conservative political belief system. If they face discrimination that inhibits their mobility, this may change. As we noted earlier in Chapter 3, Latinos and American Indians have characteristically experienced the least geographical mobility of any group and thus are likely to encounter reduced economic opportunity, especially if the U.S. economy tends to expand and contract differentially by region as it has in the recent past.

LATINO GROUPS TODAY

Under current economic conditions in the United States, some Latino groups, particularly Mexican Americans and Puerto Ricans, have faced increasing discrimination in both schooling and employment. In the port-of-entry neighborhood of Magnolia Park, a Mexican American community in Houston, troubles beginning with the oil bust in the early 1980s have escalated as blue collar jobs have disappeared in the wake of the nation's massive economic shift from manufacturing to service economy jobs on the one hand and high tech jobs on the other. While federal programs were used to create a tremendous nuclear arsenal and defense system, social programs were eradicated. For example, in 1987 defense spending in the United States amounted to 60 cents on the dollar from taxes received by the federal government. During the same period the economy foundered, thousands became homeless and job creation was limited to the service sector. While many lucrative, union-supported jobs in industry evaporated, jobs paying the minimum wage, providing no benefits and occupying under 40 hours per week accounted for the lion's share of job growth. Moreover, within labor sectors or particular industries, vast wage disparities developed with those at the top in executive jobs earning huge wages in comparison with employees at the bottom of the organization's hierarchy. These economic realities were ignored in favor of a rhetoric emanating from the White House during the Reagan and Bush administrations emphasizing hard work, "just say no," and finding success "within."

In Houston during the 1980s there was a 50 percent loss of manufacturing jobs. Accompanying this trend—not surprisingly, given overall national trends—was a 75 percent increase in generally minimum wage, no-benefits service sector jobs (*New York Times*, January 19, 1992). This pattern predominates across the United States to the particular disadvantage of recent immigrants of Mexican descent. According to the U.S. Census Bureau in 1990, 26.2 percent of such families lived in poverty compared to 18.4 percent of families representing all other Latino groups and 11.6 percent of non-Latinos in the United States. Put another way, the median incomes for these groups also varied considerably with the median Mexican American household income at $8,874 compared to $9,861 for all other Latino groups and $11,885 among non-Latinos. These income figures are particularly discouraging when combined with the continuous decline of median family income for Latinos. While the Latinos suffered a decline of 5.7 percent between 1979 and 1988, black family income increased by 2.5 percent and white family income by 1.8 percent. Finally, the National Council of La Raza reported in 1988 that 50 percent of all Latinos had not completed high school compared to 33 percent of African Americans and 20 percent of whites in the United States.

The discussion here has highlighted the variation among members of a particular social category—Latinos. It has also shown how socioeconomic factors cannot be separated from a discussion of race and ethnicity. How long Central American refugees can cherish the American dream of upward mobility by dint of hard work and individual effort in the face of current social and economic conditions is not clear; prospects at the moment are not bright for Latino Americans generally.

ASIAN AMERICANS

In his lyrically written narrative of the history of Asian Americans, *Strangers from a Different Shore*, Ronald Takaki (paraphrasing Joy Kogara) shouts, "Their history bursts with telling," referring to the Asian peoples who, by the year 2000, will make up 4 percent of the total U.S. population. He is referencing the 1,079,000 Chinese, 1,025,000 Filipinos, 766,000 Japanese, 634,000 Vietnamese, 542,000 Koreans, 526,000 Asian Indians, 70,000 Hmong, 161,000 Cambodians and 169,000 other Asians who have come to U.S. shores since 1965. At that time federal legislation, the Immigration Act of 1965, allowed Asian immigrants and refugees to enter the United States on a non-quota basis, the first such opportunity for this population since the early 20th Century. While Latinos are a rapidly growing ethnic minority group in the United States today, proportionate to their numbers, the Asian American population is growing even more rapidly. For example, between 1970 and 1980s while the Latino American population grew by 38 percent, the Asian American population expanded by 143 percent (Takaki, 1989).

Why is the Asian American story a "history bursting with telling?" Takaki asserts that, of all groups who helped forge U.S. society, Asian Americans are those most often excluded from this society's written record. While researching documents including ledgers and account books kept by early Hawaiian and California farmers and landowners, Takaki was struck by orders written by these individuals for "bonemeal, canvas, Japanese laborers, macaroni, Chinamen" (Takaki, 1989). The easy commodification of human labor under the frontier's embryonic capitalism, demonstrates how "planters systematically developed an ethnically diverse work force as a mechanism of control." In Hawaii, for example, white landowners during the 1850s "used Chinese laborers to set an 'example' for the [native] Hawaiian workers. Managers hoped the Hawaiians would be 'naturally jealous' of the foreigners and 'ambitious to outdo them.'" (Takaki, 1989). This strategy was identical to that used by industrialists in Chicago and other northern cities during the 1920s and 1930s who hired newly arrived African American migrants from the South to break the union. The representation of "Orientals" as less than human was commonplace; they were a reserve employment pool to be used in backbreaking agricultural work and manufacturing including, most notably in the Chinese case, the construction of the transcontinental railroad line. Chinese, in fact, were 90 percent of the entire transcontinental railway workforce during the 1880s, although the living conditions and wages they received were on a scale lower than those received by white railroad builders (Takaki, 1989).

It is not surprising that historians also have slighted the contributions of Asian peoples to the development of U.S. society. Takaki notes:

> Many classics in the field of American history have also equated "American" with "white" or "European" in origin. In his prize winning study, *The Uprooted*, Harvard historian Oscar Handlin presented to use the book's subtitle—"The Epic Story of the Great Migration that Made the American People." Bret Handlin's "epic story" completely left out the "uprooted" from lands across the Pacific Ocean and the great migrations from Asia that also helped to make "the American people." (Takaki, 1989, p. 7)

We agree with Takaki's observation that such accounts of the story of our nation's past do damage to us as a people: "Eurocentric history serves no one. It only shrouds the pluralism that is America and that makes our nation so unique and thus the possibility of appreciating our rich racial and cultural diversity remains a dream deferred" (Takaki, 1989).

Chinese Americans

The passage of many Asians to the United States has generally borne the face of both political and economic motivations. The development of California after the 1848 treaty with Mexico was largely predicated on that state's importance as the acknowledged link to Asia and particularly to China. Gateways were soon opened to immigration from distant shores across the Pacific (see Takaki, 1993). At this time political adversity in China included the British Opium Wars as well as localized rural conflicts. This situation made the United States a desirable destination. According to Takaki, "Many migrants were also fleeing from the turmoil of peasant rebellions such as the Red Turban Rebellion and the bloody strife between the Punti (Local People) and the Hakkas (Guest People) over possession of the fertile delta lands" (Takaki, 1993).

In addition to both British colonialism and local political skirmishes, the Chinese suffered a host of economic disasters during this period including floods and crop failures, particularly affecting rice farming. Under these adverse conditions, the lure of *Gam Saan*, "Gold Mountain," compelled the migration of numbers of Chinese, mostly men, to America which was seen as a land of limitless opportunity. The comparison of these earlier Chinese immigrants with those who have recently faced inhuman conditions in the foul holds of ships bound for U.S. shores is striking. Like their counterparts in the nineteenth century, today's young (mostly male) arrivals from rural places in China emerge from the most desperate conditions suffered during their passage with smiles that demonstrate how profoundly optimistic they remain about the good life.

Many from China in the nineteenth century made the passage across the Pacific to California through the credit-ticket system. This system entailed the negotiation of a loan from a broker for the cost of transportation to the United States. The loan with interest was then paid off from the salary earned as a laborer in the mines or, most notably, on the transcontinental railroad. Takaki urges that we see this passage not as stereotypes and popular mythology would have us believe but rather as a journey engaged by those who freely desired a better life. A popular folk song of the time captures the spirit of these passages:

> In the second reign year of Haambring [1852], a trip to Gold Mountain was made. With a pillow on my shoulder, I began my perilous journey. Sailing a boat with bamboo poles across the sea, Leaving behind wife and sisters in search of money, No longer lingering with the woman in the bedroom, No longer paying respects to parents at home. (Quoted in Takaki, 1993, p. 193)

Although California was the recipient of the greatest influx of Chinese immigrants, a surprisingly large number settled elsewhere throughout the United States: By 1870 there were 63,000 Chinese in the United States. Most of them—77 percent—were living in California, but they were elsewhere in the West as well as in the Southwest, New England, and the South.

The Chinese constituted a sizable proportion of the population in certain areas; 29 percent in Montana and 9 percent in California (Takaki, 1993). Although their initial reception was relatively warm, when Chinese laborers in particular industries became so numerous as to be a threat to white American privilege, repression through taxation, unfair wage structures and exclusion became the norm. Far from passively accepting these conditions, members of the Chinese American community readily adopted strategies to compete for fair economic conditions.

In 1880, fruit pickers in Santa Clara County went out on strike for higher wages. After the 1882 Chinese Exclusion Act reduced the supply of farm labor, Chinese agricultural workers demanded higher rates for their wages (Takaki, 1993). By organizing themselves as members of labor unions, many Chinese-Americans succeeded in bargaining for more equitable pay. Other strategies included the formation of associations such as the Chinese Six Companies. These associations initially served the economic networks of Chinese merchants in San Francisco, but subsequently became the focal point for rising Chinese political activity in the latter part of the nineteenth century. The passage of the Burlingame Treaty in 1868 assured the "free migration and immigration" of Chinese to the United States as visitors, traders, or permanent residents and the right of Chinese in the United States to enjoy the same privileges, immunities and exceptions with respect to travel or residence as others (Takaki, 1993).

Nonetheless, Chinese immigrants in the latter part of the 19th century faced harsh conditions of economic, social and political repression as a result of the blatant racism that accompanied their competition for scarce jobs with increasing numbers of immigrants from Ireland, Italy, and Central Europe. Many saw the importance of settling in colonies that would serve as communities for residency, recreation and trade. In addition to the Chinese Six Companies organization, *Tongs* or secret societies also were formed as centers for promotion and protection. Less popularly recognized beyond the Chinese community, but nevertheless an important source of Chinese identity, *Tongs* were associations that arranged the passage to the United States for members of families, clans and villages, organized temples, clubhouses and social centers and generally assisted the staged migration of thousands from China to the United States. They served other purposes as well, transmitting letters back to remote areas in China, overseeing the administration of the credit ticket system, and assisting with all phases of adjustment to the new country. From the white majority perspective, these organizations contributed to stereotypes of Chinese Americans as mysterious, clannish, and engaged in illicit business activities.

In the case of recent Chinese immigrants, the full picture is clear only when we consider the differences between the "old" and "new" immigrants and the worlds they inhabit. Prior to the passage of the 1965 immigration legislation, Chinese immigrants to New York had expected to return to their native land. Most of these "sojourners" were males who had left homes in the rural provinces to seek their fortunes, after which they planned to rejoin their families in China. After the passage of the immigration legislation, the nature of the Chinese immigrant population changed rather dramatically.

Because the 1965 legislation abolished the "national origins" quotas in favor of a system of preferences "whereby immediate relatives, skilled and unskilled workers, refugees, scientists and technical personnel were listed under different categories of preference," "some eighty-five years of bias against the Chinese" (Wong, 1987) was finally addressed. More than 200,000 individuals of Chinese ancestry currently reside in New York, approximately half of them in Chinatown, the rest in Brooklyn, and in the Jackson Heights, Flushing, and Elmhurst sections of Queens. Many more individuals with professional degrees and experience, including "some extremely wealthy individuals from Hong Kong who have fled with their capital" have altered the social and economic landscape of New York City (Wong, 1987).

Not surprisingly, the language spoken in New York's Chinatown, particularly the language utilized by shopkeepers and their customers, has changed along with the population. According to Bernard Wong (1987) whose fieldwork has involved him in the Chinese community in New York for more than 15 years,

> Before 1965 Chinatown was dominated by people from Kwangtun Province, mostly from the county of Toysan. Not surprisingly, although people from Kwangtung still make up more than half of the population, there are also many people from North China, Shanghai, and the cities of Hong Kong, Fukien, and Taiwan. Standard Cantonese, as spoken in the cities of Hong Kong, Macao, and Canton, is now the lingua franca of Chinatown. Speakers of other dialects such as Mandarin, Fukiense, Shanghainese, and Hakka have to learn the Cantonese dialect of Chinatown in order to communicate with shopkeepers and coworkers. Mandarin speakers, however, are more likely to be understood in Chinatown today than before 1965 because many young Cantonese also learn the national language (Mandarin) and because Chinatown has many Mandarin-speaking immigrants from Taiwan and mainland China. (Wong, 1987, p. 245)

Language differences in the New York Chinatown community are rampant, contributing to the difficulty many new immigrants have in communicating within the Chinese enclave. It is not surprising that Dan and Mei, whose vignette we will encounter in Chapter 5, each of whom spoke Mandarin in addition to their native dialect and English, made an easier adjustment than other family members who experienced tremendous frustration and unhappiness in their new country, handicapped by language issues and the inadequacy of the social service system to address their concerns.

Chinese Americans have been enormously successful in many respects and along with other Asians have, in fact, suffered from being labeled the "model minority." As in the 19th century when Chinese laborers were hired to replace "unruly" and unionizing "others," the "model minority" in contemporary U.S. society is often used as a call for a renewed commitment to the traditional values of hard work, thrift and industry. The appeal of the "family values" of Asian Americans generally was particularly strong during the Reagan and Bush era.

In their comparative study of Chinese, Korean, and Anglo children, Schneider and Lee (1990) learned through interviews and lengthy written responses that both Chinese and Korean children were aware of their parents' high expectations for their academic success, associated the achievement of good grades with their parents' honor, pride, and happiness, and had their high academic expectations reinforced by their classroom teachers. Nonetheless, many children felt burdened by their designation as a "model minority," avoided social activities in favor of studying alone and assumed tremendous pressure to achieve beyond their parents' status. Chinese, Korean and other Asian groups are thus often identified as "middle-man minorities" that function as a buffer between Anglo society and the minority groups who occupy the bottom rungs of the ladder. Teachers, they say, are the key to eliminating the stereotypes that lead to such rigid hierarchical patterns of achievement.

Other Asian Immigrants and Refugees

In the current migration flows, Filipino Americans constitute the largest Asian immigrant populations. During the decade of the 1980s approximately 450,000 Filipinos arrived in the United States. While the pattern of settlement in the United States was similar to that of other Asian groups, what is perhaps most distinctive about this population is their status as professional workers. Indeed, the Philippines has been the major source of foreign-trained nurses now at work in the United States. Following the 1965 Immigration Act, quotas of immigrants from Asia were eliminated and channels were created for the relatively easy flow of skilled, well educated workers as immigrants. The Philippines has maintained close and extensive ties with the United States for more than 100 years through trade agreements, foreign assistance, and the establishment of military bases. During the Vietnam War, the Philippines was seen as a strategic location for both the staging of troops into Southeast Asia and away from the battlefield. The development of an educated medical force was encouraged with a resulting expansion of nursing education facilities in the Philippines. Today, more nurses and their families who wish to do so are actually unable to migrate to the United States, a source of frustration for many. In this case as in others touching upon the lives of Asian groups, activism and the more vocal presence of ethnic-professional interest groups on the U.S. scene is likely to be important in the near future (Wei, 1995).

AMERICAN INDIANS

If there is any doubt that ours is a nation capable of massive genocide, the case of the once numerous tribal groups of American Indians surely should serve to remove it. Demographers, ethnohistorians, anthropologists and sociologists have written eloquently and persuasively about tribal groups whose devastation throughout our history speaks to the horrors of a colonizing force. Five centuries of systematic and wanton destruction throughout the United States have decimated a once thriving indigenous population.

Based on his exhaustive research, the demographer Russell Thornton (1987) calculates that "the aboriginal population of the Western Hemisphere circa 1492 numbered at least 72 million and probably slightly more" (Thornton, 1987). The population of the area corresponding to the coterminous United States was, of course, smaller—in the range of approximately five million at the time of Columbus' arrival. There are widely varying estimates of American Indian population size at this time and during subsequent periods of U.S. history. In part these variations can be attributed to the methods used by demographers to judge these figures. In large part, however, estimates are affected by what Thornton and others term "political bias."

Proponents of a "pro-European" characterization of the settlement by Anglos of the continental United States tend to be guided by far smaller estimates of the size of the indigenous population, regarding "Europeans as colonizing a vast land with fewer than 1,000,000 [such] people, and the subsequent demise or decline of the sparse native population . . . not seen as a tragedy of great magnitude" (Johnson, 1983, p. 137). It is, nonetheless, readily apparent from the analyses of the demise and virtual disappearance of native peoples, that forces for their destruction both originated in and were propelled by events stemming from the arrival of European colonists in the years following Columbus' voyage. We turn to an account of these events next.

The decline of American Indian populations in the area equivalent to the coterminous states was nothing short of a disastrous "demographic collapse" of a once numerous and varied population. It is important to recognize that "American Indian" is a label "at odds not only with the geographical facts, but also in its implied uniformity, with the subjective perceptions and sociological realities of the inhabitants themselves." Not surprisingly, the distinctions and differences among Indians were lost upon the newcomers from Europe, who regarded European civilization as embodying high culture and intellectual achievement in addition to religious and political power. By contrast, inhabitants of the New World colony were seen as subhuman, of less worth than the animals Europeans brought with them.

According to demographic analyses, the population of more than five million American Indians present in 1492 had declined to 600,000 by 1800, the date of the first reasonably accurate census, and was further reduced to 250,000 by the beginning of the 20th century, a decline of approximately 1.25 million per century over the four hundred years in question. With the enhancement in the 20th century of American Indian political resources and power, the native populations have begun to rebound. However, this relatively recent phenomenon is overshadowed by the four centuries' long devastation by disease, warfare, genocide, removal and relocation, and attendant destruction of native ways of life (Thornton, 1987).

Historians and demographers have characterized early European colonizing activities as principally a medical conquest of the indigenous American Indian peoples. Thornton (1987) describes the results of their destruction by epidemics of small pox, measles, the bubonic plague, cholera, typhoid, venereal diseases, respiratory disease, and other arthropod-borne diseases such as malaria and yellow fever. The resultant devastation was cataclysmic:

Diseases that Europeans brought from their continent—along with those brought from Africa when they journeyed from there to this hemisphere—created a demographic havoc among American Indians for several reasons. The foremost reason was that the introduced diseases found among American Indians a virgin territory to grow, spread and kill. (Thornton, 1987, p. 46).

Native populations had no immunity to the diseases carried by Europeans and were rendered all the more defenseless by the fact that diseases infected large numbers at the same point in time. In addition, native medical practices, coupled with non-existent European medical care, accelerated mortality rates.

While depopulation by disease raged, elimination of American Indian peoples was also fueled by what many have termed genocide in the name of war (Thornton, 1987). Although strife had almost certainly characterized Indian affairs prior to European settlement, the loss of life in warfare involving firearms and European battle strategies was accelerated during this period of colonization. In 1894 a body representative of the United States government, the Bureau of the Census, claimed:

It has been estimated that since 1775 more than 5,000 white men, women and children have been killed in individual affairs with Indians, and more than 8,500 Indians. History, in general, notes but few of these combats. The Indian wars under the government of the United States have been more than 40 in number. They have cost the lives of about 19,000 white men, women and children, including those killed in individual combats and the lives of about 30,000 Indians. The actual number of killed and wounded Indians must be very much greater than the number given, as they conceal, where possible, their actual loss in battle and carry their killed and wounded off and secrete them. The number given above is of those found by the whites. Fifty percent additional would be a safe estimate to add to the numbers given. (U.S. Bureau of the Census, 1894a, pp. 637–638, Quoted in Thornton, 1987, p. 48)

In the period from 1775 to the present, Thornton estimates that as many as 500,000 Indians were killed in both intertribal wars and wars with Europeans. One can only speculate about the number of dead as a result of massacres, bounties and other stratagems which can only be characterized as genocide—the systematic murder of a people whose misfortune was to inhabit lands coveted by the white man.

Removal and relocation and the attendant destruction of the ways of life followed by American Indian populations further contributed to their decline. Although massive relocation of tribal groups began as early as 1534, involving Seminole peoples in Florida who were dispersed by the Spanish, forced migration intensified following the Indian Removal Act of 1830. According to Thornton:

The most notable of the removals involved the Southeast's so-called Five Civilized Tribes in the early 1800s (whites called them civilized because they had accepted some non-Indian, that is European or American lifeways). The most infamous was the Cherokee removal of the late 1830s; as a result of it the Cherokee may have lost almost one-half of their population of about 20,000 mostly because of high death rates in transit or thereafter. (Thornton, 1987)

Our discussion of the lot of the American Indian has emphasized the genocidal nature of the contact between white newcomers and the indigenous population resident in what is now the United States. It is critical to understand this painful and shameful account in order to grasp the nature of the educational system through boarding schools and other coercive means subsequently thrust on native peoples. We will turn to that dimension of the native experience in Chapter 5 when we take into account structures and processes that characterize American Indian education.

AFRICAN AMERICANS

If this book had been written 20 years ago, this chapter might have discussed the political history and world view of only one group—African Americans. Prior to 1980, census data did not differentiate between Anglos and Latinos, categorizing individuals of both white and Latino origin as "white." Chinese and other Asian groups were generally viewed as a "model minority" whose relative success in "adjusting" to instructions and practices of U.S. society placed no pressure on institutions such as the school to be aware of their circumstances. Furthermore, advocates such as Takaki, the social historian, had not achieved voice and recognition. However, African Americans, first as Negroes and later as blacks, have been identified as a social, political and demographic category since at least the first national census in 1790.

Despite our nation's historical emphasis on freedom from political, religious and other forms of persecution, from its earliest settlement voting rights mirrored the British system "of restricting the franchise to those who owned property, namely freeholders" (Jarvis, 1992). From colonial times, qualifications for voting rights were based on particular features including gender, age, religion and length of residence as well as property ownership. Specific colonies instituted particular restrictions on voting. For example, Jews were not allowed to vote in New York and South Carolina and were also denied the ballot in Massachusetts and the Plymouth colonies. Moreover, convicts, debtors, servants and those under guardianship were similarly disenfranchised. Jarvis estimates that, as a result, no more than 15 percent of our nation's colonists in the late 18th and early 19th centuries were even eligible to vote and, of this number, only half regularly participated because of their perception that electoral activity was the province of the wealthy.

Race was an explicit category in state constitutional mandates in two of the colonies, Georgia and South Carolina. Voting regulations based on race quickly became the operating principle following the institutionalizing of slavery:

... voting based on race soon became the norm as the number of Africans increased dramatically following the institutionalization of slavery. It is important to note that the first Africans brought to this country, specifically to Jamestown, Virginia in 1619 were not slaves but indentured servants. As a result, the blacks during the period prior to the Revolutionary War had the right to own property, attend Church, pay taxes, and exercise the franchise like other colonists. (Jarvis, 1992, p. 19)

Despite their initial status as indentured servants, blacks, because of their color, less easily moved to the position of freedmen than whites. In addition, strict slave codes ultimately prevented the easy movement of blacks or even casual interaction among locally situated groups. They could no longer vote (except in Tennessee until 1834 and North Carolina until 1835), hold public office, give testimony against whites, possess a firearm, buy liquor, assembly freely (except in a church supervised by whites) or emigrate to other states (Jarvis, 1992, p. 19).

The institutionalization of slavery was complete with the abrogation of virtually all rights, let alone the right to vote, seen during these times, as we have stated, as the privilege of the propertied classes. By the time of the Civil War, the nation's population of free blacks had increased from 108,435 in 1790 to 488,000, approximately 11 percent of the entire black U.S. population. Yet, despite their freedom, this group was denied participation in the young nation's political life. Even after the movement to abolish slavery altogether achieved success with the passage of the Fourteenth Amendment in 1862, the rights of citizens as well as legal and political equality were still denied to blacks. Two dimensions of the black experience galvanized African Americans as a people. The first was the long migration from North to South after both World Wars and the second was the Civil Rights and Black Protest Movements covering the period from the late 1950s to the mid-1970s. We will examine these next. Also of great significance is the current rise of black feminist thought casting important light on gender issues as they connect with race and social class (Hill-Collins, 1991).

The Long Migration

African American scholars have been careful to be very precise in describing the black experience in the United States. It's fair to say that no other group except for American Indians in our nation's history has had so difficult a struggle to achieve an equal footing with white Americans. It is, therefore, an exacting task to define the distinctive features of the African American culture. African American scholars speak from many different positions on the question of their identity as a people. Wilson Jeremiah Moses, a Black Studies scholar writes: "As a Black American, I came from one of the most experienced of American 'ethnic groups' at being American" (1990, p. 25). Moses grew up in Detroit during the 1950s in an urban enclave that included Italian Americans and German Americans. His parents had both migrated to Detroit after World War II, his mother from Tulsa and his father, a Morehouse College graduate, from Atlanta. In declaring the roots of his own biases as a scholar, Moses recounts the influences on him from boyhood of his family, neighborhood and, most of all, his religion, not Afro-American Protestantism but (as he terms it) Italo-American Catholicism:

> Sensuality and martyrdom as DuBois knew were not cultural traits peculiar to Black Americans. The Black American religious experience must be understood not only in terms of its roots in revivals, the frenzy of storefront preachers or even the political sophistication of its educated minority. Black religion is all of those things, but a good deal more. It is the symbol of interaction between several African American religious traditions, but it may also represent a point of interaction with white hyphenated Americans. Reflecting on my own interactions with German and Italian cultures taught me that I was closer than most of them to the American religious traditions, although I did not know it then. (Moses, 1990, p. 24)

Moses' account of the forces that shaped his view of the world is on one level a highly personal statement, but it also illustrates the importance of particular institutions—the church, the neighborhood and the family—in African American life.

At the time of their experience in slavery, black Americans were members of numerous tribal and national groups. The conditions of that "peculiar institution," however, forced this population to take on a common identity. In Moses' terms, "Ancient ethnic distinctions between the various imported peoples were destroyed at the same time that acculturation to European ways was occurring" (Moses, 1990, p. 27). Second and third generation members of slave communities had been acculturated by the modification of both their language and their native religious institutions. By the end of the 18th century, black Americans spoke English reasonably well and had accumulated at least a veneer of Christian attitudes, but this veneer overlaid a set of beliefs and religious practices derived from African roots.

When debating the technicalities of characterizing African Americans as an ethnic group, a racial group or as a nation, Moses argues that the black American experience continues the "seemingly contradicting themes of political separation and cultural assimilationism within a messianic myth" (Moses, 1990, p. 27). Because of the caste-like status accorded to African Americans, as Ogbu describes it, there has always been considerable ambivalence among African Americans as to their political aims and strategies. Moses argues that "the fact that separatism so often asserts the exceptionalism of black American values and culture" is a result of this ambivalence. Further, "while Black Americans today are almost entirely acculturated linguistically and while most of us who are religious have been religiously acculturated by some degree, the majority of Afro-Americans have not been and for the foreseeable future will not be integrated into American social life despite their acculturation" (1990). Complete social integration will not occur soon because neither blacks nor whites see what Moses terms "racial amalgamation" as desirable. Since this is the case, African Americans have entered the middle class at a lower rate than other groups. Moses argues that resistance to "amalgamation" by which he means the formation of interracial families has come from both sides—both blacks and whites have maintained strong boundaries. Many would argue that Moses overlooks the particularly vehement racism that has permeated this society's relations with groups of color, particularly blacks and American Indians from the start.

1910–1920

The migration of African Americans to the North between 1910 and 1920 was assisted by economic and social "pushes and pulls." During this 10 year period, the black population in cities such as Detroit, Cleveland, and Chicago increased dramatically while states in the South such as Georgia, Mississippi, and Alabama found themselves without the backbone of their rural labor force, an experience that was to be repeated some twenty to thirty years later following World War II. Detroit's black population, for example, escalated from 5,000 in 1910 to 40,800 by 1920. Similar patterns characterized other northern targets of black American migration. The migrants were pushed North by the hard conditions of tenant farming and the attendant lack of opportunity for a better future. Takaki points to other, more subjective reasons for this vast migration: "Most of the Blacks who were moving North belonged to this post-Civil War generation, restless, dissatisfied, unwilling to mask their true selves and accommodate to traditional subservient roles" (Takaki, 1993). W.E.B. DuBois who himself crossed and recrossed North-South boundaries during this period noted "the South laments today the slow, steady disappearance of a certain type of Negro—the faithful, courteous slave of other days with his dignified . . . humility." Yet, as we have seen in Moses' account of his own life, the institutions of family, religion and neighborhood, in addition to Moses' status as an African American, create complex and often contradictory individual orientations. The African American experience clearly yields a complexity of distinctive features.

Rather than finding a Promised Land in the North, however, many African American migrants at this time and later received a hostile reception. Chicago provides all too clear an example. Chicago's black population grew from 30,000 in 1900 to more than 109,000 by 1920. Access to housing was the most explosive issue. According to Takaki, newspaper accounts of the time served to fan the flames of hostility between African American migrants and those they encountered in the neighborhoods of Chicago:

> The Black migration to Chicago sparked an explosion of white resistance. "A new problem, demanding early solution, is facing Chicago," the Tribune warned. "It pertains to the sudden and unprecedented influx of southern Negro laborers." The newspaper depicted the newcomers as carefree and lazy: "In a house at Thirty second

and Wabash eight or ten Negroes were lying about on the floor, and one was picking a banjo and singing a song the chorus of which ended 'Mo' rain, mo'rest,/Mo' niggers sleep in de nest." Determined to repel this Negro invasion several hundred white residents organized the Hyde Park Improvement Protective Club, which announced that Blacks must live in the so-called Districts and that real estate agents must not sell homes to Blacks in white blocks. (The districts which are now white, a leader of the organization declared, must remain white. There will be no compromise). (Takaki, 1993, p. 390)

Despite these difficulties, the majority of African American migrants did well economically and in other ways. While most were employed in manufacturing jobs, the work was generally better regulated and certainly better paid than sharecropping had been. Although employers frequently used tactics of hiring blacks to break strikes by all-white unions, solidarity was at least approached with the formation of the AFL-CIO. In Harlem a black literary Renaissance flowered in the 1920s and 1930s, enriching both the African American community and the wider society with new and exciting forms such as jazz and the blues.

1945–1978

World War II was a crucible for men and women of all backgrounds. The hopes for a dream no longer deferred were perhaps strongest among African Americans who believed that the struggle against totalitarian regimes abroad would mirror the defeat of racism in the United States. Ralph Bunche, a prominent African American spokesman during this period, argued that "there should be no illusion about the nature of this struggle. The fight now is not to save democracy, for that which does not exist cannot be saved. But the fight is to maintain those conditions under which people may continue to strive for realization of democratic "ideals" (Quoted in Takaki, 1993, p. 395). Nonetheless, blacks serving in the Armed Forces were generally posted to segregated units abroad while at home occupational and housing segregation persisted.

An early manifestation of what became the hallmark of the subsequent Civil Rights and Black Power movements was the proposed march on Washington in the early 1940s, organized by A. Phillip Randolph of the black-dominated Brotherhood of Sleeping-Car Porters. The march never materialized. Faced with the potential embarrassment of a demonstration in the nation's capital during a period immediately prior to official U.S. entry into the war, President Roosevelt's advisors developed policies to assure equitable employment practices under Right to Work legislation. This new policy which ultimately led to the employment of one million blacks during the war years was, of course, also ultimately imperative to the nation's successful war effort. By 1945 blacks constituted 8 percent of all defense workers. These job opportunities functioned as a magnet, pulling half a million blacks from the South between 1940 and 1945.

In the years immediately following World War II African Americans achieved a strong political voice through organizations such as the NAACP, whose mission was to redress the wrong of past discrimination through a political program aimed at removing barriers to racial integration and asserting America's basic freedoms. One of the first barriers to fall was in the realm of education where the principle of "separate but equal" facilities and resources had held sway from the time of the *Plessy V. Ferguson* high court decision in 1896. This premise was struck down by the *Brown* decision in 1954. The action in *Brown* was followed by an assault on the principle of separate public facilities. In this instance, Montgomery, Alabama was the site for the quiet protest of Rosa Parks.

> I didn't get on the bus with the intention of being arrested. ... However, I felt that I should take the stand because segregation was very oppressive and very cruel, especially being on the buses with some drivers. Not all of them, but those drivers who just insisted on ... carrying out segregation. ... To my knowledge it was the first time that practically the entire community of African Americans ... we put the bus company out of business for quite a while ... And I think that was very significant (Thornton, 1995, 1, 2).

The nation's gaze was riveted on Montgomery over the next weeks as moving photographs and stories of Montgomery's hard working blacks walking to their jobs or riding in taxies owned by others in the black community strongly affected the national conscience. These events also catapulted Martin Luther King, Jr. to national prominence with his stirring support of the Alabama protesters. Thus was born the Civil Rights Movement and a series of "other crossings," as Takaki describes them.

Despite the momentous achievements of the Civil Rights Movement and the subsequent Black Power Movement, many structural economic foundations of racial inequality remain. While many blacks found opportunity in the North and in New South cities such as Atlanta and New Orleans, many others found their passage blocked by overt discrimination in hiring and more covert forms of repression in institutions such as the school. The segregation of African American and other youths of color in our most economically impacted inner cities is all too apparent in the periodic and intense riots that have torched cities such as Los Angeles in 1965 and again in 1992. Persistent patterns of unemployment, unfair housing practices or geographic isolation create what Jonathan Kozol (1991) has called "dead zones" and eventually culminate in what William Julius Wilson terms the persistence of an "underclass" of ghettoized individuals. It is not the isolation and despair alone that create incendiary and explosive conditions, but it is also what Kenneth Clark described thirty years ago in *Dark Ghetto*. Of youths confined to the ghetto Clark wrote in 1965:

Those who are required to live in congested and rat-infested homes are aware that other young people have been taught to read, that they have been prepared for college and can compete successfully for white-collar managerial and executive jobs. (Clark, 1965)

What has created a difficult social climate at the twentieth century's end is the disappearance from such neighborhoods of legitimate African American business ventures that formerly served to buffer ghetto youth and to link them with jobs and resources. Far from seeing these circumstances as entirely hopeless, it is our view that communities at the grassroots have tremendous strength and resourcefulness. In this book's final chapter, we will turn to a discussion of some of the most promising local level activities and programs that capitalize on community cultural ties, including local institutions and leaders.

AN INVISIBLE MINORITY: APPALACHIANS

While the influx of Appalachian people from rural areas to Midwestern cities following World War II was nearly as great as Irish and Italian migration in the late 19th century and in sheer numbers much greater than the current migration of Asians to U.S. shores, urban Appalachians continue to remain a largely "invisible" minority. Internal migration, massive as these shifts may be, is not as dramatic or exotic as an influx of peoples from distant shores. Although a number of migrants have left the inner city core neighborhoods in which they and their families initially settled, many have remained.

The issues here facing urban Appalachian children and their families include social service and educational needs that also require culturally sensitive structures and focus to best address their lived experiences. Such structures should be community-based, accessible, and responsive rather than centralized, remote, and bureaucratic. These issues may not be apparent to those unfamiliar with problems of rural–urban migration. They involve cultural identity, rural–urban transition, and changes in family structure and livelihood strategies—all of which in combination create different kinds of stressors. Our assumptions about intervention and support service needs for urban Appalachians living in Cincinnati and other cities such as Columbus, Cleveland, and Detroit are predicated upon a set of harsh realities including: (a) Appalachians have the highest school dropout rate proportionate to their numbers; (b) Appalachians have been excluded from federally-funded job training and placement programs. In proportion to their presence in the eligible population for these services, this lack of access to jobs is dramatic; and (c) Appalachians in-inner city neighborhoods live in the poorest housing, are often slow to take advantage of health and prevention services, have a high incidence of female-headed households, teen pregnancies, and substance abuse.

In the section that follows, I (Borman) provide a background discussion of Appalachian migration and its impact upon the cities receiving the migrants and upon the migrants themselves. Special attention is paid to Cincinnati, the site of my 14-year research program with urban Appalachian children and youth.

Background: Mountain People in Cincinnati

Cleveland and Cincinnati, in addition to pulling African Americans from the South, drew 705,894 migrants from the Appalachian region, an area covering 497 counties across twelve states. In the 1950s, the automation of coal mining and the development of alternative fuel sources drove 1,569,000 more from the Kentucky and West Virginia coal fields. Finally, during the 1960s, an additional 592,000 streamed to the same cities that earlier waves of migrants had targeted. Tom Wagner and others who have examined the effects of this massive movement of people from rural to urban places have speculated that this huge demographic shift has gone largely unnoticed because this mass of 3,000,000 migrants were white and their migration internal to the United States.

While a relatively large number of first generation urban Appalachians reside in Cincinnati at the present time, many thousands more are the children and grandchildren of those who initially migrated to the city in the 1940s and 1950s. In order to profile current demographic data for urban Appalachians in the Cincinnati Metropolitan Area, I rely upon the recent work of Obermiller and Maloney. Their research provides data on age, patterns of residency, family status, education, occupation, and income for urban Appalachian and other groups.

In 1980 and again in 1989, Obermiller and Maloney surveyed residents in Greater Cincinnati (Hamilton County) through the University of Cincinnati's Institute for Policy Research (IPR). On the basis of respondents' self-identification, three comparison groups were drawn to include white non-Appalachians, black non-Appalachians, and white Appalachians. The researchers estimate the latter group constitutes approximately 40 percent of the county's population. In 1989, 61 percent of Appalachians surveyed were women, a demographic feature the researchers attribute to the higher mortality rate of men in this aging population. Patterns of long term residency in the urban area indicate the stability of Appalachian respondents whose average length of residency was 31 years compared to 29 years for African Americans and 32 years for non-Appalachian whites. Over the nine year period, both African Americans and Appalachians have clustered more heavily in the central city than in the suburban fringe areas. Whereas 31.4 percent of the Appalachian respondents were city dwellers in 1980, by 1989 44.4 percent lived in the city. A similar proportion of black residents also inhabit the central city, leading the researchers to conclude that the city is becoming inhabited by an overwhelmingly black and Appalachian population.

Not surprisingly, given the enormous economic and occupational shifts that have occurred over the last 20 years, employment growth for urban Appalachians from

1980 to 1989 was concentrated in low-level service industry jobs. The expansion of the service sector has paralleled the decline of manufacturing in many cities in the Midwest. Thus, for urban Appalachians surveyed, the number reporting employment in sales and clerical jobs grew 14 percent as did the number of laborers and service workers (+12%). Declining numbers (–17%) reported employment as craft persons and operatives.

Once they arrived in the cities, migrants followed a well documented and strategic pattern of settlement in port of entry neighborhoods. In Cincinnati, for example, migrants relied on networks of established kin to provide entry to the workplace. This livelihood strategy is consistent with patterns of cooperation and interdependence characteristic of mountaineers. Migrant workers recruited kin to jobs in the city during the manufacturing boom years resulting in the employment, according to some estimates, of as many as 70 percent Kentucky-born workers in some Cincinnati plants. Settlement in Cincinnati occurred in neighborhoods such as Lower Price Hill and Over-the-Rhine adjacent to the highly industrialized Mill Creek Valley where jobs were literally within walking distance. In the 1940s, 1950s, 1960s, and 1970s, work was in factories and small sheet metal and machine tool shops that generally required little or no experience or training. In the 1980s and 1990s, urban Appalachian youth remain economically marginalized. During the 1980s, unskilled work in manufacturing jobs was increasingly scaled back due to automation and the general decline of manufacturing jobs in an increasingly service-based national economy. The result has been periodic or chronic unemployment. Thus, many third and fourth generation urban Appalachian families remain isolated and out of work.

Youths in enclaved urban Appalachian neighborhoods are particularly vulnerable, attending schools that maintain patterns of socioeconomic segregation. Although socioeconomic status defined by parental income and education is generally a strong predictor of alienation from school reflected in the dropout rate, the relationship is by no means perfect. In Cincinnati, for example, the dropout rates of some urban Appalachian neighborhoods are even higher than their socioeconomic ranking relative to other city neighborhoods would suggest. In one such case according to 1980 census data, a relatively highly ranked neighborhood (17th of 44) in terms of socioeconomic status had the eighth highest dropout rate in the city.

Discrimination persists in the current job market for urban Appalachians. In cities such as Detroit, Chicago, Cleveland, Columbus, and Cincinnati with large urban Appalachian populations alongside established white groups, urban Appalachians without the benefit of middle-class origins and a college education do not acquire jobs and income equal to other whites. According to a political and economic analysis of job mobility and labor market conditions, neither cultural differences nor migrant status alone or together account for this outcome. Rather, Appalachians are excluded in order to reduce the competition for jobs "reserved" for native, non-Appalachian whites.

There is, of course, competition for jobs especially during hard times. However, discriminatory employment patterns result in the monopolizing of good jobs by middle-class workers who possess the necessary traits and behaviors assumed to be required for specific jobs and lead to the creation and maintenance of job shelters. The promise of good employment remains elusive for urban Appalachian youth whose repertoire of skills and behaviors places them at odds with employers' biases toward those who display a more "appropriate" demeanor. Employers desire docile, "responsible" workers who do not have strong obligations to kin, the problems associated with young families of their own, and whose approach to life is less spontaneous and engaged than that of many urban Appalachian and black youths. In their survey of youths in Baltimore, Providence, Cincinnati, and Detroit, McCoy and McCoy determined that, of those of school age but not in school, 49.2 percent were Appalachians, 46 percent other ethnics (including Latino and Polish youths) and 4.7 percent were black. For the most part, Appalachians and other white ethnics had simply dropped out of school while a large minority (25%) of blacks had disrupted educational careers due to criminal convictions that resulted in their incarceration and withdrawal from school.

CONCLUSION

In this chapter and in the one preceding it, we have narrated a complex story of demographic shifts, and of opportunities taken and created through political action, economic entrepreneurial activity, persistence and spirit. We fully recognize that the passages of those groups we have described here are partial and have excluded the equally important stories of other groups. Because we have principally focused on traditionally disenfranchised groups whose struggles for equity continue today and upon new immigrants whose relatively recent odysseys are unfolding, we have excluded with regret others' stories. For example, we have not narrated the powerful saga of Japanese Americans whose internment in camps during World War II, demonstrates the difficulties faced by a people whose enclaved life ways in "strategic" cities made them easy targets for suspicion during this period. Their history also exemplifies the strengths and capacity for adaptation to and mastery of a harsh political, social and economic climate that characterizes the experience of all of the groups we have considered.

More recently, immigrants from the former Soviet Union and other Eastern European nations such as Poland have come to targeted locations in the United States, specifically to locales where migrants in previous generations have gone. In the case of Polish immigrants, Chicago is a preferred destination as it has been since the mid-19th century. New arrivees quickly locate relatives, friends, residential communities, and institutions such as churches and social service agencies who have long worked with Polish immigrants. It is our hope that you will seek out information on these and other groups whose histories are of interest and importance to you, either because you share a similar heritage or because in your work and in other spheres you have frequent contact with such individuals.

Chapters 2 and 3 have set the stage for the vignettes that follow in the next four chapters. By documenting the enormous demographic shifts and changes in our population since the 1965 immigration legislation, these initial chapters have taken stock of the social, political, and economic trajectories of those whose collective histories in the United States have included the search for place, opportunity, and dignity. Consistent with our framework for understanding children's school achievement, we have provided detailed profiles of newcomers and other groups, taking the position that social structural and sociocultural realities must be understood before teaching and learning opportunities can be developed. What is most notable, indeed remarkable, in each group's experience is the creation of political, social, and economic successes despite isolation from the mainstream. This capacity to create both symbolic and real community ties is a topic we pick up in this book's concluding Chapter 8.

4

Schools and Communities: Vignettes of Recent Latino Immigrants and Refugees

In this and the next three chapters, we examine a number of vignettes drawn from the fieldwork of educational anthropologists, sociologists, and language researchers whose work has taken them into the communities, families and schools of recent immigrant, refugee, Native American, African American, and urban Appalachian peoples. Chapters 4 and 5 have been organized to consider the more recent arrivees, those who are likely to have stronger lateral ties to villages and communities in distant lands than to places in the United States.

The 11 vignettes are not parallel cases because researchers in each instance undertook their work with different questions, somewhat different methodological strategies, and various theoretical orientations in mind. For example, Jim King and his colleagues in "The Power of Ritual and Language" are guided by questions that probe the intergenerational use of Spanish among members of an extended family in the Cuban American community of Tampa. They are also interested in exploring the impact of the *Quinceañera*, a rite of passage into womanhood, upon Maria Teresa, an adolescent with a middle-class background who is the focus of the vignette. In their analyses they utilize both linguistic and sociolinguistic markers to point out differences between the first generation (Maria Teresa's parents) and the second generation in their use of English. By contrast, Pamela Quiroz's vignette, "Community Terror Creates Attachment to School," is a study of violent behavior in and outside school as it affects adolescent Puerto Rican youths. This vignette focuses upon the *social structure* of the school and the community and how these interact and diverge. Both analyses, despite their differences in focus, provide windows on lives in progress.

While the 11 vignettes vary in their emphases upon the child, family, community, and school, each examines school achievement-related experiences of particular children, adolescents and adults. Some, such as the "Dan and Mei" vignette, emphasize the family context while others, such as the "Community Terror Creates Attachment to School" vignette, focus more on the school setting. The children, teachers, parents, and other adults in each vignette are located in a particular set of nested contexts in the same manner as Bronfenbrenner (1979) describes the ecology of children's development. Thus, each vignette is framed with a description of economic and social structural conditions confronting families whose lives are embedded in particular communities. The impact and importance of each ethnic group's collective social, economic and cultural history is also presented. Each vignette is contextualized at its conclusion by a brief discussion of salient aspects of the case study.

These three chapters illustrate the varieties of experience which characterize the collective American experience, suggesting strategies for constructing more favorable learning environments for children's development by allowing room for cultural variation. Each group whose story is imbedded in the following vignettes has experienced its own unique form of staged migration, political, economic, and linguistic oppression, alienation from the "mainstream," and pride in a particular set of achievements, intergroup conflicts, myths, folklore, and other aspects of the group's culture. Nonetheless, each group has made accommodations to the larger society's culture to create new possibilities, especially for its children.

THE LATINO EXPERIENCE

The 35 million members of the Spanish-speaking communities in U.S. cities are aware of the critical nature of educational achievement and persistence in school. A survey undertaken by Bauer (1989) focused on Milwaukee area Latinos who identified educational limitations as the major problem facing their community. Because decisions to group children according to their perceived ability to succeed academically are generally tied to students' performance on placement tests given in English, Spanish-speaking students with limited English proficiency are at a distinct disadvantage in the sorting and tracking process that occurs from early in a student's career. As a consequence, students with limited use of English may, in fact, be categorized as mentally retarded and assigned to special education classes;

rarely do traditional methods used for assigning students to academic groups work to identify Hispanic youngsters as gifted and talented.

Since most Latinos live in urban areas in the United States, they are likely to reside and attend schools in resource-poor neighborhoods, exacerbating problems associated with access to an academically rich curriculum. There is little question, therefore, that a program designed to identify and foster talents among low income, urban dwelling Latino students can make a dramatic difference in these students' lives.

Hispanic students appear to suffer ill effects from placement in limited English-proficient (LEP) classes. Unfortunately, placement in such classes frequently ensures that students will be stigmatized as inferior in academic skills in comparison with others who are not in such classes. The fact is that Hispanics are regularly placed in low ability or mentally retarded classes and are consistently underrepresented in classes for the gifted and talented. Not surprisingly, many Latino students become disaffected and eventually leave school as dropouts. Moreover, those that remain are frequently denied the opportunity to enroll in courses needed to be admitted to college including coursework in math and science. Such was the conclusion of researchers in Chicago who studied the impact of track placement on students' course enrollment (Fernandez & Velez, 1985).

In this section we will examine the fieldwork of three researchers, Concha Delgado-Gaitan who conducted a long-term ethnographic investigation of the Mexican-American community in Carpenteria, California; Pamela Quiroz whose fieldwork in Chicago examined the Puerto Rican American experience, particularly the activities of Puerto Rican gang members most of whom still attended high school; and Jim King and his colleagues who have had ongoing access to Cuban families in the Tampa Bay area for several years and document the *Quinceañera* or "Quinse," a Latin American celebration and ritual celebrating the passage into womanhood of the Latina adolescent. Although each researcher asked different questions during the course of these projects, projects which were in turn located in very different sites, the studies share a common focus on people whose native language is Spanish, whose children clearly benefit from programs and rituals that recognize the value of Latin cultures, and whose families in most cases have tangential relationships with the schools but strong roots in their communities.

VIGNETTE #1: COMMUNITY RESOURCES ENHANCE CHILDREN'S LEARNING: MEXICAN CHILDREN IN CARPINTERIA, CALIFORNIA
by Concha Delgado-Gaitan

Mexicans who have immigrated to Carpinteria, California during the past twenty years know a very different community than those who came earlier. Many persons of Mexican descent came to Carpinteria in the early 19th century when immigration laws were more relaxed and the economic incentive to seek better opportunities was strong. Descendants of this migration wave constitute the present-day Mexican American family population in Carpinteria. The first generation cohort shares this history. The agricultural industry in Carpinteria was an appropriate "fit" for Mexicans who had the desired skills and motivation. It should be noted that the Chumash Indians had resided in Carpinteria since the 16th century and were hunters and fishermen; this left ample opportunities in agriculture for Mexicans.

The total population of Carpinteria did not exceed 1,000 residents until the mid-1940s. Predictably, employment differentiated ethnic groups, as did different geographic boundaries. The Mexicans took different jobs and resided in neighborhoods apart from the non-Latino population. This is generally true for most heterogeneous United States urban areas.

Lemons and avocados were the principal crops worked by Mexicans in the Carpinteria area. By 1950 the *Bracero* program had brought in a new migration of Mexicans to work specifically in agriculture. Dutch, Japanese, and a few Mexicans owned ranches which employed Mexicans as laborers. This cohort of men did not bring their families because they were obligated to return to Mexico after their contracts terminated. Many men, however, married local women and raised their families in Carpinteria.

Mexican workers were valued, but that did not grant them equal status in the workforce or in housing, social activities, or the schools (Menchaca & Valencia, 1990). Institutionalized segregation was active in the schools until the early 1970s. According to a newspaper article from a nearby town, Santa Paula, the Carpinteria school board segregated Mexicans because they were classified as Indians, and the State of California had ruled that isolating Indians was lawful:

> School authorities of Carpinteria have caused considerable interest in all parts of the state with their decision in declining to accept the ruling of U.S. Attorney General Webb that schools cannot segregate Mexican, Chinese, Japanese and Indian children . . . The Carpinteria school board takes the ground that children of Mexican born parents are Indians . . . In Santa Paula the Mexican situation is handled in a tactful manner, school authorities believe. Many of the Mexicans are going to school in the Canyon and Ventura schools situated in their own sections of this city . . . the school situated in their own districts takes care of the majority of the Mexican children, and special courses of study have been arranged for them. They are said to be happy in their own schools. (*Santa Paula Chronicle*, 1929; cited in Menchaca & Valencia, 1990, p. 240)

Under the guise of this interpretation of race, the schools could legally segregate Mexicans into the Aliso School, which became known as the "Mexican School." Children who attended the school at the time it was segregated recount the low expectations of their teachers: "I remember being in the eighth grade and before that I was in low reading groups; it was a real shock for me because when I was in Catholic school I was a very good student. Anyway, I did something silly and I turned in a terrible assignment. My teacher, who was the only Chicano teacher in the school, said to me, 'Jose, this is not like you and I expect a lot more from you.' I felt so embarrassed and from that point on I began taking note of what I did and performing better. I guess I felt that I had someone who cared about how I did in school."

Jose was fortunate to have had a teacher who communicated clearly her higher expectations. However, most students faced constant ridicule simply because they were Mexican. Mexican children were constantly reminded by the Anglo community that they were inferior not only in school but also in community affairs. An incident cited by one of the parents, Mr. Mendez, illustrates this point:

> If you ever brought *tacos de frijoles* to school, kids made fun of you so even though you loved to eat them more than any other food, and so you tried not to bring them. We were mostly Mexican but still it was like people already knew that being Mexican wasn't good enough. Anyway, one Saturday some of my friends and I went to the Tradewinds Theater and most of us could not afford the money to buy popcorn and other goodies, so we took our own snack from home. So we were outside the theater waiting to get in and along comes Jesús, this kid riding on his bike. He hit a rock and flipped over and his lunch bag flew open and out come the tortillas and beans. I can still hear the comments ridiculing that kid. All I could think was, "sure glad it wasn't me."

Mexican children who had attended the segregated school and are parents in this study graduated from the high school by the time efforts were undertaken by the school district to provide equitable education. In fact, the climate for change in the schools was created in part by the same students who had come through the segregated school experience and had gone on to become teachers. Two of those teachers (Mendez & Islas) participated in the study. In the early 1970s the federal government made funds available to create a bilingual program for limited-English-speaking students. Carpinteria used these funds to create a bilingual program and preschool. The children who took advantage of these programs had parents who had immigrated more recently. For the most part, these children were born in the United States to parents who were predominantly Spanish-speaking. The current generation, who immigrated during the past 15 years, arrived in Carpinteria at a time when the schools and the community had changed the district's segregationist policies. The bilingual preschool and bilingual program in the Carpinteria schools began to tug at the ethnic and language awareness of the educators. Since the inception of bilingual programs for Spanish-speaking students, educators have become more conscious of the educational needs of these children.

After federal funds were exhausted, the school district was not able or willing to assume financial responsibility for continuing the bilingual programs alone. As a consequence, the direct benefit to students, provision of teacher training, and the resources of teacher-assistants were lost. All of these components had supported teachers' effectiveness in working with Spanish-speaking students and teachers' assistants.

By the mid-1980s Spanish-speaking students were no longer making the academic gains which had initially characterized the school district's bilingual programs. The one exception to the declining quality of programs that addressed the needs of Spanish-speaking students was the Bilingual Preschool Program. The teacher in charge of this program provided a rich curriculum (in Spanish) and also had created a strong relationship with the Spanish-speaking families and the community.

When the children left the preschool, however, few resources existed to help Spanish-speaking parents to bridge the connection with the school. As Spanish-speaking children moved up the academic ladder and learned more English, parents were distanced from them and the schooling process (Delgado-Gaitan, 1990). Some parents reported that by the time a child reached junior high school, they felt as if they were "living with a stranger." Parental knowledge about the schooling system is seen as an essential ingredient to the effective socialization of their children, and the impact of this factor in the home provides a powerful link between the family setting and social institutions as we discussed in Chapter 1. Immigrant families were the focus of the first part of the Carpenteria study beginning in 1985. These Spanish-speaking families experienced high isolation from the school because they lacked information about its operations and expectations. This phase of the study occurred prior to the organization of the parent group and helps to explain the changes in family interaction after the family's participation in a community organization. The distance between many of the families and the school created problems for children's schooling.

For example, prior to the parents' involvement in a parent group, the Chapa family had an only son who was in preschool at the time. This posed problems for his parents because he said only that he did not like it and did not elaborate. Both parents tried to convince him that preschool was a fun place and that his friends there valued him. Although Mr. Chapa had become active in the Bilingual Preschool Program by attending meetings about the goals of the program and believed strongly in encouraging his son in the preschool, family interaction with his son at home differed from what was later observed when their daughter was born and the parents became active in the community organization. Manuelito was the object of affection and caring from his parents. Verbal interaction was comprised largely of commands and requests and responses pertaining to the immediate activity. The amount of verbal interaction seemed minimal. Messages were conveyed to Manuelito through nonverbal communication. He was to play, obey his parents, stay in close proximity and to depend on his parents. On a typical Saturday afternoon in the Chapa household, Mr. Chapa returned from the nursery, where he worked overtime on Saturdays. Prior to leaving to coach his soccer team, he ate lunch which his wife had prepared. Their son, Manuelito, in the yard, waved a twig in the air and aimed it at birds on the tree near where he stood. His mother called him to eat lunch with his father and Manuelito ran inside the house. To prevent interfering with any potential interaction, I sat outside the kitchen with an ear to the screen door.

Mrs. Chapa heated tortillas and proceeded to serve Manuelito from the pots on the stove. *"Toma, mi hijo."* (Here my son.) *"Gracias, mami."* (Thank you, mommy.) Mrs. Chapa left the kitchen and went into the bedroom. Mr. Chapa and Manuelito remained in the kitchen. Manuelito sat swinging his leg at the edge of the chair as he ate. A couple of minutes later, he appeared to be half standing and half sitting while he continued eating. Mr. Chapa noted, *"Sientate bien y come."* (Sit down correctly and eat.) Manuelito sat and continued swinging his leg. Upon completing his lunch, he got up and walked out the back door. Mr. Chapa continued his lunch and a few minutes later, he came out the back door looking for Manuelito who had resumed swinging his twig in the air and poking the ground with it. *"Manuelito, voy al futbol y regreso mas tarde."* (Manuelito, I'm going to the soccer game, and I'll return later.) Manuelito dropped his twig and ran to stand close to his father and asked to go. *"Quiero ir. Quiero ir."* (I want to go. I want to go.) *"No, hoy no."* (No, not today.) Mr. Chapa got in his car and left. Manuelito resumed shaking his twig for another five minutes and walked inside. He picked up a shoe-box of toys, lay down on the rug in the living room and proceeded to examine the collection without a word. His mother walked out of the bedroom with two armfuls of laundry. *"Vamos, mi hijo. Voy a la lauvandería."* (Come on my son. We're going to the laundromat.) Manuelito quickly stood up and followed his mother to leave. She looked at me and apologized for having to leave to do her work and jokingly said that I too could accompany her if I wished. I accepted.

Manuelito jumped into the back seat while Mrs. Chapa stuffed the clothes in a plastic bag and put it in a basket in the trunk. On the trip to the laundromat, I refrained from conversing with Mrs. Chapa, as I had done other times when conducting interviews, so as not to interfere with the potential interaction between her and Manuelito. Upon arriving in the laundromat, Mrs. Chapa removed the clothes from the trunk, and Manuelito remained in the back seat until his mother gave him permission to get down. *"Ya, mi hijo, vamos."* (Ok, my son, let's go.) Manuelito got down and slowly walked to the door while his mother held it open. He was preoccupied with a string which he wrapped around his fingers. *"Pronto, mi hijo."* (Hurry, my son.) Mrs. Chapa called out. Inside the laundromat, Mrs. Chapa's head turned frequently and kept one eye on her laundry and one eye on her son as he walked around the laundromat tapping each of the machines as if he was taking inventory. When she finished loading the machines, she grabbed her purse and took Manuelito's hand and sat him down with her. He continued twirling his string on his finger and stretched it as if to measure objects around him. Mrs. Chapa opened her purse and took out a *"fotonovela"* (romance novel in Spanish). This scenario continued for an additional hour.

Year 1 in Carpinteria: Literacy in the home and school

The Spanish-speaking community in Carpinteria has been quite isolated from the white mainstream group. Children of Latino background had attended the Mexican school up to the early 1970s. The change of political climate in the 1970s brought with it awareness and funds for special programs for educating linguistically different students.

One of the programs which Carpinteria implemented was a bilingual preschool where the teacher, Betty, changed the lives of many Spanish-speaking children in the school district. Betty spoke Spanish and knew the culture of the families and the community well because she too was Latina and lived in the community. She made the parents co-teachers with her in a way that helped the parents learn to assist their children in the home, and she also made them accountable to her for helping in the preschool. Most of these parents, all of whom were immigrants from Mexico, had no more than a fourth grade education in Mexico and held jobs as agricultural workers in the nurseries.

Betty trained the parents by showing them how to read books to their children. She insisted that they converse with their children by making time to do household chores that involved children. By allowing children to help in cooking, washing dishes, shopping, and other household chores, parents could use a great deal of language.

My interest as an ethnographer began in the homes with the question of what literacy practices existed in the home. I followed children from the classroom who were placed in different levels of reading ability. Teachers suspected that the students who were in more advanced reading groups in the classroom had parents who read to them.

Year 2—Parent involvement

To better understand the literacy practices of the community I presented data on home literacy activities to a large group of families. The families participated in ethnographic analysis and, in the process, became aware of the variance in experience with the schools. In the process, some of the more experienced families became more familiar with the needs of the Spanish-speaking community and began to organize a parent group for families to support each other.

The parent organization, *Comite de Padres Latinos* (COPLA), then became the focus of the research to help me learn how parents taught themselves to deal with their children and the schools as they struggled to adjust in a different culture. Parents cared about their children's education a great deal; there was never any question in their minds about this:

> We as Latino parents do not have the formal schooling it takes to help our children in all of their school work but we have our life experience and that's a very important teacher for our children. We have that to share with them and in that sharing we get

to share with them how important it is for them to take advantage of their schooling—because as their parents we educate them.

Year 3—A literacy intervention phase

The parent organization, in collaboration with me, designed a project to assist the parents whose children were underachieving to read with their children at home. The literacy intervention phase was designed with three theoretical premises:

- That all literacy is based on specific social practices.
- That children become empowered through interaction with parents about the story text that utilizes their personal experience.
- That intervention involving families must consider the home as a cultural niche.

The more that parents read with children, the better readers they become. During the reading activity with children, parents teach more than the mechanics and strategies on reading. Parents teach sociocultural knowledge based on their own experience. They convey values, a world view about their position in society and a sense of confidence that they are important enough to receive their parents' attention.

Following Paulo Freire's (1987) concept of liberation based upon his work on literacy with Brazilian peasants, Alma Flor Ada attempted to have parents learn how to motivate their children to read by utilizing four questioning strategies, reflecting on their own experience and liberation (Ada, 1988). To understand how to apply this knowledge (knowing one's status and experience in society) and applying it by teaching their children to do the same thing, the adults use primary experience in examining text. Put another way, adults are able to teach their children how to reflect on their own experience in relation to a story book if the adults themselves practice with written text of interest to them. Alma Flor Ada's work shows how Spanish-speaking children and their parents become empowered when they learn to interpret literature in relation to their own experience and reality.

We extended the premise of becoming analytical readers and reading for meaning by having parents and children decide their own questions and interaction during their story reading session. Four types of questions framed the interaction between adults and children: descriptive, personal interpretative, critical, and creative. Descriptive questions solicited factual recall, for example, "What did the female elephants wear?" Personal interpretative questions asked the reader to think about personal experience in relation to what was read, for example, "Have you ever felt that you were prevented from doing things that others had permission to do? How did you feel?" Critical questions revealed the child's ability to analyze the text in terms of a sociopolitical perspective, for example, "Could the male and female monkeys have divided the work and responsibilities better?" Creative questions prompt the reader to think about ways to resolve questions similar to those in the story, for example, "If you had been one of the female monkeys, what could you have done to improve the situation?"

The results of this intervention phase were quite successful except for the questioning strategies which were taught to the parents. This part was too academic for the parents, and they were often confused by the hierarchy of the questions. It became clear to me that the hierarchy of questions was designed by Flor Ada for the teacher's use and, thus, these questions created a cultural conflict with the way in which parents naturally interacted with their children at home. Parents were not accustomed to such formal types of interactions; they might have benefitted more by becoming aware of their own processes and using their own forms of interaction to initiate discussion about the literature books.

Years 3–7—Organizing Latino families/COPLA

Beginning with the child's early socialization into the family, parents interact closely with their children. They regale them with stories about family members as well as other cultural narratives. As children enter school, parents change the focus of their interaction with them. To a great extent they assist children in their home tasks in their own language. Parents communicate with the school in order to understand how and whom to contact. Many successfully negotiate the school culture in spite of their language difference, but since the COPLA organization was formed, they have found more support with other parents and have also learned what schools expect and how to communicate with them.

In a meeting Mrs. Avila epitomized the group's sentiment about their participation in the system and the system's perception of time. One parent commented (translated from Spanish) "What the schools say about us is that we don't know how to organize ourselves, that we're always late to meetings and that we don't support each other."

> Mr. Mendez said, "It's true. Lot of that is true but not all the time." "No, you're right," added Mrs. Mendez, "for example we got here on time today and it was the director that did not get here to open the door for us. We also do attend to our children's needs by going to meetings when the teacher calls us or by attending open house. The problem is that sometimes I get shy about getting to the school because I don't speak English and I know other Spanish-speaking parents who also shy away."

Another parent jumped in the conversation:

> But that shouldn't hold us back from asking for information for our children. If we need to know about our children then we need to ask in our language and find someone who can understand us. Nothing should hold us back from getting the most for our children.

Parents in Carpinteria organized themselves for the purpose of supporting each other and, in conversation, shared historical experiences—in their former country, in Carpinteria and with the schools. The conversational process that parents organized was what I termed a "critical reflection process" in which the parents shared their common experience as Mexican immigrants in this community and their cultural knowledge which they believed was the wealth they had to transmit to their children. During the critical reflection process parents discussed cultural limitations which had been imposed on them as well as practices which they recognized had previously limited their involvement in their children's education.

LESSONS FROM THE CARPINTERIA VIGNETTE

What lessons can we learn from this case? How did parents' collective migration experiences in addition to such issues as language attrition promote their solidarity and enhance their children's well being? In what ways did they experience alienation from the mainstream, pride in their accomplishments and intergroup conflicts? How did myths, folklore, and ritual figure in their daily lives?

In the Carpinteria case, the migration experience became an important touchstone that parents explicitly invoked in their conversations with each other. Delgado-Gaitan terms this "a cultural reflection process" that parents used to share common experiences, reinforce, maintain and legitimate their cultural knowledge. This same strong sense of shared experience was later an effective springboard to political organizing. The political, economic and linguistic oppression experienced by these families was apparent in the kinds of employment initially available to them and the low regard accorded their jobs as agricultural laborers. Stereotyping and ridicule attended children's experience in and out of school. Further, language attrition became a paramount concern for the first generation of immigrants who created COPLA largely as a vehicle for maintaining the language. Subsequent generations—the sons and daughters of the first settlers in Carpinteria—sustained the climate for change by becoming teachers in the community. However, for many of the first generation, the passage of their adolescent children from the family into the larger culture was marked by their experience of "living with a stranger" as their own children inhabited spheres in and outside the school that were both unfamiliar and threatening to them.

As with virtually all of the groups considered in this volume, the Mexican immigrants who participated in Delgado-Gaitan's study, were, at various points in their lives, very isolated from the Anglo mainstream. This isolation derived from at least three sources: the economic and residential cleavages that separated the immigrant farm workers from middle class and wealthy Anglo citizens in Carpinteria; the separation of Latino children from their Anglo peers in school until the early 1970s; and cultural stereotypes held by Anglo children that fueled their negative responses to and harassment of their Hispanic age mates.

This vignette considers the experiences of Mexican immigrant families and their children in the context of a relatively small city in a southern California coastal agricultural area. Delgado-Gaitan's extended field work over the course of several years allowed her to understand and analyze the development of a strong parent-organized and governed body, COPLA, that successfully promoted parents' interests and those of their children. Although her initial research question focused on literacy learning in the family, like Shirley Brice Heath in the Piedmont-area communities of Trackton, Maintown, and Roadville, over a 10 year period Delgado-Gaitan also developed a thorough understanding of the historical, political, social, and economic constraints and opportunities presented to immigrant families in Carpinteria. Additionally, she worked with families to familiarize them with the language of the classroom. These actions allowed Delgado-Gaitan to become a community-based advocate for the families she researched and thus could promote and represent.

The isolation of immigrants from the mainstream is no accident. Workplaces, schools and other settings are often organized to exclude or marginalize groups that are not valued in the society. Thus, economic, residential and school grouping practices are patterned responses to groups perceived as threatening. As Louise Lamphere and others who have conducted close ethnographic investigations of newcomers' experiences in U.S. institutions such as schools and workplaces argue, these factors are rooted in the social structure of this society. Most important in the experience of newcomers are their interactions in the context of major institutional settings including workplaces, schools, community organizations, rental housing complexes and retail businesses where immigrants and their U.S. citizen neighbors come into regular contact (Lamphere, 1992).

VIGNETTE #2: COMMUNITY TERROR CREATES ATTACHMENT TO SCHOOL: PUERTO RICAN HIGH SCHOOL STUDENTS IN CHICAGO
by Pamela Quiroz

The Chicago School District is one of the largest metropolitan school districts in the United States with 407,241 students. The school system operates a total of 553 schools including 478 elementary schools and 75 secondary schools. Its schools are among the most racially and ethnically diverse in the United States. The racial/ethnic composition of the school district is 11.3 percent Anglo, 54.9 percent African American, 30.4 percent Hispanic, 3.2 percent Asian American and Pacific Islander, and 0.2 percent American Indian. During a recent year (1994), 79 percent of the students came from low-income (AFDC) families. Of all the limited-English-proficiency students in Illinois, 50.8 percent of them live in Chicago, and they comprise 14.2 percent of the district's student body.

During the last seven years, three important legislative events have thrust the Chicago Public Schools (CPS) into a process of renewal. In 1989, the Chicago School Reform Act shifted the primary responsibility for the education of students from central administration to the local level. The intent was "to make the individual local school the essential unit for educational governance and improvement, and to establish a process for placing the primary responsibility for school governance and improvement in the hands of the parents, community residents, teachers and the school principal."

In 1991, the state legislature passed the Illinois Public School Accreditation Process which requires schools "to provide evidence, over a period of time, on the extent to which students are meeting standards for student performance based on the State Goals for Learning and the extent to which all students are being served . . . as documented on a School Improvement Plan."

Because progress was limited and accountability weak, the Illinois legislature in 1995 revised the school governance plan by giving the Mayor of Chicago and the CPS central office expanded powers to work with failing schools, install new leadership or even close troubled schools. It is now felt that an infrastructure is needed to support local efforts through training school councils and principals and establishing a system of incentives and accountability.

The new structure provides a school reform board of trustees that consists of the president and four members. The Chief Executive Officer and Chief Education Officer preside over the system to create a community of learners that places "children first," according to District rhetoric. Major changes in management include the following: the Office of the Chief Instruction Officer manages all instructional, academic, and athletic programs, as well as the categorical funding which supports these programs; the Office of Professional Development is responsible for instructional, noninstructional and administrative training of all employees; and the Office of Accountability is charged with review, evaluation and analysis of school performance in order to break down barriers to achievement.

As of November, 1995, the new team had negotiated a four-year contract with teachers, streamlined and reduced central office staff, begun to deal with waste and mismanagement, planned a four-year balanced budget, and established education regions to support students, teachers, administrators, families, and communities. Funding has been allocated to improve student performance by such avenues as extending the school day for academic and extracurricular purposes and tapping into community resources.

The School Community Context

The high school that is the focus of this vignette has maintained a relatively stable Hispanic enrollment (82–86%) since the 1970s with the majority of its students

Puerto Rican. Low-income enrollment in this high school is 65.1 percent of its student population, and the high school graduation rate is 35.5 percent. Moreover, compared to schools nationally, this school's American College Test (ACT) percentile ranking is 1. This means that less than one percent of high schools nationally scored below this school on the ACT. In sum, the statistical indicators of this school reveal all the characteristics of an inner-city high school serving impoverished students.

The socioeconomic status of the Puerto Rican community in the school's neighborhood mirrors the national figures for Puerto Ricans illustrating that, relative to other Hispanic populations (and particularly Anglos), Puerto Ricans are more likely to live in poverty, have lower labor force participation rates, and lower education rates (Hispanic Policy Development Project, 1984; Stier & Tienda, 1991). Their difficult economic situation is largely attributable to the growth of the service sector economy where Latinos are underrepresented and the decline in manufacturing jobs where they have been overrepresented. Thus, Latinos have experienced the loss of industrial work without important gains in other sectors of the economy. As poverty increased in the neighborhood, so did crime. In the early 1980s, the neighborhood in which this high school is located was considered to have the highest juvenile homicide rate in the country, most of it attributable to gang activity (Spergel & Curry, 1988).

The initial focus of this study was to examine the school-related decisions that students make, such as which activities to get involved in and the extent of time and effort to invest in such activities. How such institutions as family influenced student decisions in this direction was also of interest. In what follows here I provide an illustration of contextual effects on students' educational experiences and decisions.

Throughout the academic year, and particularly during the interview process, two major issues surfaced when I discussed the "problems" of the school with students and staff. Gangs and the students' neighborhood environment were both mentioned as interfering with the schooling and learning process. Gang membership is typically associated with boys' dropping out of schools, as was the case at Lares. However, in addition to the gang influence in the environment outside school, many gangs and their members remained *in* this school, often disrupting the school's *internal* environment. Thus, I focus here on those students *still in school* who are either members of gangs, have friends or relatives involved with gangs, or for whom gangs have had some effect on their educational process. In addition, the effects of homelessness are also examined, primarily through the interviews I conducted with students and also as recorded in the interviews and insights of teachers and counselors. What emerges is a view of children, certainly *at-risk*, who are coping with these influences in ways which often utterly compromise the learning process.

Lares High School

Lares High School enrolls approximately 2,900 students and has a staff of 181, 141 of whom are teachers and nine of whom are counselors. The newly formed "Local School Council," an advisory group representing the school's community, was the school's sole governing unit. This body had formulated school policy that considerably expanded the administrative staff. A new multicultural curriculum was also being developed, along with several other changes simultaneously being attempted during the year I undertook this study (1991–1992). In connection with these changes, teacher in-service workshops on the awareness and reduction of prejudice took place, and a cultural center was established to heighten students' awareness and appreciation not only for their own culture but for other cultures as well. Concomitant with the advent of these structural changes were changes in the student body. One pronounced change was the increasing influence of gang activity within the school. Lares High School has approximately nine identifiable gangs in the school including names and colors. Although there is no way to be certain, estimates suggest that between 50–75 percent of all boys in the school are identified in some way with a gang.

During the course of the 1991–1992 school year I interviewed 30 students. These interviews ranged from 40 minutes to several hours, with an average interview taking three hours. Although all students were selected on the basis of gender, 16 of the students were selected based on ability grouping, gender, grade level, and ethnicity. Both Mexican and Puerto Rican students were included. These 16 represented high and low performing freshmen and juniors. Specifically, two females and two males in high and low ability Freshman English; and two females and two males in high and low ability Junior English were included. Close to 20 percent of the staff was interviewed during sessions lasting approximately 80 minutes. In addition to the interviews, I also observed four English classes at intervals throughout the school year along with a Puerto Rican History class and, occasionally, a freshman social studies class. I was provided an office on one floor of the eight story building, known throughout the school as the "Vietnam" floor—this was because it was the area in which gangs sequestered themselves into different niches, frequently leading to violent encounters. I was also invited to attend numerous faculty and administrative meetings, school functions, in-service sessions, parties, and the like before, during, and after regular school hours. Having done research in a number of inner city high schools, I was somewhat surprised to find no evidence of the stereotyped "burned-out," recalcitrant inner-city teacher.

Throughout the days that I worked in the school I would not only ask about issues of concern but would also be sought out to discuss the problems facing the school. Inevitably these discussions always returned to the two major concerns of the school, gangs and the students' external environment. I choose the word "external" since it was not simply the family that was mentioned but the neighborhood, larger community, and even societal conditions that were often perceived to be transgressing on the school and its members' attempts to engage in their schooling activities and in-school learning.

Lares High School appeared to be a magnet for the local gangs whose activities inside the school were an extension of those outside the school. Without exception, students, when asked either what some of the problems were at Lares or if they could change anything at Lares what would it be, responded with "the gangs." Some could not, and others would not, elaborate on just how or why the gangs troubled them, and most admitted having friends who were in gangs. But most students talked in matter-of-fact tones about exactly how gangs affected them in school. According to Alfonso, a 17 year old sophomore who had transferred to Lares after attending school in the East:

> In New Jersey and New York you got the same thing, you know, but you don't get em like here, . . . there they jump you once and they saw you got hurt and that's it. They won't bother you no more . . . But here, you know, it just keeps on . . .

Different frustrations were faced by Sal, a 19 year old senior and art scholarship recipient:

> There's people bugging me, you know . . . they do come up to me and, you know, they do talk to me and stuff like that. Especially since I draw, they like, you know, they want people to draw gang symbols for them, you know . . . Well when you look around the school you can see all the graffiti and uh, and especially in the washrooms and there's a lot of drugs going on . . .

Finally, Jose, a 17 year old junior, points out how annoying he finds the presence of gang members in school:

> There's a lot of gang bangers hanging next to the escalators, if you went by sometimes they snatch your chain, throw a pop can, or an egg, hit you, or things like that . . .

Perhaps the most disturbing element in these statements was the matter of fact, prosaic manner in which all students accepted the situation as beyond their control: "It just keeps on"; "a lot of drugs going on"; "snatch your chain, throw a pop can, an egg . . . things like that." I was moved and shaken by the presentation of such dramatic events as simply "school business as usual."

Teachers and counselors also discussed how gangs created havoc throughout the school:

A physical education teacher remarked:

> The gangbangers are usually the ones that don't dress. They intimidate the kids . . . So they're afraid to go in the locker room to dress. They dress in the washrooms and then they come . . . or they don't come at all . . . Who's gonna admit that they're afraid

cause they [the gangs] ask em to buy them stuff, pop out of the pop machine, or they say, "give me part of your lunch". . . Now the kid that's out on bail for murder, he says to me, the teacher, "so what! I'm up on trial, what the fuck are you gonna do to me?!" Well, he's really right. I'm watchin' him every minute so that he doesn't do anything to anyone else!

A counselor observed:

Well, the gang activity has been incredible in the schools. It's just gotten so big that I can't . . . I wish I were literate enough to tell you exactly how many kids are . . . the name of each gang but we have a highly integrated population . . . It's a real pressure on these kids. It's a real pressure on guys. I'd say being a young man in a school like this is a real test . . . We have fights in the lunch room every given time . . . ah . . . Maybe a few weeks ago, we had a fight, and the same day there was one on seventh floor cafeteria, one on five, and one on the other . . . many times, more than not, it's related to a gang thing, and I've seen them sparring in the halls, doing their gang stuff at each other and oh it's. . . .

Clearly, school personnel are aware of the gangs, ascribing much negative behavior to gang members who are represented as threatening and intimidating to other students. Gang members are recognized by their ritualistic confrontations: The exhibition of gang signs and symbols (their "gang stuff") and half-serious sparring in the halls. Although much gang violence is constrained at Lares, public expression of the gang sometimes deteriorates into actual fighting. It seems obvious that school personnel lack power and authority to protect either students or themselves from gang activity.

Gang membership dramatically affects the lives of students at Lares. Laws are broken in the community, and police are called. Territories are challenged, and fights occur between gangs. Although much of the trouble outside the school is seen as a community problem, these activities also cause school problems, in that gang fights out in the community are often followed by both attackers and their victims meeting at school. A temporary cessation of warfare may well end inside the school in renewed violence among the same boys. In fact, gang violence occurs spontaneously and adjacent to or on the school premises, the corner of the school building or the athletic field. One freshman boy described having to fight frequently in school, being shot at on his way to school, witnessing a stabbing on his front porch, and finally, having to modify his class schedule in line with his brother's to allow their father to drop off and pick up the two boys from school safely. Here is how Ephraim describes life in his neighborhood:

Where we live at, there's this building, right? And they always taking drugs and having gang fights. Yesterday, we were to church, right. And my father said he was watching TV and he heard somebody throw like a little rock. And he heard that, like somebody threw a little rock at the window, and they just started shooting. He thought that they were shooting us. He said he went outside barefooted . . . he thought that they shot us.

As in the cases of Alfonso, Sal, and Jose, Ephraim related his experiences in a manner devoid of the emotions usually attached to events of this sort. His flat, off-hand narration was a moving and convincing characterization of the effects of gang activity on the lives of those who happen to be nearby when the gangs confront each other. Students' statements about gang activity were rather bland statements as opposed to expressions of excitement, terror, or some other emotion.

Gangs affect the high school students of Lares in a number of ways. The subtle ways in which gangs may affect school learning, as well as the daily process of life in school itself, include the psychological effects of fear of physical aggression, embarrassment and shame especially with respect to the school's reputation. Without exception, students told me that Lares had not been their first choice. They would have preferred schools with stronger academic programs, closer to home and, most importantly, schools without violence. Most talked about the necessity to modify class schedules; to not participate in some classes such as gym; and to give up their lunch periods to avoid being harassed or facing threats of extortion.

Still, gangs remain part of the neighborhood and part of the school. We know quite a bit about why gangs persist in impoverished communities, but we know very little about the existence of gangs in school. Why are gangs hanging out in school rather than on the street? One answer is that school is where the action is—gang members can hang out together, recruit new members, keep an eye on the enemy, sell drugs, and meet girls. In addition, school is probably the safest haven around. Inevitably, some gang members acquire some formal school learning, although acquisition of knowledge does not appear to be sufficient reason for gang members to remain in school. Rather than being the *goal* of gang members who stay in school, an education is a latent consequence of remaining to pursue some other activity more meaningful to individuals in the gang. Despite their persistence in school, several arguments can be made for the expected exit from high school by gangs. Indeed, many students, both gang members and others, choose to leave, approximately 64 percent of Lares' students fail to graduate or leave before graduating.

One explanation for attachment to the school is that the gang may provide a structure that allows both primary and secondary relationships to coexist. Perhaps gang members require attachment to their primary group in an alien situation that establishes only secondary relationships with those engaging in day-to-day school activities. This indeed does seem to be the case, and gang membership constitutes the support system for members and its recruits that other opportunity structures provide for different groups of students in high school. The gang within the high school setting provides many benefits, such as those present in friendship or even family relationships, while simultaneously providing training for both legal and illegal careers. Gangs have become a part of the structure of the school. In fact, although it is not formally recognized, gangs are part of the school's reality—a latent extracurricular activity.

At school, members are able to exhibit gang membership and celebrate it without the constant violence that celebrates it outside or on the street. The violence within the school is more controlled and contained. Probably nowhere else can a number of gangs converge in one setting where each can express, display, and celebrate its membership without fear of being seriously hurt. The school has become the one place where gangs form a "convention"—where they find affirmation for the actual existence of the institution of the gang itself.

Homelessness

The function of the gangs at school as providers of primary family relationships is better understood when considering the second issue which inevitably arose in discussions with school staff and students. Not only gang members, but many other students as well, experience *homelessness*. I am using the term homelessness here to include the conventional understanding of the concept where one is without a place of residence. The term also is used to refer to the lack of basic primary group membership, where *home* transcends the physical to include ties to significant others such as the family. This is a broader use of the term and one which I find useful in describing my conversations with students and teachers at Lares.

It is the concept of home which provides young persons with a sense of self, belonging, community—the foundation which enables them to establish other relationships, both primary and secondary. The realization that one belongs and is accepted is integrally and inextricably tied to this concept which transcends the physical. It is this kind of homelessness, the absence of both special relationships and physical location, that is part of the reality of many (if not most) of the students' lives at Lares.

Teachers, staff, and students described living situations which fall under this rubric of homelessness: Students whose parents either abandoned, abused, or threw them out of the house; students who left the nuclear family to live in an extended family member's home and ultimately in a friend's family's home; students cohabitating with peers/friends; and students who are entirely without a place of residence or shelter. While the family traditionally has provided shelter for children, sometimes the nuclear family lacks sufficient resources when other factors are involved. Many students described constantly moving (some with their families) both between states and within the same neighborhood. In fact, few described having lived in the same home for more than a few years.

Homeless students

Albert, a male junior describes his family's economic decline and structural transitions when his father lost his job in New Jersey, forcing them to move from their working class neighborhood to live with extended family in Puerto Rico.

My parents decide to go to Puerto Rico, you know. So they said all right, they did that, and . . . um . . . they um . . . got divorced. So my dad moves over here, you know. Dad was over here, then while she was over there and you know . . . um . . . I don't know. I moved here . . . my dad lived here, and I decided to move here on my own . . . so I worked . . . paid my way . . . and just came over. . . . Then she (mother) came and brought my brother and sister. Now we all live in the same house. Yeah . . . he stays in his room, she stays in hers, you know, but we all live together.

In explaining why she did not apply to college, Nilda, a senior also gives us insight as to the effects of the home on her educational trajectory:

My parents were like, "we might have to send you to Texas." And you know, I don't wanna go, cuz you know here is where my friends are. But then my . . . mom came out, you know, saying that she needed me . . . And my father, he isn't gonna go. He just decided to stay here, so we're gonna, my mom and my brothers and sisters and me, we're gonna go. I'll have to work and help mom out with the kids . . . My father, it's like, you know, "leave me alone, don't touch me . . . If you have something for me, come and talked to me, but other than that, get away." I mean, we're suppose to be his kids, and you know, then he treats us like, like we're just one of those weirdos from the street.

Finally, Maria, who has difficulty in school and is considered to be emotionally troubled by her teacher, explained to me that there are four Marias in her family: mother Maria, grandma Maria, sister Maria, and Maria. It is only in our third time speaking together that I am told about her family.

Cause you know, they're not really my parents . . . they're my aunt and uncle . . . and my cousins . . . so I don't get along with them . . . my mother left me with them when I was a baby . . . and then she took off.

Teachers and counselors offer additional insights to situations that are sometimes so bad that it takes them months to understand the circumstances. An English teacher offers two such examples:

I talked to the godfather of this girl yesterday. He came to get her grades. She made all F's because she's been absent a considerable amount of time. But she probably cut class. He told me yesterday her mom's an alcoholic. Her stepfather is too, and that she now lives with her 21 year old aunt who is expecting a baby, who does not have a husband, and she's a high risk, which means she's had serious complications. He says he has never seen anybody live in such poverty-stricken conditions like this. There is sometimes so little food in the house to keep them going. She used to come once in a blue moon. And one day when she came, I looked at her and I could see how nasty she was. Personal hygiene was seriously impaired. She had all kinds of little cotton balls and things in her hair and she hadn't had a chance to brush it out and she got lice. And her clothes were not as clean as they needed to be . . . Many times when I would talk to her she would smell of urine. And she was a big girl. She must have been 5'8". I found out, finally, through a little detective work with Youth Guidance, that she lives in an abandoned building on the third floor, which is the crack floor for all drugs that are being sold in that area. And her mom and everybody else in the building is on it. All the money that they get from wherever goes to drugs. I decided at that point I'd shut up . . . such extreme poverty. With situations like this the question is not why doesn't she come to school more often but why does she come at all? This last question is one for which I have no answers.

Children can be made homeless as a result of many different kinds of experiences. The effects of being without a physical residence are obvious. The effects of being without a home in the sense of lacking a nurturing environment are less obvious. Even when a child remains with the nuclear family and that family is often forced to move, there can be negative consequences which play out in the schooling process.

In sum, two major issues surfaced in my interviews with students and staff at Lares, the problems of gangs and of homelessness. Usually these issues are examined as problems in the community, external to the school. However, it is more useful to recognize that these issues are not "out there" but very much a part of the schooling process. As such they should be considered an integral part of any examination of inner-city secondary schools.

LESSONS FROM THE CHICAGO VIGNETTE

Unlike Delgado-Gaitan's work in Carpinteria in the previous vignette, Quiroz's research in Lares High School was principally concerned with life *inside* the school. Quiroz provides a grim picture in their own words of students' lives both in and outside school, lives that are haunted by the specters of gang violence and home-lessness. Rather than positioning herself outside the screen door of the Chapa family household as Delgado-Gaitan did to listen to the family's lunchtime conversation, Quiroz's vantage point on the lives of the participants in her study is from the corridors, classrooms and her office in "Vietnam," the floor of the school most associated with gang violence. This difference in perspective or vantage point prompts Quiroz to be concerned with such questions as What impact does gang violence have upon students' feelings about and achievement in school? and How do teachers perceive their students' lives? Like Delgado-Gaitan, Quiroz also changed her research focus over time. Her original agenda addressed questions about how students made decisions about taking part and investing time in school-related activities.

Most of the students at Lares with whom Quiroz spoke would have preferred attending another high school with a better academic reputation and with less violence and gang activity. Ironically for many, particularly the gang bangers, school seems to serve as a refuge, almost a safe haven from the lawlessness and violence of the streets. As much as gang violence contributed to students' sense of futility and frustration on a daily basis in the school and in their neighborhood, for many students it was their household situation that ultimately set the most ironclad limitations on their school attainments. In discussing "homelessness" Quiroz refers to conditions created by family hardships and stresses related to migration, divorce and separation, drug use and joblessness. Teachers, while sympathetic to the impact of these unsettling circumstances, were not involved in direct ways in their students' lives, perhaps explaining why they were not suffering the burnout Quiroz and others associate with teaching under such conditions as those that characterize life at Lares.

While the Chicago Public School district has been engaged in restructuring its schools, the impact on Lares seems negligible. Schools such as Lares in Chicago are overwhelmed by the culture of the streets and the economic and social circumstances of the students who attend them. Schools and communities faced with high levels of delinquency, in addition to pervasive joblessness and family discord, lack the institutional resources necessary to create environments conducive to comfort and security much less high academic achievement. It seems beyond the capacity of traditionally organized schools and school systems to address and meliorate such circumstances—a point to which we will return in the concluding chapter of this volume.

VIGNETTE #3: YOUNG CHILDREN AND THE CONSTRUCTION OF SCHOOL SUCCESS AND FAILURE: A HONDURAN REFUGEE STUDENT IN "LAKELAND," WISCONSIN

by Marianne Bloch, Jay Hammond Cradle, Carolyn Dean,
Miryam Espinosa-Dulanto and B. Robert Tabachnick

Social and Cultural Context

In 1989, our research team identified three groups of children from three different ethnic groups who were beginning to attend public school in a moderately large city in Wisconsin we call Lakeland; the population of Lakeland is about 170,000. The school district population was approximately 80 percent European-American in ethnic heritage, 11 percent black, 5 percent Asian-American, 2 percent Latino and 1 percent "Other." We observed children at home and in their local community neighborhoods as well as in their classrooms across the first three years of schooling (grades K–3). Here, we focus on culture, class, race, gender, and language as complex, interrelated factors that appeared to affect children's success in the beginning years of school.

Case studies of three schools were carried out during this period. Two of the schools were selected because each had been recently involved in a court-ordered integration plan. While both schools, Greendale and Lakelawn, enrolled more than 50 percent European-American children, Greendale had a large black population

(33%) while Lakelawn had a large Hmong population (28% at the beginning of our study). Similarly, while the third school, Oakhill, had a majority of European-American children, it had the largest Latino group of children in the city—children who had recently immigrated from Central America, Mexico, or who were first-born Mexican-American United States citizens. We hoped to study small groups of black children in Greendale School, Hmong children in Lakelawn School, and Latino children in Oakhill School in both home and school contexts. We wanted to study children's primary language use at home and at school, as well as family and school expectations for children before they began school and during the first several years of school, as well as the organization of home and school curriculum, teaching, and learning. Finally, we were interested in what parents, other community members, teachers and other school personnel said about and to each other, with special attention to discourses and practices that influence the children.

Schooling and Its Context

Children's learning is frequently viewed as that which happens only within the classroom, with peers, with teachers, and the "curriculum." Our perspective by contrast takes into account each child's history, both within school over time and within family and community. Further, each child has a unique constellation of characteristics; therefore, intra-group (for example, differences between the Hmong children) as well as inter-group differences (e.g. between black, Hmong, and Latino children) are important. Similarly, as noted throughout this volume, the three schools, their staffs, and children's teachers must be viewed as carrying particular cultural and social histories that, like children and their families, are also nested in the socio-cultural and political/economic contexts of the broader society. From these vantage points, the stories we tell about individual children are contextualized within the stories of their different schools and communities and cannot be directly compared because of the uniqueness of these multi-layered histories. The histories of the Hmong, as recent voluntary immigrants to the United States or as political refugees after the Vietnam War, is quite different from the history of blacks in the United States and the history of different Latino groups, some of whom are/were voluntary immigrants while others came as political refugees. Ogbu's framework fits the intragroup variability we have seen in our study. We believe that broad macrostructural factors related to class, race, ethnicity, and gender are critical to how children's success and failure become part of their constructed identity within schools and communities. Here we give a heavier emphasis on the local construction of identity, and power relationships in the construction of "truths" about children.

The following is a portrait of one "alien," "foreign," "minority" child and his dealings—success and frustrations—in the two places—school and home—in which he spends most of his life. Rafael, as well as the rest of his family and many other immigrants in the United States, was born in Honduras. During the 1980s they fled from the civil war that engulfed their country. They came to the United States searching for a better life and dreaming of having a safe place to live. We can begin Rafael's portrayal with his "trip" to the United States.

> Maria [Rafael's mother] reached the U.S.-Mexican border with her two kids. There she bought a rubber tractor tire to cross the river. She put both kids inside the tire and she kept swimming and pushing it with all her heart. When she heard the choppers, she had to immerse herself while calming her kids, who were very scared inside the floating tire. Maria and her kids succeeded in crossing the river. Then they had to walk a long distance until they could catch a bus. Meanwhile, the kids were starving and tired, but she could only offer them a small snack she brought with her and beg them to keep walking. Manuel (Rafael's father) was waiting for them in a small town and, after joining him, they came to Lakeland.

Neither of Rafael's parents had many years of formal education or a command of English that could allow them to search for skilled and better paying jobs in the United States. Both parents searched and found jobs in cleaning, construction, and other manual jobs. Maria eventually found work as a school aid. The schedule was much better than that of her former jobs, permitted her to earn a little more money and gave her much more time to spend with her children and at home. Still the family economy was always strained. However, both parents were working and not on welfare or on any kind of economic aid program. They lived in a subsidized apartment-complex and their neighbors included blacks, Asians (refugees), Hispanics/Latinos and poor European-Americans.

In Rafael's family Maria had an important role as mother and head of the household. She was the one who brought the children to the United States while Manuel waited for them. It was a dramatic moment in which she alone was protecting her children. Furthermore, in the United States, Maria was the one who took care of the home, the children, and also worked long hours outside. Rafael's parents had been together for a long time, but had never married. Manuel used to work little and also had a drinking problem. The couple had many problems. Maria stayed with Manuel because he was the only one in the family who held U.S. residency. Consequently, he was the only one formally allowed to sign the apartment lease, make phone contracts, and the like. By the fall of 1992, Maria and her children worked out their immigration papers and now hold U.S. residency. Manuel and Maria broke up, and Maria married a black man from the United States. Rafael's family portrait is far from the European-American middle class family ideal. His family structure is in distinct contrast with the idealized version of the mainstream. Unfortunately, it is the American family value that is held by most in the school setting. As a consequence, Rafael, as well as other children of color, must confront and determine family reality *vis á vis* the predominant European-American middle class ideology regarding family structure and values.

During the course of Rafael's family's "adjustment" to U.S. society, linguistic competence played a major but uncertain role. On the one hand, English proficiency is an important and powerful element in accommodating to U.S. society. On the other hand, for Maria, maintaining Spanish language mastery is also a very crucial issue.

I noticed that, within the household, both parents talk among themselves and to the kids in Spanish. The children basically talk back to their parents in Spanish, but they also use a few words and idiomatic expressions in English. The children definitely use English among themselves. Maria expresses that it is important that her children don't forget how to speak in Spanish. She does not allow them to forget it, and the most important things in their home are spoken in Spanish.

Rafael not only rejects acknowledging Spanish, but also identified himself as a Latino at the school. However, Rafael also sees that one more language gives him at least a modicum of intellectual power. Above all, he has the ability to affirm or correct the teacher, yet he holds the only power he has in the classroom by silencing his Spanish proficiently.

[Teacher] greets in Spanish by saying "Today is Thursday" (*Cueves*) in Spanish. [She] asks who knows what that means. No one answers. [She] calls on Julio and Rafael to help out. Rafael looks down, smiling, says he doesn't know what "*cueves*" means. [Teacher] says, "Thursday. Today is Thursday." [Thursday in Spanish is *Jueves* not *Cueves*].

Rafael changed his name to Raymond. This act illustrates the dual course of identity he and many other children of color pursue. The home-culture and values are not usually the same as those of the mainstream. Moreover, those values are considered deficiencies, and children are socially ostracized in school because of their "lack of language"—English or their understanding of rules. On the other hand, the school environment reflecting mainstream ideology represents a major source of social pressure against home-culture and non-mainstream family values.

Rafael is a very intelligent child with high self-esteem. Why should he be treated differently and be less well regarded because of his background? Rafael respects both places, home and school. His desire for the same respect and recognition for his background (i.e., family values) from the school seems quite reasonable. By changing his name perhaps Rafael believes that he can create a buffer that allows him to negotiate his identity in a less confrontational manner. One of the first grade teachers recalled what happened when Rafael did not know how to deal with the school environment, when the rules were still unclear to him and when he still called himself Rafael.

[Teacher] I think Rafael is a very sharp kid. Very smart kid. . . . He's pretty squirrely, too, but he was kept in Head Start for an extra year because when they tried to screen him for kindergarten he climbed under the table, and over the table, and all over the room, and it was recommended that he have another year of pre-school, so he stayed in Head Start and I think that year to mature did help him.

While changing his name in kindergarten helped him cope with the school environment, Rafael was still considered to be a "squirrely" kid in first grade. "Teachers were trying hard to understand the different experiences he brought from his neighborhood and from his home-culture. In addition his mother had developed strong communication skills and worked with Rafael's teachers." "[Rafael's mother] was very supportive and I [teacher] know she checks every night to make sure that he's bringing [Rafael's behavior chart] home, and he's very conscious of the fact that he needs to bring it." In this way, Rafael was not alone; school and home were helping him to find his own path within the school environment.

Rafael's portrait, then, is judgment of what Rafael is or will be. It is remarkable in fact that the same institution that makes and treats Rafael as different because of his Latino heritage, when it becomes personalized, through individual teachers or in a specific school, gives him the "benefit of the doubt."

> Teacher: The biggest problem that we had . . . that Rafael had this year was stealing, and that was a very aggressive action on his part, and I was real concerned . . . was really tough to deal with. But I think we finally got through to him . . . .

> Interviewer: How did you deal with Rafael?

> Teacher: I try not to embarrass anybody in that situation because I know that all children have that desire to want something that someone else has, and especially if the children around you have more than you do. I think that's really tough and that can happen in this school. Unfortunately [stolen things] were always in his backpack or desk, and so what happened then, the other children began to accuse him. That was pretty upsetting, and Rafael talked about the fact that people were beginning to think of him as a thief . . . I think that's what finally turned him around.

The first grade teacher and the school allowed Rafael to make mistakes in the same way that other children are allowed to do. Both Rafael and his teacher, in conjunction with parental support, worked things out and Rafael "turned around."

UNDERSTANDING RAFAEL'S VIGNETTE

This excerpt of Rafael's school experiences and from his everyday life illustrates that Rafael is still a small child who needs to create structures to understand and construct his own identity. This will, in turn, affect how he is perceived and will allow him to learn more about the mainstream culture, values, and rules. Together the institutions of school and home have worked to support Rafael in becoming fairly successful in school. The ways in which he, at a very young age, must interpret his worlds, and try to bring them together, or behave differently in each, underlines again how truly bright he, and how many others like him, need to be. It also underlines, however, the fragility of the institutional discourses and constructions of children's identity and behavior when children are linguistically or racially "different."

VIGNETTE #4: THE POWER OF RITUAL AND LANGUAGE: MARIA TERESA TAKES HER PLACE IN TAMPA'S CUBAN COMMUNITY
by Jim King, Mary Alice Barksdale-Ladd and Richard Alvarez

Maria Teresa Martinez is 15. Over two hundred friends have come to celebrate her "Quinse." Like many other young women of Hispanic descent, Maria joins the "world of adults" in this scripted ritual of passage. Along the way, Maria and her parents, Zoila and Manuel, have spent considerable time, energy, and money to make this evening special for Maria Teresa and her friends.

In the large rented hall, Zoila and Maria Teresa greet their guests in gowns made for this occasion. Maria Teresa's 14 female attendants all wear matching aqua dresses. Their partners and Manuel all wear black tuxedos. Only Maria Teresa and her escort dress in white. It is her night, and all of us focus on her. After several rehearsed dances (*"La Quinceañera y sus Parejas," "La Quinceañera y su Papa"*), after hors d'oeuvres, drinks, and dinner, Maria Teresa makes her "Quinse" speech to the group of family and friends that have assembled. On the printed program, the sentiments made in her speech are recast. *"Les demos las gracias a todos aquellos que con su participación han hecho de este día uno muy especiál para Maria. La Familia Martinez."* (Thanks to all who participated and made this a very special day for Maria. The Martinez Family.)

Later, Zoila, told us how proud she felt of Maria, her performance, and the success of "their Quinse." That night Zoila had suggested to Maria Teresa that she should write out her speech so that it would be just right. She was concerned about Maria Teresa's nervousness, as the "Quinse" speech "must be made in Spanish." Maria Teresa simply said "I'll just wing it." And she did, without hesitation or mishap.

In this vignette, we want to highlight some of the unique aspects of Cuban-American lives in Tampa, and how Cuban-Latin heritage impacts on beliefs and practices associated with literacy and schooling. Readers should know that Maria Teresa and her parents, Zoila and Manuel, are our leads or centers. But we have also included information from several other Cuban-American informants.

The Place of Ritual as a Cultural Signifier

That Manuel and Zoila could provide this special evening for Maria Teresa is significant in this social context. They are members of an upper middle income group, with a family of limited size. With a strong sense of responsibility to their family within a larger sphere of the Cuban community, Manuel and Zoila's concern over Maria Teresa's intention to "wing it" makes sense. Both Maria Teresa and her parents recognize the importance of the ritual performance of a Spanish speech. But Zoila has a functional competence with Spanish, and fears that her daughter's command of the language may not be up to the task. She is also concerned about the impact of nervousness, something Maria Teresa seems not to possess. But the two remain connected at the ritualistic level.

Rituals and ethnic identification also figure in the intergenerational passing of literacy and how it is shaped. For Manuel, the situation is more complex than whether or not he is Cuban. It seems more important to know how many generations of the family have lived in the United States. To some degree, one's distance from immigration is a measure of Cuban influences.

> It's about how close you are to Cuba. Take Zoila. Her mother was born in Cuba, and her father spoke Spanish and Italian. Yet, Zoila knew some English before she went to school. She didn't have a Quinse like this one. I was born and raised in Cuba. In some ways, I was closer to Cuba because of that. Now we both speak English OK. But we often talk in Spanish at home. So, if Maria Teresa speaks Spanish, it is because Zoila's family and my family speak Spanish. We are both in some way Cuban-American.

Zoila remembers that she knew English and could speak it when she began kindergarten. "English wasn't a problem in kindergarten." Yet, learning to read English did present a problem. Zoila remembers being confused by the variation between English and Spanish correspondences between graphemes and phonemes. "What a letter said in reading it wasn't like what I heard at home. And besides, later on I realized that certain things they [her parents] said weren't right. They said shair (/s/) instead of chair (/c/) or sherry instead of cherry. How about beige (/j/) instead of beige (/z/)."

On one hand, English becomes emblematic of adjusting and fitting in. It functions as a check. But literacy also works in the same, or similar, ritualistic valuing. That is, its importance to Zoila is representational more than functional. First, the acquisition of a second language (English) is a benchmark for school readiness, but the use of English as an academic tool was not part of her home experience. Second, learning literacy in school had functional aspects within the school classroom, but since neither English nor Spanish were used much at home in reading or writing, literacy also assumed a ritualistic importance as a signifier of learning. From the perspective of her parents, Zoila was learning two new languages, English and literacy. Yet, the two came home from school in one package.

Zoila carries a respect for language. She talks about saying things the right way. She became aware of the differences when her friends started commenting on the way she talked in upper elementary grades. Now she wants to "say it right," and reports being embarrassed when others correct her. She is also aware of when her mother says "shicken" (chicken) and "shursh" (church).

Manuel voices at least two of his beliefs about language and its social representation. He indicates that speaking both Spanish and English is not a problem and that having two different ways of talking and thinking is a good thing. Yet there is a cost. He wants to be able to do each without inflection or influence from the other language. His view of language competence includes a certain amount of what others think of his performance of language.

"I felt funny speaking Spanish in Madrid," Manuel confides in an interview. "I figured that they [Spaniards] could tell I was Cuban." Similarly, Zoila's embarrassment about her mother's confusion of an alveolar affricate (/c/) and an alveolar continuant (/s/) signals Zoila's valuing of uninflected English. And realizing that there are systematic interference patterns between languages seems irrelevant. "I know we Cubans all do the same thing [with English]. But the idea is to get it right." And "I want to say it the proper way." Manuel thinks before he responds. He considers his words. In addition to a careful representation of a complex idea, he adds a layer of monitoring both syntax and orthography.

Literacy as performance and ritual is also evident inside the Spanish speaking community in Tampa. Zoila's mother recalled that her work in one of the cigar factories was also informed by the richness of literacy. While rollers spread tobacco leaves, chopped them, and produced cigars, "the reader" sat in a pulpit-like raised cubical, and read in Spanish. "*La Lectura*" read newspaper bulletins, and novels into minds, while the hands made cigars. "*La Lectura*" brought new worlds into the cigar factory and kept the rollers working in their places.

Knowing Your Place: Relativism on the Inside

The three generations of Cuban-Americans that live in West Central Florida at this time represent an important shift in Spanish culture and Spanish language use. The oldest group, the grandparents, remain dominant Spanish speakers and talk to each other in Spanish. Yet, they are also fluent and at least functionally literate in English. Talking is often translating between Spanish and English. Grandparents ask "*Como se llama . . .*," as they turn away from their English-speaking friends and toward their adult children who will supply the missing piece of English. The children, who are themselves parents, are bilingual also. But their dominant, or most frequent, language is English. While they are able to speak fluent Spanish, it is with concentration and effort. Much like their parents, they often struggle with "*Como se llama . . .*" But unlike their parents, they are looking for the Spanish word. The youngest group, Maria's generation, "know of " Spanish. They know Spanish labels for objects. They use some Spanish in greetings and in ritual exchanges, such as expressions of insult, humor, and slang. They do not use Spanish spontaneously. Nor do they often talk with their Spanish-dominant *abuella* or *abuello* in Spanish.

Because of a rich cultural network, older generations lived day-to-day without needing much English. To this day in Tampa, Cuban grocery stores, restaurants, hair stylists, banks, and other businesses offer Spanish speaking customers service in their native language. An informal network of plumbers, doctors, electricians, pharmacists, tile setters, exterminators, roofers, and others of Cuban descent provide their services to neighbors and friends. It is a comfortable co-existence. Spanish language and culture is ubiquitous.

People of Cuban heritage have settled in Tampa from the mid 19th century around the cigar manufacturing in Ybor City (Perez, 1980). Another enclave of Cuban-Americans eventually came to live in the small bungalows of West Tampa, where many still live. But, it would be a mistaken notion to think of Tampa's Cuban-American population located exclusively in any part of Tampa—although there are Cuban-dominated neighborhoods. The city is permeated with people of Cuban descent, and the cultural impact is part of the city's heritage as well.

Learning in Place

Manuel's grandmother claims to have learned spoken English from daytime "stories" (or soap operas), yet she remained unable to read and write in English. This story about his grandmother is emblematic. In one sense, Manuel celebrates the ingenuity of his *abuella*, who with limited resources managed to learn a new language while caring for a home. In contrast, he smirks at her choice of content— soap operas. Similar stories echo through the family. He remembers his father's hard work in composing a letter in English to his brother in New York. There were frequent requests for spelling help. This was a hard task. But when the letter was completed, Manuel remembers his brother's laughter at the "mistakes" still contained in the letter. The give-and-take between speakers and writers seems to come from a valuing for both languages.

Because Cubans in Tampa are a long-standing, relatively financially secure group, their use of nonstandard English or of Spanish is contextualized, understood in unique ways, by both insiders and outsiders. To better understand the patterns we have presented so far, and to introduce others, we include descriptions of Manuel, Zoila, and Maria Teresa as they remember their coming to an English language place.

Manuel's Learning in a New Place

Manuel is proud that his daughter has chosen to continue the tradition of "Quinse." He thinks it is like a number of similar customs that are eroding and hopes that Maria will continue with Cuban social practices. When he was slightly younger than Maria, Manuel remembers that his life was less self oriented, and more one of serving his family. He tells a story about a time when he had first come to the States:

> In Cuba, I could sit back and relax. But here, they [his parents] wanted to buy a car, so I'm dealing with a dealer. A guy wearing a weird suit and a loud colored tie and talking real fast. I'm trying to make deals, something I've never done before. Not even in my own language. Now I'm doing it in English. I was afraid to say the wrong thing. And if you know my father, when it comes to making deals on a car . . . he would say "No! You tell him that!" Oh God, I remember a time when my father would tell me "You tell him this, that, and the other!" And I just couldn't get myself to cuss at somebody who was older than I was.

Manuel sees these differences between his life and that of his daughter as natural and developmental, part of adjusting. He wants it to be better for his daughter and sees much of the change from the perspective of his own experiences as a first generation immigrant.

> As the oldest, I had to do a lot of stuff my brother wasn't expected to do. [When] we had to hook up the phone, I had to go out there and do the paper work. It was a lot of pressure. I was almost forced to go out and learn things, do things, because nobody else could do it. Going on vacation, I had to call and make reservations in a hotel. I was so embarrassed to make mistakes, to say the wrong thing.

A real difference in reasons for learning are evident in Manuel's stories. He remembers his learning from a sense of responsibility as a major player in the welfare of his family. His ability to speak English was a required skill for his role as family translator. As the interlocutor for his father's business deals, Manuel felt the weight of this linguistic responsibility in concrete ways. His desire for his daughter's appreciation of that same capability cannot be seen as having consequences that are so dramatic.

Manuel's memories of school in Cuba are of success, achievement, and satisfaction. He liked school in Cuba. "I was real good in school." In our interview, Manuel mentions "I was good in school" repeatedly. Hearing his stories about the differences in school experiences on either side of the "plane trip," the need to establish his credibility as a learner is easy to understand.

> In Cuba, I used to read books by Jose Martín. There was a book called *La Epocha d'Oro*, (*The Golden Age*), and it was written by Jose Martín. I used to read stories out of that. My father had a cousin that was like a poet, who used to write stuff and give me books. I used to really enjoy that. Maybe because my father used to like that, too. And it was something that we could share. I remember reading *Moby Dick, 20,000 Leagues Under the Sea*, and sports things that they have in Spanish. They used to have things like Batman and stuff like that in Spanish.

Manuel's memories of his reading center on rich, complex, and sophisticated texts. He talks rapidly, proud of what he could do in Cuba. He remembers himself as more of a reader than a writer.

> I remember writing in Cuba. Not too much. I don't think I ever liked to write. I don't think I would have done a lot of writing, even in Cuba. I was pretty good in school, in all my classes. But I don't think I really liked writing.

Yet, his "not really liking writing" is a much different situation than not being able to do so after the "plane ride." In both writing and reading, Manuel differentiates before and after Cuba, and sets the demarcation at the day of his trip and, later, at the first day of school.

> Leaving Cuba was just like any other trip. And leaving was everybody's idea of a good thing. But it's weird, you know. You wake up, get on a plane, and 45 minutes later, you are in a different world. Your bed you slept in, your toys, your clothes, your language, the foods you're used to eating . . . everything's different. Forty-five minutes! There was no gradual change. Forty-five minutes and I was in Miami. I can still remember the air smelled different.

"Breathing the air, I could smell it . . . the difference." After a summer of relaxing, adventure, and getting along, Manuel faced his first day of school in the United States. ". . . the reality of school hits you pretty hard when all of the sudden, they drop you off at the school door and say 'Here you are. Go for it!'" Manuel's anxieties are joined by fears with causes other than newness and the unknown. After being successful in Cuba, he now faces school as the "other," and the rituals that the school visits on him as other have little to do with how he sees himself as a learner, but much to do with the new school's construction of "who he now is."

> In Cuba, I was so good. I used to represent my school in talent things, stuff like that. All of the sudden, you come here and you have to learn your A, B, C's and 1, 2, 3's all over again. It was so embarrassing, almost degrading for me. To sit there and read this book with a whole page and just a couple of big letters on it. Things like you did in first grade.

Living in this new place, and with many relatives and friends in Cuba, Manuel recognizes that he had a real opportunity for writing. Yet, there was something that kept him from using this new opportunity for real writing.

> I would [try to] write for the longest time, just sitting there. My mother would say "Don't you want to tell them about _____?" But it had already happened for me, you know? I might have mailed a few, but not so many.

In addition to his separation from his friends and family in Cuba, Manuel begins to experience a similar rift in his relationship with his parents. As he acclimates to the demands of an English thinking classroom, and as he complies with his parents' needs for his mediation of their new language and culture, Manuel shifts in his relationship towards his schooling. From a position as accomplished at school and valued for his academic performances at home, he became one seen as less accomplished at school and valued for his functional relationship to the culture by his parents. The school taught from simplified and demeaning texts attributable to a confusion between his limited knowledge of English and his competence with literacy. In contrast, at home he was valued for the very ability the school perceived him as lacking—the ability to be a broker between two cultures and two languages. His parents spoke Spanish exclusively and relied on their son for negotiating their new environment.

> I was on my own in school because they didn't know much about school. They would ask "Have you done your homework, have you done your homework?" But they couldn't tell if I did or didn't do it. And if I had done it, or tried to do it, they couldn't help me with it. Thirty years later and he [father] still doesn't know. I'm still translating for him.

His classroom experiences were constructions of performance. Not knowing what was "really going on," Manuel developed coping strategies that would at least give the appearance of participation.

> . . . During the first year, I would wait and see what books the other kids were pulling out . . . after the other kids caught on, they would all take out a different book, just messing with me.

Although at least some of the other students had also placed the wrong book on their desks, they had done so to ridicule Manuel, undermining his confidence in himself as a student. Manuel maintains that he learned more English during the summer following his first attempt at sixth grade than he did in the classroom. His contention makes sense given the chilly classroom climate he describes. Language is learned through frequent use; however, classrooms are often construed as places where children raise their hands for permission to use (and practice) language, and where turns to talk are contested among 20 to 30 students. In the summer Manuel has an additional seven hours each day to learn English. Nonetheless, the decision was made that he repeat the sixth grade.

Manuel has some ideas about how second language acquisition works and why he had such difficulty. Some of his understanding sounds like a critical stage theory of language acquisition, embedded in a sociological framework.

When I was young, and the grown ups got together, I used to listen to their stories. We were not allowed to break into the conversation . . . My father's mom lived with us. She used to tell me stories . . . The younger you are the easier it is [to learn English]. Around 10, 11, 12, 13 is real bad . . . Or, if you're older and you already had your education in Cuba, [then] you just have to learn the language. But I was caught in between. I didn't have one *or* the other. I started all over again and it really put me back.

Manuel sees his own competence with English in developmental terms and in specific applications:

I started talking at first. Then reading. After a couple of years, I could understand what others were saying, but I would have to explain what I was trying to say. My vocabulary was so limited that I found myself saying "Well, you know it's like that thing that you use for ____." You know, that kind of stuff.

He also understands interference between languages. Speaking English meant a long path toward understanding and making himself understood. His issues are in lack of correspondence between Spanish and English and the amount of work required to use them in integrated ways.

It's frustrating to know what you want to say in Spanish and you have to translate it. Maybe [the frustration] is something that happens in second language. You would talk to me in English. I would listen in English. I would have to translate it to myself in Spanish. Answer in Spanish [to myself]. And translate it back to English. It slows you down. It's confusing. It's time consuming. I think it happens in second language. If it makes sense, that's the thing. It has to make sense to me in Spanish.

Zoila in the Meaning Space: Waiting for Understanding

At the "Quinse," Zoila was wearing a dress she had made especially for the evening. The dress, the evening, her daughter—all special. This is also a first for her, as her own fifteenth birthday was not marked by a "Quinse" of such extravagance. With Manuel's closeness to Cuban customs, with their family together, the tradition was embraced. Moving between the old and new has been a defining characteristic of Zoila's life. While her father spoke some English, her mother spoke none. Her mother had come to the United States from Cuba looking for work. She found a job and a husband. Zoila's father was born in Florida from Cuban and Italian parents. So he grew up speaking both Spanish and Italian. He knew English as well. Her mother was Spanish-speaking in Zoila's childhood.

I translated a lot for my mother. If Dad was there, he could handle it. But at the store and other places she and I would go . . . She could understand some [English] if we spoke slowly. But I remember as a kid going places and her not being able to understand.

Like Manuel, Zoila interpreted for her mother outside the home. But inside the home, Zoila's family spoke Spanish.

> Even though Dad could speak English, at home we never spoke English. We never spoke English. My mother would say "If you would speak English here, I might learn some." When she would try to say something and wouldn't get it right, we'd say 'Forget it. We'll just talk in Spanish.'

There are parallels between Zoila's and her mother's learning of English. Zoila compares her lack of patience with her mother's attempts at English with her own in school. She describes a tension, a space between speakers that stretches the sense-making out, while the other waits, struggles and gulps for understanding. But classroom teachers for Zoila didn't always say "Oh, forget it. We'll just talk in Spanish."

From a perspective of goal attainment, one can argue that Zoila productively learned English because she was required to do so in these instances of classroom communication. Yet, such a view does not capture the daily effort and struggle Zoila endured to make sense of her experiences and receive a meaningful payoff. A similar argument can be made regarding the separation of languages between home and school contexts. While Zoila may not have been confused by her parents' use of nonstandard English in a Spanish-speaking home, she also did not benefit from any reinforcement of English speaking, from modeling by others, and from witnessing her parents' use of English literacy.

> My mother didn't read to me because she worked at night. When I was little, she was working, so I watched TV with my Dad. There wasn't a lot of reading. He used to tell me stories of when he was a kid. Mom never sat down and talked with me. [She] was always at work. So the only times I learned English was from TV.

Her mother came to the States and found the work she wanted. That left Zoila's father to care for her. The expectation that he should read to her was not so great as that for her mother. Yet, it was from a combination of TV viewing and interaction with her father about events and experiences in her life that taught Zoila any English she knew before going to first grade.

> I learned English in first grade. I remember Martin Smith making fun of me when I didn't understand. I would ask "What does that mean?" I never forgot that. Kids would communicate and I would communicate a little, maybe because I watched TV, but sometimes they'd say words and I'd have no clue what was going on.

She goes on to explain her experiences in subsequent grades:

> In first, second, and third grades I had teachers who were bilingual. I remember that [having bilingual teachers] was easier because they figured I was just like from another country, too. And they tried to help me. They could translate something for me if I needed it.

In this case, Zoila views her metaphoric "being from another country" (and consequently, another language) as an advantage because such a designation allows her to get help from her teachers like other kids from another country. This is the very designation that traumatized Manuel's first years in U.S. schools. The teachers' use of bilingual instructional methods appears to have been limited to spoken language only. Zoila's first experiences with written Spanish occurred when she took Spanish in school. "I never learned to write Spanish until I took Spanish in school. So, a lot of what I can say in Spanish, I can't write. I learned Spanish from speaking it." As a second and third generation member of her mother's and father's families in the United States, Zoila had many experiences that prepared her in at least some ways for her school years. Living in the culture of the school, speaking some English at home, starting English language schooling at a young age, and having bilingual teachers appear to have helped her in school. Little preschool experience with written language, Spanish or English, created some limitations to her acquisition of school based literacy learning.

In effect, Spanish is relegated to functioning as an oral language in the second generation. When parents reason that their Spanish-speaking children will learn English as well as reading and writing in school, Spanish literacy is minimized. Also given the fact that some parents are not frequent readers and writers, there is an even greater chance that Spanish will be seen by the children as an oral language and English as both oral and written. The chances increase for a split between oral and literate cultures.

Maria Teresa Inherits Her Place

Both Manuel and Zoila made sure that Maria Teresa was educated in ways that would minimize the difficulties that they had experienced as students. She attended parochial elementary school and now attends a public high school of her own choosing, where she is an excellent student. Her story is best told in her own words. We have included the transcript of her interview with only minor editing and the removal of the interviewer's questions.

> [My] first language was Spanish. I started English in nursery and prekindergarten. The lady in nursery spoke Spanish, so that was easy. If I didn't understand in English, she would speak to me in Spanish. I knew I couldn't start first grade without English because I wouldn't be able to read. Once I started school, I didn't have a problem with

English. I took pre-K and kindergarten to learn it. I didn't have any trouble understanding teachers or like that.

I don't remember being read to. But my grandfather told me about Cuba, and my grandmother would talk to me, but not read to me. They didn't really know English, so they couldn't read to me. When I came home from school, it wasn't hard, because I liked speaking Spanish. Now, I don't really like it that much. I've lost a lot of Spanish. I can't speak as well as I used to. My pronunciation isn't as good either.

Now I like English better. But I will speak to my friends in Spanish if they'll understand. And I'll even speak in Spanish to someone who doesn't understand a word of Spanish. I get mixed up. Another problem I have is spelling. I remember in third grade I couldn't spell very well. My teacher said it was because I speak Spanish. And that was my fault or my problem. I still can't spell.

When I was little, I never read or wrote Spanish, or even learned the alphabet. It was just that I spoke it, and that's all I heard. It's hard now. When I was little, we had Spanish 30 minutes a week. But it was a joke. We colored pictures. And now, it's hard in Spanish. They give you a whole page, and there's 20 questions and that's your exam. It's really hard because I've never really had to read it. It's my first time to read We also have a diary and I have to write a paragraph. It's so hard. All of the audio exams I can understand.

Everybody in my class says "Oh, don't study. You're Spanish." And they expect me to know everything and I don't. Some of them probably know better because it's their third year taking Spanish. It's my first and I'm the youngest in the class. That doesn't help. I've never written or read Spanish until now. Now I even have trouble speaking it at home. They [Maria's family] don't correct me. They just think it's funny. So, I get really frustrated and I don't speak to them. They say "Speak in Spanish so we can understand." And I think to myself "Why bother if you're going to laugh at me?"

I write well in English. I get good grades in writing. I can't do the parts of speech—like a direct object, an indirect object. Just let me write. And now we're doing the same thing in Spanish. I don't like this in English. I can't do it in Spanish.

I didn't really want the "Quinse." My Mom has been talking about it since I was eight. I got to the point where I thought "I don't want it. I don't care." But as it got closer, I started getting excited about it. I'm glad we did it now. It's like *La Noche Buena* and all that stuff. I'm glad we keep all those traditions. It's supposed to be that now I have all these privileges, like I'm allowed to speak to boys and shave my legs. But, of course, I've already been doing that. But, I'm glad I did [the Quinse].

Maria Teresa is in many ways highly representative of her gender, age group, ethnicity and social class. As a young woman, still struggling with issues of identity formation in adolescence, her awkward pronunciation in Spanish is a source of embarrassment and works to inhibit her use of the language in social situations. As an adolescent member of a middle class family still highly attached to a Latin and Cuban heritage, her participation in the celebration of the "Quinse" is important both symbolically, signifying her assumption of the rights and responsibilities of womanhood, and culturally, affirming notions of family solidarity and tradition associated with her household.

Understanding Our Place

In this section, we interpret what Manuel, Zoila, and Maria Teresa have shared. We frame their ideas against a backdrop of waves of Cuban immigration and Florida educational policy that has affected and continues to affect second language learners. Our place includes the agenda that the three of us bring to this analysis. Richard is of Cuban descent, Jim's life partner is of Cuban descent, and Mary Alice teaches in a program that trains bilingual and multicultural elementary teachers. We all see our positions as advocates and certainly more than detached interviewers. As people who write text like this and as teachers who value education, we have reason to be careful about what we interpret as "literacy," "competency," and "efficacy." One way we hoped to monitor our valuing was to include the participants in all stages of the process.

Situating this Study

Because Cuba is located only 90 miles off the coast of Florida, there have always been Cuban-Americans in Florida. Large groups of immigrants have entered the state and become citizens during two time periods. In the 1950s, and especially after the overthrow of Batista's government in 1959, large numbers of Cubans immigrated in advance of Castro's government. Many of these émigrés came with considerable resources and entered this country with some measure of political influence. Later, in the 1980s, several waves of Mariel refugees came to the shores of Florida. These Cubans did not come with any significant support, financial, political, or social. In fact, they may have eroded the positions of Cuban-Americans already settled in Florida. In 1994 another wave of refugee Cubans floated to Florida. For the first time, they were greeted by restrictions which reflect the growing resistance in Florida, and in the United States generally, to additional Cuban immigration.

The greatest number of Cuban-Americans are found in the Miami metropolitan area. According to Perez (1980), Miami is home to 40 percent of the U.S. citizens of Cuban descent. Here, ethnic neighborhoods, businesses, and schools maintain a Cuban identified culture and Spanish literacy traditions. In other areas of Florida, Cuban-Americans are less isolated from mainstream Anglo lifestyles, and in some ways, face greater challenges to the preservation of Cuban cultural and Spanish language and literacy traditions. Manuel, Zoila, and Maria Teresa are representative.

Variable Tolerance

For this family, Spanish functions as an oral culture and is valued as an aspect of Cuban heritage. In contrast to the family's steady state perception of the importance of things Cuban, the valuing of Cuban-American culture and Spanish language by Florida's schools can be seen as fixed to a pendulum. The metaphor of a pendulum suggests that there has never been complete acceptance nor has there been complete intolerance.

During the period in the 1960s, when Manuel and Zoila were elementary students, classroom instruction in schools occurred in English. As speakers of highly accented English, Manuel and Zoila were merely tolerated in their class-rooms and received little help to ease their transition from Spanish into English. By the end of the 1960s, political pressures had moved the pendulum in the direction of broader acceptance and support of second languages learners. The federal Bilingual Education Act was passed in 1968, providing funds for teaching content in native languages to language minority children while they simultaneously learned English. A 1975 ruling in the U.S. Supreme Court (*Lau vs. Nichols*) established the legal obligation that public schools provide special programs for children with limited English proficiency. When Maria Teresa entered school, she inherited the benefits of these proactive policies. Maria Teresa's transition from a Spanish-speaking home to reading and writing in English in school was eased as a result of in-place bilingual education.

However, during the very years of Maria Teresa's school experience, there has been a great shift toward intolerance. In the early 1980s, a large wave of immigrants from Cuba entered Florida at Miami. Later named the "*Marielitos*," and the event the "Mariel Boatlift," these immigrants, many of whom had working class back-grounds, were seen as troublesome, prone to criminal activity, and, in general, less desirable immigrants than previous groups who had emigrated from Cuba. Con-tinuing reports that suggested that these new immigrants had been Cuban prisoners and residential mental patients persisted and contributed to a xenophobic climate in much of Florida. As a result of the "Mariel Invasion," over 13,500 Cuban children entered the Miami public schools in a six month period.

At this time, no doubt buoyed by the public reaction to the economic costs associated with the new wave of Cuban immigrants, various groups under the rubric of "U.S. English" successfully campaigned for English as the official language of Florida. The official English language policy made clear what may have been only implicit before; Cubans, as represented by their language and culture, were an unwelcomed minority. The public school community responded in kind and re-pealed teacher certification options in bilingual education in that same year. Teacher certification in bilingual education has never been reinstated in Florida. For newer immigrants who face schooling as Manuel did, without English and without English resources, the State of Florida has promised little in the way of support. The well planned transition made by Maria Teresa may also occur for other Spanish speaking children, but it will be good fortune, not good planning, that will allow it.

While the policy and public pendulum continues to cut its arc across the culture, it is within Cuban-American families that the continuity of language and tradition has been sustained. Education has a tradition of importance in Cuban culture. It is not uncommon for families of Cuban descent to do without other material comforts in order to enroll their children in parochial schools. "[Cubans] flourish because many Cuban parents are greatly concerned with transmitting to their children their language and culture" (Perez, 1980). The commitment to nonsecular schooling, combines what is for many Cuban-Americans a significant trinity: family, love of God, and education. It is important to point out, however, that respect for tradition and maintenance of rituals may have unexpected effects when the young children enter school. Many Cuban-American parents have maintained an expectation for Spanish at home, and for English at school. Because of situationally defined reading (such as the daily newspaper) and virtually no writing, children are socialized into an oral Spanish culture.

In Maria Teresa's childhood, books had little impact. Since Spanish literacy is apparently valued by Cubans and by Cuban-Americans in Spanish contexts, it is important to ask why these parents did not attempt to engage their own children in this world of Spanish speaking readers and writers at home. First, in all likelihood, her parents were themselves not highly skilled in literacy. Their own limited involvement in reading and writing may not have prepared them to anticipate reading with children. Second, without frequent need for and use of literature and writing, they may not have had strategies for, or awareness of, engagement with books, and the potential benefits of Spanish *or* English literacy to their children's schooling success. Not knowing what to do relative to "English literacy," these parents chose not to "interfere."

Researchers who work within first and second language acquisition and first and second literacy acquisition have confirmed that competence with native literacy facilitates acquisition of literate competencies in a second language (Harste, Woodward, & Burke, 1984; Teale, 1986). However, what researchers come to know and what parents already know are often not the same sets of information and usually not related in how they were learned (Heath, 1983). Cuban-American parents' decisions to avoid interference with school practice is not unique. It is a patterned response to sensing that one has been excluded from the mysteries of school practice. If Manuel and Zoila had known that preschool literacy experiences in Spanish would have enhanced English literacy learning for Maria Teresa, would they have provided them? Likely. Reading to Maria Teresa in Spanish honors literacy knowledge that Manuel brought from Cuba. It would have helped them connect their own literacies (Spanish *and* English) with those of Maria Teresa and, through her, to the school. For this to be a productive experience, the same kind of multiple perspectives on literacy need to be in place in the classrooms.

Resources in a Place and a Half

During the seventies, Cuban-Americans were termed an "economic miracle" when compared with other groups of Latin heritage who were living in the United States. And while the relative advantages that Cubans have enjoyed have eroded during economic downturns, they still maintain what can be seen as an enviable status.

Cubans are more likely than other Hispanic groups to hold college degrees and have unemployment rates lower than the national average.

Yet, Perez (1980) recommends caution in assuming that Cubans uniformly attain the American dream, suggesting that: ". . . the economic achievements of Cubans in the United States have often been exaggerated because of the rags-to-riches success stories of a few individuals" (p. 258). In contrast, most of "Cuba's aristocratic and traditionally wealthy families, although they retain certain prestige among the immigrant group, have lost status as well as wealth" (p. 258). More to the point of Maria Teresa's "Quinse," Perez (1980) writes:

> Upwardly mobile families have attempted to adopt and preserve the trappings of upper-class life in prerevolutionary Cuba . . . The society pages of Miami's Hispanic newspapers are filled with descriptions and photographs of increasingly lavish social events. Weddings and birthdays (*particularly the traditional 15th birthday for girls*) are occasions for successful families to display their new wealth. (p. 258, emphasis ours)

Explaining the Cubans' relative and economic advantages in the United States is complex. In addition to the factors of individual agency, particularly the personal resources brought to the immigration process and recycled in the economic support structure of enclaved Cuban-American communities, Perez (1980) also suggests an additional, intermediate, factor of Cuban family structure as instrumental in Cuban success. The Cuban family facilitates upward mobility, with more workers per family, low fertility, and multigenerational family structure. Manuel and Zoila are more able to provide for Maria Teresa and her brother because both parents work outside the home, and their family size is four members.

Yet, Firmat (1994) suggests that the current structure of Cuban culture that has facilitated success is one with a short half life. He calls the current generation of Cuban-Americans "the one-and-a-halfers" (p. 4). The 1.5 generation, that is Manuel and Zoila, are members of neither culture, Cuban *or* American, but are both simultaneously. So positioned, they are "tradition bound but translation bent" (p. 5). The parents of the 1.5 generation have little choice. They are Cuban. In contrast, the children of the 1.5 generation are American. For them, Cuba is a narrative, a memory of their parents.

Firmat sees this positioning as one having the potential for true biculturation. Unlike acculturation or transculturation, biculturation implies an equilibrium that is constantly shifting. It can be seen as an empowered stance, with some degree of prerogative for the participants. But this gift is first a bit of fate and, once accepted, becomes prerogative. Firmat suggests that acceptance is gained through stages of adaptation. The initial, or, in Firmat's terms, "substitutive," stage replicates the cultural scene that has been left behind, such as in the creation of a Little Havana, with the intent of preserving the sense of "we are still there." A second stage of cultural destitution incorporates estranged and disconnected immigrants who reason "we are nowhere." Finally, an institutive stage assimilates immigrants (or perhaps their sons and daughters or grandchildren) to a sense of "here we are." For Firmat, the acquisition of institutive assimilation signals that "these are the last days of Little Havana" (p. 17). The group is now invested in the institutions and practices of their adopted culture. By extension, Manuel and Zoila represent a particular moment in Cuban-American culture that causes an "occasional urgency" for its own half life, or expiration date.

From Another Place: Hillsborough County (Tampa) Public Schools

In a public school in Tampa, one of the authors asked Antonio, a bilingual kindergart-ner, "Do you know your numbers?"

"Yes," he answered quickly. "I know *all* of 'em. I know 'em good. But the teacher doesn't like 'em that way."

When asked, "What do you mean 'She doesn't like them that way?,'" Antonio responds "In Spanish. She doesn't like 'em in Spanish. She wants English." He shrugs and smiles. Then, without prompting, he happily "told his numbers" to twenty in Spanish, without mishap.

The Hillsborough County (Tampa) Public School District is the twelfth largest school system in the United States and the third largest in Florida with a student enrollment of approximately 138,000. Today the racial/ethnic composition of the school district is approximately 59 percent white, 23 percent black, 17 percent Hispanic, less than 1 percent American Native, and 1.8 percent Asian/Pacific Islander. By contrast, the ethnic distribution in 1985 was 74 percent white, 20 percent black, 5.6 percent Hispanic and less than 1 percent Native American and Asian/Pacific Islander. The population of students classified as white has decreased by 15 percent, whereas the Hispanic population has increased 11.4 percent. During the same time period (1985 to 1995), the total number of students increased from 109,708 to 134,263. The percent of students on free/reduced lunch has changed significantly in that same time period. In 1985, 35 percent of the district's students were on free or reduced lunch. In 1995, the percentage grew to 51 percent. The profile of students for the next five years appears to be similar to the trend over the last 10 years. That is, the student population should increase by 8,000 to 10,000 students. Ethnic distribution should stay about the same as the present with a slight increase in black and Hispanic enrollment. The percentage of students on free or reduced lunch status will probably increase by 3 percent to 5 percent. Student achievement is measured by a number of traditional assessment tools. For example, The Stanford Achievement Test—8th Edition (Stanford-8) has been administered to students in grades two through nine in Hillsborough County since 1990. Students' mathematics scores have always been higher on average than scores in the areas of language arts and reading. In reading, percentile scores have ranged from 41 to 46 during the last seven years. The mathematics percentile rank has ranged from 46 to 56 and language arts score from 44 to 54.

As with any large urban/rural school system, the district has its problems as well as its strengths. Some of the district's problems include a building program that cannot keep pace with student growth. The student population in the district increases by 2,000 to 3,000 students annually and has done so for the last 10 years. Another issue of concern is the funding of the school district and the questionable equity of the funding formula. A third area of concern is school safety and the increase in drug use and violence within Hillsborough County.

A major district and state initiative is implementation of recent state-wide accountability legislation. This legislation has been endorsed by the district's school board and addresses seven major goals. These goals deal with readiness to start school, progress in school, graduation, safety, and staff training in line with the state's school reform agenda that is in turn aligned with Goals 2000, the Clinton Administration's plan (See Borman, Cookson, Sadovnik, & Spade, 1996).

The district is undertaking a program of school restructuring that focuses not only on local school governance in ways similar to the Chicago reform agenda but that also addresses the delivery of instruction. In line with its major school restructuring goals, the district is moving towards a Pre K–5 elementary, 6–8 middle school, and a 9–12 high school configuration, and has recently installed magnet programs for the International Baccalaureate in two high schools, an Academy of Health Professions, and a Technology Magnet at the middle school level. The district is also considering a magnet school for the performing arts.

The Hillsborough District has tried to eliminate grouping and tracking of students where possible, although ad hoc grouping for students with skill deficiencies is still practiced. Another area of strength in the district is the increased number of parents who are actively involved in the schools. Each school, by law, must have a School Improvement Team (SIT). This team is made up of various stakeholders including students, parents, and members of the business community. Currently, an average of seven parents serves on the SIT at each participating school, up from fewer than three per school in 1993. The District reform agenda, nonetheless, does not target issues of concern to the large and growing Latino community except, perhaps, for its focus on local school governance.

LESSONS FROM THE TAMPA VIGNETTE

Unlike either the Carpinteria parents whose collective power and authority in the eyes of the schools derived from their political organization or the Puerto Rican families in Chicago whose day-to-day struggles with economic issues, drug-related problems and personal survival stand in the way of their engagement with the schools and their children's education, Manuel and Zoila, Maria Teresa's parents, use the "Quinse" and other family rituals to mark important milestones and maintain family solidarity. The Martinez family has the economic wherewithal to provide such entertainment for their close friends and family members. By observing the ritual of the "Quinse," Maria Teresa incorporates a strong sense of her ethnic and religious heritage as an important component of her identity. With the distance from the immigration experience increasing over time for this family, such celebrations take on heightened importance as strategies for retaining Latin culture and Cuban influences. Important questions addressed in this research include How are celebrations of family culture important in maintaining ethnic solidarity? and How important is it for schools to organize instruction around the use and appreciation of languages other than English?

The observation of the *Quinceañera* occurs in families retaining ties with a Spanish heritage marked by strong connections to the Catholic Church. In its report on a *Quinceañera* celebration in Houston for a young woman of Salvadorean background, *The New York Times* (February 1, 1996) notes:

> If this centuries-old Latin American tradition both marks a young girl's passage into womanhood and celebrates her innocence, it also highlights the powerful role that age-old rituals play in modern American society. The Quinceañera, celebrated from Mexico to Argentina, is as much a family statement, a reaffirmation of its cultural identity and its unity in a new world as it is an overblown birthday party.

In addition, the *Quinceañera* provides the Latin community involved in the celebration a chance to reaffirm itself in cultural terms, confirming its strength in "a place and a half."

Nonetheless, in many Florida school districts, including Hillsborough County, parents lack a strong presence in the day-to-day operation of their children's schools, and language attrition (in the case of the Spanish language) is likely to weaken children's attachment to the culture. Schools and school districts must weigh questions about the value of programs to strengthen children's competence in using languages other than English for their community's students and their families. In Dade County (Miami) Schools, one school's curriculum incorporating the active use of Spanish in instruction with a high powered academic program attracts the interest of parents and children from a range of ethnic backgrounds. At Coral Way Elementary School in that district, teachers collaborate across grade levels to present curricula in the areas of social studies, mathematics and literacy using both Spanish and English as the languages of instruction. Parents of the Anglo students attending the school see their children's future success as citizens tied to their knowledge of other cultures as well as to their skillful use of the Spanish language in a local society where they are already the minority population.

PUTTING THE IMMIGRANT STORIES IN PERSPECTIVE

The four narratives included in this chapter tell the stories of immigrant Latino families, children and communities in the United States. These cases are suggestive of the diversity of experience that characterizes different groups who share elements of a Spanish heritage. Taken together, then, these three cases have by no means told the entire story. Missing from consideration here are the stories of Central and South American immigrants (many of whom are actually political refugees) whose heroic passage to the United States is told in the film "El Norte" and, among other places, in the accounts of Suarez-Orozco that we referred to earlier in Chapter 2.

Also missing are the stories of migrant workers and their families who follow the seasonal planting and harvesting of crops across the United States. On average, migrant farmers work 30 hours a week, earning wages that yield salaries of less than $4,000 a year. Their lives are extremely harsh, resulting in an average life expectancy 30 percent shorter than that of the average American. Norma Nunez and her husband Julio are a young couple with eight children who have recently decided to settle in Wimauma, Florida and give up the harsh migrant farm worker family life (*St. Petersburg Times*, May 9, 1996). According to reporter Lara Wozniak, the Nunez family is representative of families who work eight hours a day picking everything from tomatoes to cucumbers and often bringing their preschool aged children into the fields with them simply because they have no other options:

> There are no easy answers for the Nunezes, one family among hundreds in this east Hillsborough . . . [County] community . . . For them, affordable child care is a tough thing to find. While there are at least five government-subsidized facilities around Wimauma, the waiting lists are long. Without adequate day care and a head start on learning, the cycle of poverty becomes even more difficult to break for these children. Many not only fight poverty and hunger, but also face a language barrier and a harsh political climate that doesn't embrace their existence even if they are legal U.S. citizens.

The community of Wimauma plans a center to serve 100 children, making only a small dent in the number of children eligible for such services. Not surprisingly, the most frequent reproach launched at such service providers is that the center will be used by illegal immigrants. The response to such criticism by the director of a nearby mission is telling: "He notes that officials don't deport immigrants during harvest season, nor do employers refrain from taking Social Security payments from the workers' checks. So he asks, why not educate the children while they are here?" (Wozniak, 1996). As long as we persist in lumping all newcomers into a similar category and referring to them as having no legal status, speaking languages that have no currency in our nation's social and economic life, and present in the United States to take jobs that should rightly go to others who have been here longer, it is difficult to see how any other reaction will be forthcoming.

5

Schools and Communities: The Asian Experience

Unlike most Latino immigrants, with the important exceptions of those leaving war-torn countries in Central and South America, many Asians who settled in the United States between 1975 and the early 1990s were refugees seeking asylum from political, religious, and ethnic persecution. Whereas migrants leave one country for another for a complex set of personal, political, economic and religious factors, refugees generally must leave or face serious reprisals. Refugees, unlike migrants, are accorded a number of rights upon their arrival in the United States including permanent residency and the right to work in the United States. In addition, they are able to qualify for public assistance and other resettlement services. Not surprisingly, the United States is more likely to grant asylum to refugees from nations with whom the United States is in conflict than to those from nations with whom relations are cordial. According to Gold (1992):

> [In 1975, the U.S.] . . . gave 80,000 Vietnamese the security clearance required for refugee status in only 3 months. In contrast, two years after 12,000 persons fled Chile's rightist coup, only 26 had been cleared to stay in the States. (Gold, 1992)

Thus, Vietnamese refugees, including the Hmong—tribal people from rural mountainous regions in what formerly constituted South Vietnam—are more likely to

123

gain entry into the United States than refugees from despotic governments such as Haiti's under the dictatorship of Papa and Baby Doc Duvalier. The image of the Haitian boat people, most of whom futilely sought asylum throughout the 1980s and early 1990s, attests to the U.S. government's selectivity in determining which groups are provided status as refugees.

In his study of Soviet Jews and Vietnamese refugees, Gold points to the host of variables on which refugee groups may differ and which make a difference in determining how refugees organize their communities and adapt to the social, economic, and other dimensions of life in U.S. society. These variables include refugees' past experience in business and community life in addition to the presence of earlier groups of immigrants, refugee, co-ethnics, and their socioeconomic status or statuses. All of these elements help to define the ecology of the refugees' experiences in their new society.

From 1975 through the 1980s, 1,214,500 refugees settled in the United States. These individuals constituted 20 percent of all immigrants during this period. By far the largest number were Vietnamese and other Asian refugees, many of whom settled in Northern and Southern California. The stories that follow are told by Li-Rong Lilly Cheng who uses an ethnographic narrative style different from the field studies of Delgado-Gaitan and Quiroz that we have just considered. Cheng abstracts qualities of personal experience to weave together the stories of Dan and Mei, and Ming, and Washington and his family; the former Chinese American refugees, the latter, Hmong refugees.

Like all groups who have experienced social inequalities, Asian refugee families exemplify divergent, but fundamentally difficult, experiences after their arrival in the United States. The cases here provide narratives of the multi-faceted historical, cultural and linguistic barriers that face foreign-born families and, in particular, their children, in contemporary American society. Although the studies are different—the first portraying the fragmentation of a traditional Asian family in the wake of attempted assimilation and the second an example of the common misinterpretation of cross-cultural codes and behavior—they share commonalities, bringing to light real-life examples of the pain and struggle of social integration.

VIGNETTE #5: ISOLATION FROM HIGH ACHIEVING PEERS: THE STORY OF DAN AND MEI, REFUGEES IN LOS ANGELES
by Li-Rong Lilly Cheng

The stories here are neither fictional nor garnered from a reference book, but rather are the real-life situations of people I know well. The loose narrative style in each is meant to convey, as plainly as possible, the "real-life" facts. I will conclude each study with some suggestions as to how the process of mainstreaming might be less of a strain on both the individual and the family, and how it might be possible for families to access mainstream American culture and language while simultaneously maintaining a strong sense of cultural/linguistic heritage.

Family Background

Dan, an artist, left China as a refugee more than 10 years ago, leaving his two and a half year old daughter, his 65 year old mother and his wife behind. Feeling personally and politically stifled by the government of the People's Republic of China, he applied for a visa at the U.S. embassy and left, at the first available opportunity, for the United States. Doing so placed him on a black list of dishonorable Chinese citizens, forbidding him to ever return.

Like many of his peers, Dan met Ming in the countryside when they were both student laborers during the Cultural Revolution. She married him against the strict wishes of her parents, who disowned her for violating traditional rules of filial piety. Dan was considered "black," making him the worst kind of person in Ming's parents' eyes. When they moved back to the city of Shanghai shortly after their marriage, Dan assumed care of his ailing mother. An artist herself, specializing in embroidery, Ming worked in a neighboring city while Dan was in America, coming home only during the holidays to spend time with her daughter. Mei grew up speaking Mandarin at school and Shanghainese at home with her grandmother, from whom she received the majority of her support and socialization. Dan wrote to them frequently and kept in touch by calling them a few times a year. Despite their separation, they forged a sense of familial identity that sustained and unified them.

After six years of waiting, Dan was able to be reunited with Ming and Mei. Ten year old Mei was captured immediately by the allure of the "American" image propagated by television and, consequently, spent most of her days watching TV. She enjoyed going to the malls and window shopping. She very quickly adapted to the Southern California way of dressing. Ming, on the other hand, could not understand English and found support in the company of other Mandarin-speaking artist friends. This marked the initial split between the "old" world and the new, between the radically different interests, needs and desires of members of the same family.

After many months of searching, Ming found a job doing illustration for a fabric manufacturer and, after being hired, spent her days drawing patterns. She worked long hours and often worked on the weekends. She had minimal interactions with people and had virtually no opportunity to communicate with English-speaking people.

Mei's School Experience

Mei quickly found friends in her neighborhood which was primarily Mexican-American—identifying with them, perhaps unconsciously, as other marginalized but "Americanized" children. Within six months, she was able to speak English fluently and in one year, she almost stopped speaking Mandarin altogether.

At school, Mei usually went with the same group of friends. They were very supportive of her. She even learned to speak some Spanish. She attended English as a Second Language Program (ESL) and learned oral English very fast. In general, school work did not seem too difficult for her since she was a very good student in China. The two subjects that she had difficulty with were English and Social Studies. Her teacher was patient with her and did not demand a lot. After two years in school, she still read very little, although she stopped reading Chinese all together. As a teenager, she spent most of her time on the phone and did not seem to worry about homework.

English Language Acquisition

Dan, in his attempt to become part of the social fabric, found the English language to be a tremendous barrier. He encouraged Mei to speak English and asked her to teach him, although he was equally concerned with maintaining his native culture. Mei became his tutor, and the two grew very close. Since Mei never really had a strong relationship with her mother to begin with, their communication was reduced to a purely functional one, focused mostly on clothing, foods, allowance, and other practical day-to-day activities and concerns.

In an attempt to entice Mei to speak Mandarin and reconnect some of the family's disintegrating fabric, Dan invited the children of his friends to come over and play with her. Mei typically says "hi" to them and then soon disappears. On the home front, Mei comments about her mother and, after her arrival, her grandmother, exhibiting a dramatically altered perception of normalcy and "intelligence" that is in accord with the American cultural mainstream. "Why can't they speak English?" she asks. "Is Grandma stupid? She doesn't know how to use the microwave; she does not know how to use the oven. She looks weird and dresses funny." With the influence of her American environment, Mei's conviction of her family's "foreignness" increases the disparity between the generations.

Estrangement

After two years of waiting with great excitement and anticipation, the much-missed grandmother arrived via New York to be with her family. When the grandmother appeared at the gate, Mei ran to her and hugged her. The moment of excitement soon turned cold however, when the grandmother attempted to communicate with Mei and Mei could not respond. The communication gap was immediately apparent and prefigured the later, more subtle differences that would destroy their once close relationship.

The following Monday, the grandmother wanted to escort Mei to school as she always did when they were in Shanghai. Mei, embarrassed by her grandmother's manner and style of dress, refused at first, but finally agreed on the condition that the grandmother walk on the other side of the street—signifying the physical and emotional separation between their two worlds. Tension soon began to build at home as Mei seldom talked to her mother or grandmother, spending a great deal of time secluded in her room or going out with her girl friends. The grandmother was profoundly disappointed at the fact that Mei's "American" transformation had caused the two to be estranged.

As a successful artist, Dan has many shows and is constantly invited to go to parties and opening nights. Ming feels awkward accompanying her husband and Mei, humiliated by the way her mother presents herself, asks Dan not to take her. Dan, again, is torn; feeling, on the one hand, uneasy about his wife's unassimilated ways and, on the other, obligated to her through bonds of spousal piety. He is heartbroken because the warm and loving relationship that Mei had with her grandmother and the closeness of the family is lost and will probably never be regained.

Dan senses the coldness of his broken home and spends most of his time at his own studio. The family breaks apart more and more rapidly. They have become strangers. His mother feels alienated and alone, spending most of her time at the apartment by herself. Her only genuine cultural connection is the occasional video tapes of Chinese programs she receives from her friends in Shanghai. Her sense of helplessness and insecurity compels her to want to return to China. Dan, wanting to fulfill his duties to his ailing mother, tries to convince her to stay.

Ming has buried herself in her work, viewing it as a means of emotional security and survival. Although she longs for the old feelings of cultural and familial identity, she too, is banned from returning to China. She is overwhelmed with a sense of hopelessness and futility, mindlessly going through her routine: working, cooking and cleaning.

Self-image: Parent, Teacher, and Peer Relations

Mei is now very successful in school both socially and academically, enjoying her popularity with both her teachers and her classmates. She speaks often of becoming a cheerleader and of the many Anglo boys on whom she has developed a crush. Getting up very early in the morning, Mei spends a lot of time curling her hair and putting on make-up. The grandmother, shocked at such a flagrant violation of traditional Chinese notions of proper behavior, cannot accept that Mei would be doing these things at such a young age.

Dan and Mei frequently spend time watching TV and Mei comments on her flat nose and slanted eyes, mentioning that she would like to dye her hair blonde. She also asks Dan when she can go out on a date. Although Dan feels such impulses are natural for the process of integration, the radical change of culture and character disturb him to the point where he is confused and cannot answer. He feels a sense of dual loyalty in his approach to raising Mei. On the one hand he desires to emulate the ideal of American freedom, for which he left China, and on the other he wishes to uphold the family's historical/cultural and linguistic heritage.

Although Mei is doing well in her classes, she still struggles with reading English. She avoids reading and finds excuses to not write. She is convinced she will be an artist like Dan and is already thinking about leaving home for college and dating boys. She has no Chinese-speaking friends and dislikes her father's friends and their children, seldom speaking to her mother and grandmother who disapprove of her behavior and want her to listen to and obey them. They say that Mei is not fulfilling the obligations of a daughter, that she is violating the traditional rules of filial piety. This criticism has driven Mei farther from her family and its culture, prompting her to stay away from home for longer periods of time, communicating solely with her father whom she feels is the only one who accepts and supports her. She now speaks no Shanghainese and claims that she does not understand any. She converses only in English. It is possible that she has yet to see, because of her naivete, the "hidden agenda" of the American beauty ideal. It is possible that she will be rejected, by boys or by the cheerleading coach, for not being the right "type" or having the right "look."

Mei often complains about her mother and grandmother, asking Dan, "How come they are not learning?"—not knowing that they are paralyzed by culture shock and are incapable of assimilating their host society's alien culture. Dan's attempt at joining the three generations of the family and linking two entirely different cultures and languages has failed. This is the cause of much personal frustration and shame. All have paid a great price for what Dan refers to as a "maladjustment to culture."

LESSONS FROM THE DAN AND MEI VIGNETTE

Had Dan arranged for Ming and Mei to study English together, encouraged Ming to go to Adult ESL School, or arranged family outings where the three of them might have had greater opportunity to communicate with one another, he might have established a fundamental linguistic, emotional and pedagogical connection among the three of them in which each became the teacher and supporter of the others. After many years of separation, the three—and eventually four with the arrival of Dan's mother—were thrown together in a completely new environment that demanded different linguistic and cultural codes. Unusual amounts of courtesy and understanding on everyone's part might have given them the space they needed to reflect on their experiences and plan strategies of adaptation.

Dan could have also provided more and earlier opportunities for Mei to play with children who, like Mei, also spoke Mandarin or Shanghainese, as opposed to allowing television to exert such an enormous influence. By maintaining the home language, Mei would have been able to speak to her grandmother, thus lifting the communicative and emotional barrier that stood between them. By being able to affirm her own bilingual/bicultural identity, Mei could have facilitated her grand-mother's passage into a new culture, easing the shock of culture/language change and acting as a model from which the grandmother, with Mei's help, could learn. These strategies, of course, assume the active work of the family as a *unit* functioning to create its own safety net.

As we saw in Chapter 3, the earliest Chinese immigrants in the mid-to-late 1800s in California formed associations that provided financial and other forms of support to members of the community. Today's Chinese immigrants and refugees are also likely to create opportunities for each other within the bounds of a closely knit community. Dan's independent status as an artist, however, may have made community interdependence more difficult to foster. Nonetheless, as we argue throughout this volume, it is important to look beyond the individual student and family context to understand the full meaning of the migration experience for the child's success in school.

VIGNETTE #6: THE STORY OF WASHINGTON, A HMONG CHILD
by Li-Rong Lilly Cheng

Different refugee families develop different coping strategies. This case study describes a Hmong family—a mother and father who are illiterate, who have different notions of "development" and "progress" than those held by the American mainstream, but who have also had to adjust to a world where conformity to the American standard of behavior is assumed.

Family Background and School Experience

Washington Cheng is a six-year-old Hmong boy. He was born in the United States and is the youngest of eight children. The names of his male siblings are Jefferson, Kennedy, Lincoln, Franklin, and Eisenhower; names chosen by Mr. Cheng because they represent great men in U.S. history. Although his parents left Laos 15 years ago and five of their eight children were born in the United States, neither Mr. nor Mrs. Cheng speak much English, still feeling ill-at-ease and displaced.

Washington has been attending school since he was four years old. He is currently attending kindergarten at Mar Vista School in Los Angeles. Generally very quiet in class, he prefers to sit in the corner instead of participating, watching the other children play. His behavior is in keeping with the guidelines of the Hmong culture in which teachers are respected as fonts of wisdom, and children are told to be humble, obedient and observant. However, because of a fundamental misinterpretation, his teacher believes his speech/language skills to be underdeveloped. When she attempts to get Washington involved in a small group activity, he remains a silent observer.

Clinical Encounters

On the basis of his reticence and abstention from classroom activity, the teacher phoned the school nurse who performed a hearing screening and found that Washington was not responding to the pure tones (part of the standardized practice in audiological examination). As a result, she sent a referral to the Health Maintenance Organization (HMO) for a complete audiological evaluation. Because the audiologist could not elicit any verbal response from Washington during the evaluation, the results of the audiology report indicate mild to moderate hearing loss. Like his teacher, the audiologist viewed Washington's speech and language skills as underdeveloped. Consequently, a referral for a speech/language evaluation was made. What neither of the testers knew, however, was that, as was often the case in the classroom, Washington was unable to understand the instructions given for the testing procedures.

Since Washington's parents could not read English, they did not fill out the form required for the test. The clinic assumed the responsibility of translating the message about the appointment and providing directions to the site of the testing. On the day of the appointment, the Chengs were not to be found at the 5:00 p.m. appointment time. Several phone calls were made in attempts to reach the Chengs with no success. The clinician waited until 5:30 p.m., deciding to go outside and to look for them. Fifteen minutes later, the Chengs drove into the parking lot, tired and apprehensive; they had been looking for the building for over 45 minutes. Washington looked frightened but did not cry. He followed the clinician with eyes opened wide, watching carefully. The clinician sensed the tension and decided to spend some time attempting to communicate with the Chengs. Mr. Cheng did not become any less anxious and said very little during the course of the visit.

The clinician asked the family if they were aware of the findings of the audiology evaluation in which Washington was found to have moderate hearing loss. Mr. Cheng replied only by saying "Yes, I heard that." The clinician then mentioned the need for a hearing aid. At this, Mr. Cheng became extremely agitated, nervously relating the following: "My daughter was found to have a hearing loss; they gave her a hearing aid. She was not hearing impaired, she did not need the aid. She is doing very well, and they were wrong about her. Washington is like his sister—very shy and does not say much. But he can hear me from a distance and he speaks good Hmong. He will learn, give him time. We Hmong people are shy." The clinician was attentive to Mr. Cheng, appreciative of his input. She spoke to Washington, asking him "How are you?" Washington answered, "April." Mr. Cheng said "He means April. He was born in April, so he was telling you his birth month."

The clinician asked more questions and gave Washington a picture vocabulary test. Washington was able to identify all the objects on the test in very clear English. The only feature he exhibited was a "frontal lisp," an attribute which Mr. Cheng also possessed.

Washington understood two-level directions and was attentive throughout the whole interaction. The results of this evaluation, in which Washington was found to have no speech, language or hearing deficiencies, suggest a number of cautions for those who teach and work with the Hmong:

- Do not make assumptions based on professional records. The child might be too shy to respond.
- Provide time and space for family members to interact and respond. Ask many questions about the family and elicit feelings. Be aware that people may be shy, fearful and apprehensive.
- Understand that a people's way of saying "No" may be an indirect one. Instead of saying "No, I don't want to get a hearing aid," or "No, my son doesn't have a hearing loss," or "No, I disagree with your findings," one may indirectly communicate such messages as illustrated by Mr. Cheng's discussion of his daughter's misdiagnosis.

LESSONS FROM THE CHENG FAMILY VIGNETTE

As is evident in this case study, many refugee families place as much, if not more emphasis, on the continuity of the home culture and language as they do upon becoming fully fledged members of the new culture. Preserving the "old ways" ensures a connection with the parents' roots even if this means that their children will be misdiagnosed, misinterpreted and misplaced. This sense of the importance of their ethnic culture bolsters the self-esteem of ethnic community members (Gold, 1992). Most feel confident that their children will learn English and "appropriate" social skills in due time and that their children will assimilate naturally without the risk of losing their native culture.

An approach to teaching that takes these considerations into account will allow those who have undergone the slow struggle of adaptation eventually to lift their voices and share their experiences of development, learning, schooling and cultural expectations. This information is important for the formation of educational policies and decisions based on careful consideration of the dynamics of cultural mainstreaming, identity survival, and a deeper understanding of each individual's linguistic and cultural background.

VIGNETTE #7: THE CONSTRUCTION OF IDENTITY IN SCHOOLS: THE ROLE OF GENDER AND ETHNICITY
*by Marianne Bloch, Jay Hammond-Cradle, Carolyn Dean,
Miryam Espinosa-Dulanto and B. Robert Tabachnick*

Mai is a Hmong girl whom we have followed both at school and home throughout her kindergarten, first and second grade years in "Lakeland." Like Washington, the young boy in the previous vignette, she was born in the United States after her parents came here as refugees. Her father studied through the fifth grade in Laos, and her mother had no formal education prior to coming to the United States. The father is now a student at a local technical/vocational college, and the mother has studied English and two years of high school here. They repeatedly emphasize the importance of education for themselves and their children.

Both Mai's teacher and her parents have expectations for her school experience which are imbedded in cultural and social constructions of learning and education and reflect differing backgrounds, perspectives, discourses, and perceptions of power. Of particular interest in this case is the perception of who is primarily responsible for Mai's education. Mai's parents assume that the main responsibility lies with those who structure the school environment. The teacher is responsible to teach, and the school officials are there to assure this happens. The teacher, on the other hand, concentrates on the learner and her efforts. Mai's parents emphasize the importance of the school officials (teachers and administrators) controlling the school environment and guaranteeing that students learn. According to Mai's father, in Laos "the teachers controlled everything," which he notes was sometimes good and sometimes not. "If the teacher was kind, the students could learn but if the teacher was mean, some of the students could not learn at all."

The teachers focus on another aspect of the situation. Mai's first grade teacher, for example, reported that Mai's school performance had declined over that year and attributed this to personal characteristics. She described Mai as "stubborn," "slow," "kind of mischievous," "refusing to talk," and practicing "avoidance" in regard to doing her school work. She notes that Mai is "shy" but that she is also an instigator of trouble among the other children, especially the Hmong. Yet, Mai was observed being asked for help frequently by other Hmong students in the classroom. The teacher's perception of Mai's declining performance was not necessarily supported by the progress report either, which indicated that Mai improved in at least half of the areas which called for improvement; in no area of the report card offered to parents was there any indication of real problems that could be detected without teacher interpretation. There seems then, to be some ambivalence on the teacher's part as to whether Mai is shy or uncooperative, slow or belligerent, and some ambivalence about how to describe Mai to her parents.

Thus, while Mai's teacher seems to emphasize indicators of progress and related personal characteristics, the parents comment on their desire for their daughter to do well and for the school and teacher to provide the structure in which this can occur. While her parents are eager for the school to "control" positively Mai's learning, they appeared also eager to understand how she was doing, and looked to report cards, and other communications with the school for such information. The divergent perspectives and ways of constructing "truths" about Mai contributed to difficulties experienced in parent/school communication and joint efforts on behalf of the child's education. They influenced both parents' and teachers' perceptions of each other as well.

Another aspect of the differing expectations of school officials and Hmong parents lies in the lack of experience of Hmong people with living in small cities and towns in the United States. The parents express their sense that in order to do well in this country, that is, get a good job and fit in, the children must do well in school. They must also be socialized into life here in a broad sense. They must learn how to operate here in ways which will make them successful and accepted.

However, the parents feel at a disadvantage in facilitating this and leave it to the schools. They realize that they themselves do not know the expectations and are not able to help their children in this way. They want to cooperate with the school but may not always know what to do, know what is expected or see things in the same way. Mai's father related that sometimes notes are sent home by the teacher. In one such instance the teacher mentioned that Mai is shy. Her father said that he didn't know what to do about that and added, "I think she will learn and get along with the other kids okay so I am not worried. We'll see how it goes. I'll follow my children's progress." This was a situation in which the father was a bit uncertain as to what response was expected. Was the teacher simply sharing her observation or was she implying that the parents should do something about this? He noted that Mai is the same way at home and like her mother in this; indeed many Hmong girls are encouraged to appear "shy" in their interactions with broader communities and with adults. However, Mai's mother is the one who takes the children to the doctor, goes to the parent–teacher meetings, and even helps to translate for other Hmong mothers.

Mai herself does take the initiative in certain situations as she begins to feel comfortable. The following is an example which illustrates this. The interviewer was outside where the children play.

Mai: "Do you have a grandma?"
Interviewer: "No, I used to. Do you?"
Mai: "Yes, she lives over there."
Interviewer: "Is your grandma nice?"
Mai: "Sometimes" (playing with the gum in her mouth)
Interviewer: "How do you say gum in Hmong?"
Mai: (after thinking for a second) "*Ko noos*." (We repeated it together several times until I got it right. Mai would say, "No, it's *ko noos*).

Thus, although Mai was also described as shy in other situations, here she is taking initiative. In terms of socialization and language learning, Mai's father feels that "the Hmong children should be separated from each other in school so they can learn [English] more quickly." When asked what he felt it was important to study in school, Mai's father said, "The teachers have more ideas, but I think English is important; English and also math." However, this presents a dilemma for the parents, because at the same time as they defer to the school to socialize and teach their children, they are also concerned about how the children are turning out and what they are learning. The parents see the children rejecting the Hmong ways or feeling unable to relate to them. Mai's father expressed this in the following way: "Hmong children do not listen to their parents as much any more. This is because of the laws here which forbid parents from punishing their children and thus, to some extent, take control away from the parents." Mai's father captures this when he commented on his brother's children who are older. "He has two daughters who only speak English at home. If you say something to them in Hmong they ask, 'What do you say?' They don't want to eat Hmong food either." He did not seem to want this to happen to his children. Therefore, while encouraging his children to do well in school and learn English, he is also teaching them Hmong at home and hopes they can know both. Even though seven-year-old Mai is the oldest of their five children, her father is already expressing his concern about these issues.

Thus, although the parents defer to the schools, to some extent they are anxious about the results and uncertain about the methods. This leaves them with a dilemma in which their role is unclear, in particular in relation to the schools. As Mai's father notes when acknowledging why he did not go to a parent-teacher conference, "If you talk to the teacher, you should have something to say. I didn't have anything." He also mentioned how busy they were, but the feeling was they did not know what input to give.

LESSONS FROM MAI'S VIGNETTE

Hmong parents experience an enormous dilemma: the desire for the children to have the advantages which they feel this society offers, accompanied with the regret over losing their Hmong identity. In addition, they perceive that the schools play a key role in helping to prepare their children for success in the United States, but also experience ambiguity as to how this is happening and what the results will be. In some ways they are proceeding in blind faith, raising their children in partial alignment with the old ways, while maintaining a loose connection with the school in hopes that they will provide for their children what is needed for a good life here.

In the two "Lakeland" (see pgs. 98–102) cases we see evidence and hear statements suggesting that children are bright. The construction of what and who children are begins to take on the form of a "problem"; there are few ways to bridge the different interpretations. In the case of Rafael, we see that the institution of the school constructs a positive view of Rafael; however, it is still clear, that Rafael's sense of himself, as he tried to bridge differences in his two worlds, is still guarded in both home and school. We see there is respect for his abilities, but still little understanding of who he or his family are, from the school-as-institution. There is a little understanding from the home about the possibilities that school can offer Mai. Children develop their own bilingual/cultural identity only with difficulty within the settings of home and school.

The two Hmong vignettes, the stories of Washington and of Mai, suggest not only the importance of discourse, identity and constructions of children, but emphasize, too, the race, class, language, and gender relations that interact with the enactment of power and constructions of "truth." It is from this perspective that we agree with Foucault's (1980) use of "regimes of truth" to describe what we see as powerful problems represented in research and for children.

PUTTING THE REFUGEE STORIES IN PERSPECTIVE

The Dan and Mei, Washington and Mai case studies provide an idea of the cultural and psychological realities of home and community contexts of the Asian-refugee family and the ways in which they shape and influence Asian students and their attitudes toward American culture and education. These cases also underscore the importance of SES, time of immigration, gender as well as ethnicity in the process of settling in that newcomer's experience. In Dan and Ming's family, Dan (rather uncharacteristically for the male head of household) took on the role of culture broker, attempting to somehow mediate the experiences of different family members. Functioning to span the family's several worlds is most often a role taken on by women in such circumstances, frequently through their contacts both in their workplaces and the community (Lamphere, 1992). Because Ming's emotional and psychological resources were limited, it fell to Dan to negotiate the new culture, a task he was unable to do well in large part because of his limited institutional connections as an independent artist and a refugee.

Neither Dan and Ming nor the Chengs came with capital to invest in business ventures for their families unlike, for example, the Martinez family whose parents came as middle class immigrants from Cuba with resources and social connections in Tampa sufficient to allow them to establish themselves in business. Contemporary Asian immigrants and refugees in communities such as Monterey Park outside Los Angeles have been able to create enormous opportunities for themselves as described in Chapter 3. This is largely because of the propitious economic climate of a community relatively open to accommodate the interests, talents and skills of the newcomers.

Nations in the Pacific Rim will play a pivotal role in unfolding our collective future as a nation. Asia, the world's largest continent, contains nearly 50 countries as well as portions of several others. It encompasses one third of the world's land mass and is home to two thirds of the world's population. Asia also has the largest concentration of the world's consumers and producers. Culturally its diverse heritage reaches back many millennia, representing a valuable resource for enriching world culture.

East Asia, Southeast Asia and South Asia have been the source of the main immigrant groups of recent immigrants to the United States, as pointed out in Chapter 2 in some detail. These areas encompass the People's Republic of China,

India, Japan, South Korea, Taiwan, Hong Kong, and Singapore—an economic powerhouse—as well as North Korea, Kampuchea, Pakistan, and Bangladesh—all political hot spots—and emerging market forces in Vietnam and the Philippines. In general, people from these nations come to the United States to seek a better quality of life, including employment opportunities. Many of their children will not be able to use English during their first few years in the United States. Interpreting people's lives is a difficult and perilous undertaking. In this volume, our interpretation emphasizes building on the strengths that individuals bring from their families and communities to societal institutions, especially schools.

Facing the Challenges

The challenges immigrants and refugees face are numerous. They are forced to make many choices that entail serious consequences, decisions that are often uninformed or made out of necessity. They come to the United States to fulfill the "American Dream," unaware of the sacrifices implicit in what might be called the Dream's hidden agenda. They want to assimilate and yet often find themselves being rejected, reinforcing their feelings of marginality and alienation. They desire to belong, yet they may be excluded because they do not meet the ideal American "requirements" of "proper" speech, "proper" appearance, and the like. They want to learn English, often at the cost of losing their home language—a loss that entails disconnection with culture and other family members. These kinds of fragmentation are common and may serve to create the kind of dysfunctional family as we saw in some of the cases we have just considered. What can we do to prepare refugees for transplanting and transformation? What lessons have we learned by working with refugee families experiencing adjustment problems? What advice can we provide to inform those who work with newcomers about language, school and literacy issues as well as the broader social context of the newcomers' world? Increasingly in many communities with an Asian presence, we can observe manifestations of a strong Pan-Asian American political movement (Wei, 1993). Seeking political empowerment through activism in arenas as diverse as educational and community development, cultural expression, alternative publications and press, and institutionalization in university-based Asian American studies programs, the movement incorporates Chinese Americans, Filipino Americans, Korean Americans, Japanese Americans, and others in an increasingly strong collectivity.

6

Schools and Communities: The Native American and Urban Appalachian Experience

In Chapters 4 and 5 our focus was upon the experiences of Latino and Asian students and their families. With the exception of the Carpinteria case, where immigrant families from Mexico have been in residence for almost 150 years, each of the vignettes considered the experiences of "new" immigrants and refugees, individuals who have come to the United States in the period following the 1965 Immigration Act. We saw that considerable variation characterizes the experiences of different Latino and Asian students and their families depending largely upon their country of origin, the family's background experiences, values and resources, and length of residency in the United States.

We next turn to a consideration of the experiences of groups whose ties to America are of long duration. In the case of the American Indian, an agreed-upon assumption among many tribes is that Indians are indigenous to the country we call the United States. African Americans, whose vignettes we present in Chapter 7, have roots in this nation that extend back to the early 17th century when the first blacks came to what is now Virginia, not as slaves but as indentured servants (Stevenson, 1996). Likewise, Appalachians trace their history to the same period when, as refugees, the earliest forebearers of many of today's city-dwelling Appalachians fled religious persecution by the Church of England. These Scots-Irish settlers migrated further into the Appalachian Mountains and the Ozarks from the coastal plains and Piedmont areas of Virginia and what is now Maryland and the Carolinas in an effort to retain their independence from governmental and religious institutions. Unfortunately, none of these peoples was allowed the tolerance or freedom we now believe all individuals should claim as inalienable rights. Their struggles to create lives in harmony with their belief systems, often divergent from the pervasive U.S. standard, demonstrate the strength of cultural and social structural systems in the face of a press to homogenization.

AMERICAN INDIANS AND THE SCHOOLS

Native American tribal people have, more than any other distinctive racial or ethnic group, suffered the almost total eradication of their cultures and folkways in the name of progress, manifest destiny and the melting pot. In his searing account of federal educational policies designed to control native populations, Joel Spring (1994) speaks of the "deculturalization" of Native Americans and Puerto Ricans, the two peoples whose native cultures have been systematically stripped from them by institutions including the schools. We have seen in Chapter 3 how native peoples were relentlessly pursued by policies of eradication and containment throughout U.S. history.

Spring's analysis of educational policy directed to the American Indian underscores the effort to contain and homogenize native peoples and their cultures. During the post-Revolutionary War period and up to the 1830s, missionary schools were established to assimilate native cultures. While native peoples were transplanted to the West, the federal government supported schools in Indian territory (what is now Oklahoma) with the hope that Native Americans would be "civilized" in one generation (Spring, 1994, p. 3). However, with the persistence of the Indian wars and the resistance to cultural assimilation of virtually all tribal groups, federal policies centered on the boarding school, a total institution in the same sense as prisons and mental hospitals, designed in this case to obliterate native cultures and languages entirely. Despite the federal government's attempts to establish Indian Schools controlled and regulated by the government, the Indian peoples themselves established schools so successfully that Congress in 1887 passed legislation (the Dawes Act) designed to "break up tribal control of land by granting land in allotments to individuals as opposed to tribal organizations" (Spring, 1994, p. 15). This effectually destroyed native control of schools and the organization of the curriculum.

By the early 1900s, boarding schools had become established as the major vehicle for educating Native American children. These schools were designed to provide training in agricultural skills and in other forms of vocational education. In his annual report of 1858, an early Commissioner of Indian Affairs, Charles Mix, detailed a plan for organizing schools on reservations to maximize native children's opportunity to learn agriculture skills and minimize their contact with whites. Mix's rationale was similar to others advanced by other policymakers who saw themselves as sympathetic to the advancement of these peoples whom they viewed as requiring "civilizing" influences.

In this context, the values, traditions and practices prized by family members are stripped of their currency as capital in the mainstream. This is the climate that persisted for Native American children until the organization of AIM (The American Indian Movement) in the 1960s and 1970s and the subsequent creation of schools such as the Heart of the Earth Survival School in Minneapolis. Such schools emphasized the importance of utilizing core native values and strengths as the centerpiece for native education. Unfortunately, schools like these are still extremely rare.

The numbers of students and their parents identifying themselves as Native Americans is increasing; 1990 census data indicate 2 million such individuals, an increase of 500,000 since 1980. The academic achievement of Native American children continues to be problematic; according to Department of Interior data (1991), student academic performance is well under national averages at all grade levels. In 1991 average standardized test scores for Native American students nationally ranged from a low at the twenty-fourth percentile in third grade to a high at the thirty-second percentile in twelfth grade. Dropout rates for Indian youths continue to be high, and the matriculation rate to higher education extremely low. The U.S. Department of Education reports that the attrition rate for Indian youth is 35.5 percent at the sophomore level in high school; many others drop out before that time.

There is considerable reason to hope that, through current national policies of self-determination in education, greater local involvement in and improvement of the education of all Native children will continue. According to Reyhner (1994):

> Self determination in education has led to an increased number of tribally controlled schools, a more active role by tribal councils in education, and reservation public schools with all-Indian school boards. Many reservation schools have large numbers of Indian teachers; *however, efforts to modify seriously the curriculum have not really taken place except in a few schools.* (p. 57, emphasis added)

Native American students, whose educational achievement is among the lowest of any ethnic group, reflect significant cultural differences between values learned at home and those regarded as appropriate by teachers. The origins of Native American school problems can be traced to the neocolonial nature of Indian education, including forced acculturation, punitive coercion in the use of English, and removal of children to boarding schools. Even under more recent and more benign conditions, however, problems rooted in cultural differences persist; some of these are quite subtle. For example, many Native American communities convey norms of cooperation in learning and view competitive and individualist activities unfavorably. Requirements that children compete with each other to achieve the right answer or deliver the best performance conflict directly with the values they learn at home; many would rather fail in school than suffer disgrace in their communities.

Nonverbal cues, by which teachers derive messages and often render unconscious judgments, are also quite different in many Native American communities than in the dominant culture. Teachers may expect children to look them in the eye and speak up resolutely when questioned. Many Native American children, however, are taught that direct eye contact is rude and disrespectful, and that they should speak softly. Such simple incompatibilities in expected paralinguistic behavior may engender misunderstandings on both sides, and may lead teachers to believe that their students are shy or avoidant, or simply do not understand. For Native Americans, and many other ethnic groups whose cultural systems differ from those of the mainstream, such incongruities contribute to disaffection with school and to lack of mutual understanding and respect between students and teachers. These problems increase the more substantive barriers to learning in culturally diverse classrooms.

The maintenance of ethnic or cultural identity is difficult for students who are taught through the medium of the mainstream culture. They often adopt bicultural identities and cope through processes such as accommodation or resistance. Resistance or oppositional behavior within school has been observed by many researchers (Deyhle, 1986; Fordham, 1991; Fordham & Ogbu, 1987; Willis, 1977). Students who adopt this coping mechanism enact cultural behaviors that set them apart from the dominant culture and provide explanations that justify their lack of academic success. African-American students, for example, define their behavior in opposition to "acting white"; Navajo youths develop skills in break dancing to offset their failures in academic endeavors. Resistance theorists view these behaviors as a consequence, not a cause, of a school system that attempts to impose a culture not accepted as a viable alternative (DeMarrais & LeCompte, 1995).

According to Dick Littlebear (1994), teachers of Native children everywhere must symbolically and literally "cross the cattle guard that separates family residences from the school." This is especially important because Indian-developed, tribal-specific curricula are virtually nonexistent (pp. 104–105). Despite their respect for teachers' professional authority, conflict between teachers and the parents of American Indian students persists. White teachers are not familiar with the development and behavior of Native children, and stereotypic views of low-income ethnic minority families are deeply embedded in school wisdom. This is changing to some extent in the American Indian case with the advent of greater local tribal control of the schools. However, not all such schools have enough parents actively involved in school governance through Parent Advisory Councils (PACs) and the like.

VIGNETTE #8: "MOM, WHAT IF I FORGET HOW TO TALK NAVAJO?": COLLISIONS OF CULTURE IN THE PUBLIC SCHOOLS
by Abbie Willetto and Margaret LeCompte

As involuntary minorities (Ogbu, 1986), American Indian children face many of the same disabling effects of cultural and racial prejudice which immigrant children encounter, even though they may never have crossed national boundaries. As they move between their native culture and the dominant culture of European Americans—especially when they attend public schools—many American Indian students confront a gap between home culture and school culture which, in many ways, is as vast as that experienced by true immigrants. They also find that racial and ethnic prejudices, as well as simple ignorance of their culture, serve as barriers to academic achievement.

Background Information

The following case studies illustrate the complex encounters experienced by Navajo students attending school both on and off their reservation. Two types of communities are considered; the first are the Navajo communities in which the children were born and the schools which serve them; the second is a white, affluent university town outside the Navajo Nation to which one of the children moved in first grade. The first case shows how cultural patterns of interaction in the home and school differ, even within communities on the Navajo Nation. These differences exist because most schools, to a very large degree, reflect European-American rather than Navajo cultural values.

The second case analyzes the difficulties Navajo children face when they attend schools outside of the Navajo Nation. Both cases illustrate the pervasive nature of school culture as well as its domination by curricula and pedagogical practices which ignore issues of diversity. The stories which follow illustrate how difficult it is for Navajo children to avoid being labeled as failures and pushed out of school, even when they have high motivation to succeed, supportive families, and past records of high achievement.

LORENCITA AT HOME, LORENCITA AT SCHOOL

Lorencita's Diverse Educational Experiences

In the fall of 1988, Lorencita entered ninth grade at the public high school 15 miles from her home. Although Lorencita had seen the outside of high school many times while attending basketball games in its gymnasium, she had never been inside the building. The youngest of 10 children, Lorencita speaks both English and Navajo, although Navajo is the language used most frequently at home. Although both of her parents understand English, her father chooses not to speak it. Her mother speaks English when non-Navajo speakers are present and Lorencita, who is very fluent in Navajo, always speaks that language at home.

The Arroyo Community Day School, which Lorencita had attended for eight years, was located safely in Mesa Edge, the tiny village where Lorencita grew up. Mesa Edge is snuggled against Rough Butte Mesa; the population of both the town and the K-8 school which served it is entirely Navajo. At the day school, students and paraprofessionals spoke Navajo. In fact, many members of the small student body and some of the teachers were Lorencita's clan relatives. At Arroyo Day School, Lorencita had been an honor student and president of the eighth grade student council.

The high school is located in Castle Rock, one of the larger Navajo communities in the Navajo Nation. Castle Rock has a population of about 6,000 people, most of whom are Navajo. Non-Navajos can live in Castle Rock only if they are employed there; most work in the school district, the tourist industry, a large coal mine, and the Indian Health Service. These industries provide housing for their employees, since only Navajos can purchase land or houses on tribal holdings. Castle Rock High School is 97 percent Navajo, though less than 10 percent of its teachers are Native Americans.

Lorencita's Experiences in School

Waiting by the bus stop with her older sister, Jane, that fall day in 1988, Lorencita felt she was leaving her family behind. She cast a doubtful glance at the clothes she was wearing—jeans, a t-shirt and sneakers. She looked at her sister who was dressed in a color-coordinated shorts outfit, and she felt under-dressed and self-conscious. Unlike Lorencita, Jane had chosen to attend the public schools in Castle Rock several years ago, after she completed elementary school. Their parents had left the decision to transfer to the two girls; Lorencita had chosen to remain in the smaller Arroyo Day school a mile from her house for seventh and eighth grade.

In Castle Rock Middle School Jane had learned about the latest trends. She had spent her summers attending special minority college preparatory classes in Flagstaff, Arizona, 150 miles to the west. By contrast, Lorencita had devoted her after-school hours and summer vacations to taking care of younger nieces and nephews at home. She enjoyed getting the little children to do games and chores as a group. Chores meant taking care of the livestock and teaching the younger children different tasks such as feeding and watering the cows, sheep, horses, chickens, and sheepdogs. She had a gift for making chores an enjoyable, cooperative activity. She could settle disputes with ease and manage large groups of children whose ages ranged from infants to 12 years old.

The school bus approached, and Lorencita's freshman year at Castle Rock High School began. Within two weeks she was behind in every class. Her reading teachers complained that she was below grade level and unmotivated; they asked that she be tested for possible placement in the learning disabled group. Lorencita's response time in class was so slow—sometimes she didn't respond at all. One teacher also requested that Lorencita's hearing be tested; because she was so unresponsive, the teacher feared she might be deaf. This news came as a shock to her family members. At home Lorencita was a responsible and integral member of the family. As the youngest of 10 children she was outgoing, spirited and feisty. Notwithstanding, in school, her academic problems were considered to be identical to those of the Hmong refugee in the Washington vignette in the previous chapter, and for much the same reasons.

A closer look at Lorencita's difficulties with the school environment revealed that she was simply uncomfortable with, and reluctant to participate in, English, the language of instruction. At her previous school, answers to general questions had been accepted in either English or Navajo. Now her teachers were mono-lingual speakers of English who employed a very traditional, question-and-answer model of classroom instruction. In this unfamiliar linguistic environment, Lorencita withdrew. Even though she could use English competently, given enough time to think, she could not respond quickly enough to teacher questions. The teachers would pass on to another student before enough language process time had elapsed for her to respond. Eventually, she was completely closed out of classroom discussions. For her own part, Lorencita thought the teachers talked too much and asked stupid questions. She knew the answers to the questions in Navajo, but she needed more time to translate them to English.

The physical size of the high school, with its complex time schedule and endless hallways, also created what felt like an unfriendly and intimidating atmosphere. The halls were filled with shoulder-to-shoulder students laughing and talking. Lorencita longed for the quiet of home. She said she probably would have left the high school if it hadn't been for her older sister, Jane. Her parents left the option of leaving school or dropping out up to her, although they certainly didn't encourage her to quit.

Over the months, Jane gradually showed her the ropes which she had learned years earlier in the Castle Rock Middle School. Jane showed Lorencita where her classes were and helped her complete her homework. They met daily for lunch during the first semester but later separated into their own peer groups. Although Lorencita did not drop out of school, and was getting C's and D's by the end of her sophomore year, her high school experience was not very enjoyable, and she was overshadowed by her older sister's honor roll status.

"WHAT HAPPENS IF I FORGET TO TALK NAVAJO?"

Wilson's Background Experiences

Two weeks ago, Wilson left the town of Castle Rock on the Navajo Nation. There he had been surrounded by family, close relatives and friends whom he had known from birth. All of Wilson's paternal relatives were Navajo; they lived in Mesa Edge and Castle Rock and were a close-knit and supportive family. Both his mother and father were Navajo college graduates, among the first in their families; his maternal grandparents also had graduated from college. His maternal grandmother, a European American, lived in a border town not far away; his mother's Navajo father lived on the Navajo Nation a day's drive from Castle Rock. Wilson's father's family lived in a culturally traditional part of the Navajo Nation and most members spoke Navajo as well as English; a few, like Lorencita's father, chose not to speak English. Wilson's mother spoke some Navajo, but not fluently. She had to learn it in high school, when her family moved from California to Rough Rock, Arizona, where her mother and father taught and she attended a pioneer tribally controlled school. Wilson's family separated while he was in kindergarten; his mother had decided to leave the reservation where she had been a science teacher at Castle Rock High School to attend graduate school at a predominantly white university. The university was located in Stone Creek, a community of about 75,000 people, more than 85 percent of whom were white. Stone Creek was in another state, more than 11 hours drive from Castle Rock. Income levels there were very high, as were the educational levels of its inhabitants. The move by Wilson, his mother, and little sister from Castle Rock ultimately broke up the marriage between Wilson's parents.

Wilson's Experiences in School

The 24 students obediently sat in the designated spots at the six tables in the first grade classroom. For the first three minutes all of the students remained silent. After five minutes the class—except for one boy—chatted in a dull roar. Wilson sat quietly at his table and did not talk. His dark brown eyes absorbed unfamiliar surroundings. All of his classmates in pre-school and kindergarten had been Navajo; now he was the only non-white student in the class. His friends were hundreds of miles away. Wilson bit his nails and tried to keep from showing how truly out of place he felt. The teacher began to speak above the first grade din about mandatory classroom procedures. At times her voice sounded as if she were shrieking in anger in an attempt to be heard. Wilson finished off all 10 nails the first day of school.

Wilson had been judged an active and gifted student by his kindergarten teacher in the Castle Rock school district; his parents were told he was doing well in school. His mother assumed that his performance in Stone Creek school district would be judged similarly, but, to Wilson on that first day in school, his former success seemed very far away. Alone and unsure about the rules for proper behavior, he continued to behave in the ways which he had grown up knowing were acceptable to his family and community and which had created success for him in the Castle Rock kindergarten.

His teacher in Stone Creek repeatedly tried to draw him into the verbal activities of the classroom by calling on him to volunteer answers. This quite acceptable mainstream practice succeeded in alienating him from educational activities for the first two months of school; Wilson did not feel ready for public performance.

Wilson's mother was aware of his homesickness. However, she herself had obtained some of her education in predominantly white, middle-class settings off the reservation. She was accustomed to Anglo schools—especially since she had been a teacher in the Anglo dominated schools of Castle Rock. She had not thought through how leaving his culture to enter another one might affect Wilson, because cross cultural experiences had been well-integrated throughout her growing up.

One day Wilson's problems became very clear. He came home with a note from the teacher which said he was "behind in his development." The teacher asserted that he didn't seem to be ready to read. She was very concerned because Wilson seemed so bright and was such an attentive youngster, so thoughtful and considerate to other children. Attached to the note was a slip to be signed, asking that his mother give permission for him to be tested and screened for placement in the "learning center," a pull-out program for children with learning problems.

With the problems now out in the open, Wilson's mother spent the next afternoon in conference with his teacher. She adamantly refused to allow him to be tested. Later she said, "I'm absolutely not worried about Wilson. And I don't want him to be labeled. I know what it feels like to be in the 'buzzards' group instead of the 'blue birds.' I didn't read in the first grade either. He'll read when he feels that he's ready." She explained to the teacher that Wilson needed more time to become adjusted to his new school and life in Stone Creek community. The teacher accepted this view and began to ask for suggestions on how to get Wilson more involved.

Wilson was the only non-Anglo child in his class. To avoid the negative stereotyping which she knew often accompanies minority children and their families, Wilson's mother decided to become very visible in his schooling so the teachers could not avoid noticing how interested she was and how much she participated in her son's education. Because the school had no formal science program, Wilson's mother began teaching a math or a science lesson on Fridays with the classroom teacher. The teacher welcomed her help and slowly stopped worrying so much about Wilson's progress. As a consequence, and because he grew more comfortable with the new school setting, Wilson slowly began to become more involved in school. Just as his mother predicted, Wilson began to read when he felt ready—suddenly, well, and with interest. In fact, his first act of reading was to read a complete bedtime story to his little sister.

In second grade, Wilson moved to another school closer to the University. Although he read stories every night to his little sister, his new teacher again described him as "on the fringes and uninvolved." What she meant was that Wilson intently watched presentations and listened to the teacher, but would not volunteer information readily. His mother once again had to convince a teacher that nothing was wrong with her son's behavior. This time, however, the process was much more difficult and at times required uncomfortable confrontations. As Wilson exited from second grade, he was reading on grade level but the teacher still felt that he "needed to become more verbal."

Linking Home, School, and Community

In the context of a Navajo community, Wilson's "withdrawn" behavior was not really withdrawn. In fact, he demonstrated behavior which is very appropriate to novice learners. Wilson came from a community where people learn from watching role models until they feel capable of competent performance.

Visual learning with little discussion is acceptable to Navajos and learners will not attempt something new until they feel confident that they can perform in a reasonably competent manner. Because the trial and error model of learning which is so encouraged in white, middle-class schools is frowned upon, Wilson would not try to read because he was not yet sure he could do it. When he had watched others sufficiently to feel comfortable with his own first attempt, he began to read fluently on his first try. His little sister now will have two role models as she goes to school—her mother and her brother, both of whom read stories to her every night.

Wilson's experience also demonstrates the cultural bias of widely used educational concepts such as "readiness." Because Wilson's teachers did not understand how Navajo children get ready to read or demonstrate that they are, in fact, good learners, he almost was labeled as a slow learner. Wilson's teachers were waiting for him to demonstrate behavior that matched their own culturally defined definitions of readiness to read. When he didn't, they prepared for the worst. In fact, unbeknownst to his teachers, Wilson was actively involved in the learning process, but was unable to verbalize what he was doing to his teachers. This misunderstanding would have had vastly different and negative consequences if Wilson's mother had not been so active on his behalf.

Navajo high school students, more often than not, fit the description of Lorencita. When their early education is delivered by teachers immersed only in the Navajo culture, these students find themselves unprepared for the rigors of contemporary school life. Even if they have attended mainstream schools all their lives—as Wilson had—their classroom teachers fail to draw upon the vast amounts of knowledge with which such students come to school, and they assume that non-mainstream responses—such as the "silence" of Wilson and Lorencita—denote learning problems or handicaps, even deafness. Lorencita's problem, however, was that the school constituted an alien culture for her. She felt uncomfortable being singled out for public classroom performance in ways which are antithetical to Navajo cultural norms. To this day her family laughingly refers to her as "*Ja'ii*," the one with the hearing problem.

Like Wilson, Lorencita simply came to school with mismatched cultural tools, not a physical or intellectual deficit. The tools of her first language and the cultural values she held did not match with the requirements for success in Castle Rock High School, though she was initiated into some of the mysteries by her sister, Jane. The linguistic fluency, conflict resolution skills, and leadership abilities she demonstrated at home remained undiscovered by the school community, no matter how much they continued to be valued and relied upon by her family and relatives in Mesa Edge.

What almost happened to Wilson and Lorencita mirrors the experience of many language and ethnic minority students who each year face misplacement in special education programs (Baca & Cervantes, 1989). Once misplaced, they often become lifers in a system which does not know how to adequately address the cultural needs of non-mainstream students.

The experiences of both Lorencita and Wilson also demonstrate cultural differences in child rearing practices in Navajo and Anglo communities (see Deyhle & LeCompte, 1994). Navajo children grow up more quickly than Anglo children. Navajos believe that their children are capable of exercising good judgment at a much younger age than do European-American parents. Hence, Lorencita's parents let her decide which school she should attend, and whether or not she should stay in school. Similarly, Wilson's mother did not interfere with his own decision about when to begin reading. She did, however, provide support by remaining quite visible in the classroom so that the teacher could neither persist in her negative judgement of his readiness to read nor treat him in ways Wilson's mother found prejudicial. European-American parents might not have been able to maintain such distance from their childrens' decisions in light of their possible negative consequence. However, lack of interference on the part of Navajo parents—coupled with confidence in their ability—seems to be an effective strategy. Wilson entered third grade as an enthusiastic participant in a new bilingual program, where the fact that he already was fluent in two languages was considered a plus. Lorencita graduated from high school in 1992 because, as she said: "I'm used to it now."

Lack of compatibility between their homes and the public schools is a critical issue for Navajo students. Regardless of where they live, Navajo students attend schools which reflect Eurocentric values of the dominant culture, rather than those of their native culture. Even within the boundaries of the Navajo Nation, lack of cultural compatibility between public schools and the home is evident. The school environment usually is identical with that of schools found in middle class white neighborhoods anywhere in the United States. Classroom teachers and district policies often ignore the strong cultural identity and highly developed stores of knowledge Navajo students bring to the school setting. In some cases, the lack of cultural sensitivity derives from simple ignorance of students' cultural background. In others, district policies overtly are directed at replacing the student's cultural affinities and identity with a more "functional" European-American orientation. The effects of these practices, whether intentional or not, are both identifiable and understandable. American Indian students often resent and resist the assimilationist attitudes their teachers convey by acting in ways which frustrate and anger unknowing teachers. They also leave school in disproportionate numbers, despite their obvious intellectual capabilities (Deyhle, 1989, 1992; LeCompte & Dworkin, 1991).

The experiences of these two students demonstrate that culturally different children really need advocates—even watchdogs—in the classrooms to assure that they are not mistreated, misunderstood, misplaced, and miseducated. They also argue for an imperative: school personnel must be knowledgeable about the cultural practices of the students they teach—especially with regard to traditional patterns of teaching and learning in those communities. Finally, recent research on American Indian children indicates that the assimilationist educational policies which the United States historically has imposed upon American Indian students not only alienate them from their own families and cultures, but act to push them out of school. In fact, students who are fluent in their native language, are *knowledgeable about their own cultural heritage, and who have close ties with culturally traditional grandparents* are those most likely to graduate from high school (Deyhle, 1989, 1991); these are the students with the emotional stamina, self-esteem, and family support system necessary for survival in the alien environment of contemporary public schools. Schools must examine their practices—both within and outside the classroom—for institutional and personal insensitivity and racism. Similarly, local communities need child advocates to assure that such practices do not continue.

UNDERSTANDING THE NAVAJO VIGNETTE

An understanding of the conditions in which individual and contextual factors interact in various ways to produce school achievement for students from particular tribal groups is critical for the sound spiritual, intellectual and physical development of Native children. Educational anthropologists have provided particularly good documentation of the Navajo in this regard. Nonetheless, as we learn from the Lorencita and Wilson cases, such knowledge does not necessarily inform classroom practice. Native children often need advocates, and occasionally watchdogs to prevent miscarriages of justice in their school experiences.

In the case of tribes in the Southeast, such as the Seminole, Mickusukee, and Cherokee, virtually no educational research data exist to inform practice. Creating academically challenging and culturally sound curricular materials; addressing tribal school governance issues; and building upon community strengths to enrich students' in- and out-of-school experiences is next to impossible in these instances. The educational system must change in order to effectively educate a heterogeneous student population; this change must be shaped and motivated by an understanding and acceptance of the variety of influences on that population (Comer, 1988; Gill, 1991; Hare & Hare, 1991; Nobles, 1981). Without a collective effort involving schools, families, and the community, there can be no effective solutions to the problems confronting the educational system's effort to educate culturally diverse children, a point we explore further in the concluding chapter.

McCarty and Schaffer (1994) describe an innovative and effective language arts and literacy curriculum for Navajo high school youth whose parents valued the stability and continuity of their community, hoping their children, while gaining at least a high school education, would also acquire knowledge and respect for their heritage and surroundings. Teachers utilized the "uniquely Indian resources of their students and communities," adapting standard texts and readers by utilizing themes and issues introduced by the students. In addition, *"Tohono O'odham* first graders examined material relevant to but extending beyond their desert community by investigating themes such as shelter, water, local village life and the concept of community" (McCarty & Schaffer, 1994, p. 129). These curricular approaches are designed to incorporate Native ways of understanding the world with pedagogically sound practice.

VIGNETTE #9: FROM MOUNTAIN TO METROPOLIS: URBAN APPALACHIAN CHILDREN AND YOUTH
by Kathryn M. Borman

There was no doubt that these . . .[urban Appalachian] mothers cared about their sons and all the rest of the children in the family. But they were just trying to make ends meet and trying to hold themselves together, trying to meet the demands of the kids and it wasn't working. They seemed very overwhelmed. (conversation with Susan Murphy, Teacher, Cincinnati Public Schools, 1990)

Background

This vignette addresses the issues facing urban Appalachian children and their families. These issues may not be apparent to those unfamiliar with problems of internal rural-urban migration. These issues involve cultural identity, rural-urban transition, and changes in family structure and livelihood strategies—all of which in combination create different kinds of stressors. Appalachians in urban places such as Cincinnati, Dayton, Asheville, and elsewhere are similar in their hopes, dreams and experiences to other immigrant and indigenous peoples previously considered in this volume. Unlike other vignettes included in this book, this one features the inclusion of the voices of teachers, neighborhood-based advocates and social workers who work closely with their clients.

In Chapter 3, I provided a background discussion of Appalachian migration and its impact upon the cities receiving the migrants and upon the migrants themselves. Special attention was paid to Cincinnati, the site of my 14-year research program with urban Appalachian children and youth. In 1991, while a relatively large number of first generation urban Appalachians lived in Cincinnati, many thousands more were the children and grandchildren of those who initially migrated to the city in the 1940s and 1950s. The researchers estimate this group constituted approximately 40 percent of the county's population. Both blacks and Appalachians have clustered more heavily in the central city, as opposed to the suburban fringe areas over the nine year period. Whereas 31.4 percent of the Appalachian respondents were city dwellers in 1980, by 1989 44.4 percent lived in the city. A similar proportion of black residents also inhabit the central city, leading the researchers to conclude that the city is becoming inhabited by an overwhelmingly black and Appalachian population.

Not surprisingly, given the enormous economic and occupational shifts that have occurred both locally and regionally over the last 20 years, employment growth for urban Appalachians from 1980 to 1989 was concentrated in low-level service industry jobs. As discussed at the outset, the expansion of the service sector has paralleled the decline of manufacturing in many cities in the Midwest. Thus, for urban Appalachians surveyed, the number reporting employment in sales and clerical jobs grew 14 percent as did the number of laborers and service workers (+12 percent). Declining numbers (−17 percent) reported employment as craftsperson and operatives.

Throughout the remainder of this vignette, I examine life in the neighborhood for both elementary school-aged children and adolescents whose criminal records and frequent school absence make them tough cases, but whose attitudes and behaviors also illustrate the strengths of this community. Finally, I consider how the school as a community-based institution can be organized and positioned to carry out its work successfully.

Community Life and Educational Issues

In describing the dilemmas of community life for residents and particularly for children and their families who live in Cincinnati's urban Appalachian neighborhoods, I will examine the dilemmas of urban Appalachian children, youths, and their families. I turn attention first to how young elementary school children negotiate neighborhood life. Next, I consider how older urban Appalachian youths and their families manage the "welfare game." I also present accounts of neighborhood life focusing on the availability and use of drugs, particularly alcohol. These accounts have implications for both educational policy and social service policies more generally.

I also examine the sense of alienation experienced by many Appalachian students and their parents. While parents clearly attach importance to their children's achieving success in school, they are ambivalent about encouraging behaviors that traditionally have supported academic success. Finally, I conclude by suggesting structures for the delivery of social services and other outreach programs to urban Appalachian youth.

I rely on several sources of information: (a) past and current research in enclaved urban Appalachian neighborhoods, (b) interviews with an adult first generation urban Appalachian, Larry Redden, who has successfully negotiated the system, (c) interviews with adolescent urban Appalachians currently involved in a neighbor-hood-based summer job skills training program, and (d) interviews with Susan Murphy, teacher of urban Appalachian children for most of her career.

Negotiating the Neighborhood in the Elementary School Years

Life in predominately urban Appalachian neighborhoods varies according to the economic prosperity enjoyed by neighborhood residents. In neighborhoods such as Over-The-Rhine, Lower Price Hill, and the East End in Cincinnati, households face severe economic constraints that place a ceiling on the amount of resources the family can utilize on their children's behalf.

Lower Price Hill's residents have settled in the neighborhood over a period of 25 to 30 years, migrating in a clearly identifiable, coherent, and consistent stream from eastern Kentucky coal fields in a manner similar to patterns characterizing nearly all urban Appalachian communities. Close kin tended to move to the same location in the city and subsequently provided shelter, support and access to jobs for kin arriving later. Among a group of 24 parents living in Lower Price Hill one named 30 relatives living in the neighborhood. Only one respondent had no relatives living close by; most had seven or more. As a result of settlement patterns and subsequent sustained interactions, children in Lower Price Hill grow up in a context of familial ties that bind them to their families and make transition to work outside the neighborhood difficult.

Contributing to the close integration and sense of isolation from the rest of the city is the neighborhood's topography. Observers regularly characterize Lower Price Hill as an urban "holler." Lower Price Hill's geography makes it an enclaved community since a steep, unpopulated hill encloses it to the north and highways, major thoroughfares, and a viaduct spanning the Mill Creek Valley surround it in other directions. Because the community has natural boundaries, children in Lower Price Hill develop a clear sense of their community. When a group of 10 children (ages 7 to 14) and their parents were asked to provide an outline of their neighbor-hood on a city street map, children responded by drawing a more circumscribed space than that drawn by their parents. All children agreed upon a core space that included frequently used social spaces such as the elementary school and surround-ing yard, the Bible Center, a social service agency housing a community council meeting room, the locally controlled community school, and other offices accessi-ble to the neighborhood.

Elaine Mueninghoff, Shirley Piazza, and I also investigated children's use of neighborhood social services to gain an understanding of their involvement in neighborhood social life during the summer months when they were not in school. Three basic assumptions guided this research. First, children who spent recreational time outside their homes were seen as gaining important knowledge about patterns of social participation in community activities. Involvement in local activities apparently generates adult satisfaction with their role in the community. A second assumption was that children who were active participants in neighborhood life were building strongly positive feelings about their neighborhood. A third assumption, following from our knowledge of settlement patterns, was that kin groups and informal friendship networks were important in determining knowledge and use of community resources by neighborhood children and youth. Therefore, their involvement in neighborhood life would not only reflect children's perceptions of benefits from such involvement but would also be highly dependent upon their integration into a network of neighborhood friendships and family relationships.

Several findings in this study bear comment. First, children have a working knowledge of their neighborhood and its resources given their responses to the boundary-drawing task mentioned above. Second, by the age of seven, children develop generally positive and strongly felt emotions about their neighborhood. In response to the question, "If you had to explain to someone where you lived, what would you say?" the youngest respondent replied, "I live over there [pointing across the street] where my cousins live." A slightly older [aged eight] child responded, "Here, the school yard by Oyler School, my house and my friends'." A 12-year-old said, "To me it's the only community I've ever lived in. It's my life." Finally, children learn of ongoing activities in the neighborhood by word of mouth. Many informal activities, street games, and the like are undertaken by children who live in the same buildings and spontaneously gather after lunch or in the evenings on street corners or playgrounds. Other activities such as events at the Bible Center are more regularized since they are scheduled at specific times. A 13-year-old newcomer to the neighborhood was representative in naming the Bible Center, open weekdays from 10 a.m. to 2 p.m., as the primary social center for children. "I met a kid down the street who brought me up here [to the Center]. So far, I've been here—two weeks—I like to play ping-pong."

The Bible Center's attractiveness was based on two features, both important to an understanding of political socialization in the neighborhood. First, the supervisor was a local resident, the 18-year-old daughter of a prominent, civically active neighborhood family who provided activities appealing to children of an extensive age range. Although the local social service agency paid her salary, the pool table and ping-pong equipment used by older children had been donated by her family. Art supplies were also available for the projects of younger children. Second, since the facility was located in the geographical center of the neighborhood, it served as a convenient place to meet other children.

In summary, children in this enclaved neighborhood were informed by their working knowledge of local geography and by word-of-mouth-information, and made use of neighborhood resources. Social services targeted for them are particularly favored but are most popular when supervision is locally-based. These findings have direct application to policies aimed at eliminating traditional patterns of school organization which are bureaucratic and centralized as opposed to site-based.

In order to understand cultural continuities and discontinuities between home and school, I and my colleagues, under the rubric of the Center for Research on

Literacy and Schooling at the University of Cincinnati, explored family and school linkages in two inner-city low-income communities. One of the communities (the East End) included many families who are third and fourth generation migrants from the Appalachian Region. The study examined patterns of relationships between home factors and student school achievement. Special emphasis was placed on understanding family literacy activities, parent discipline practices, and parent participation in school events as these were related to student outcomes.

River Road Elementary School serves a neighborhood comprised overwhelmingly of white urban Appalachian families. A total of 2,815 such individuals, as compared to 407 blacks, live in the two census tracts comprising the East End neighborhood. Most parents (76.8%) interviewed during the course of the research grew up in Cincinnati, and a majority (52.9%) own their own homes. In addition to standard SES measures, we utilized four sets of family-related variables to analyze household influences. The four are family literacy activities, parent discipline practices, parent school participation, and household composition.

I first describe related research in documenting findings on the relationship between family literacy activities and school success. Activities such as storybook reading, and experimenting with writing have been identified as providing young children with school-related knowledge that prepares them for the transition to formal education. For example, Dahl (1989) found that inner-city children who had more knowledge of written language were more successful at learning to read and write in a traditional public school kindergarten classroom. In a study of low-income Latino families, Reese and associates concluded that, "the impact of parents' educational experiences on children is mediated through particular activity settings, such as the use of literacy in the workplace, the modeling of literacy behaviors at home, the viewing of incipient child literacy attempts in a positive and encouraging light, and the scaffolding of children's learning experiences" (p. 20). Thus, considering parental educational level, household structure, or any other individual or set of family characteristics by themselves is insufficient.

Studies of the influence of household composition on school achievement concluded that mother aloneness may be more important than father absence in predicting poor adjustment to school. The presence of a second adult has beneficial effects on reading marks. What is important in understanding children's literacy learning is *how* parents and other adults in the household structure, organize and carry out reading and related activities with their children.

In considering the relationship between family characteristics and student outcomes, it is important that several caveats be kept in mind. First, not all family characteristics may be equally important in influencing children's school-related achievements. Literacy activities such as reading aloud to children or engaging in writing activities such as carrying out correspondence with absent kin may be more influential than, say, parental disciplinary styles. Second, family literacy activities vary and may be dependent on cultural variations. We saw, for example in "The Power of Ritual and Language" that Spanish in the Martinez family was used by the parents and members of their generation for many kinds of interactions. Maria Teresa employed that language during a formal celebration but did not commonly use Spanish on a day to day basis, worried that her poor vocabulary and sometimes awkward expression would embarrass her.

Variations in the use of English and other languages as well as different uses of English dialects such as Black English and "Standard" English" are important in providing cultural maps of communities. These maps are useful to teachers in performing their instructional routines in teaching reading and writing. Finally, cultural variations such as these evident in families and communities should be viewed as resources rather than deficits. We say more about this in Chapter 8.

While school and family alike value and practice such literacy activities as reading aloud, other family practices may not be recognized and valued. This may further alienate children who are most vulnerable to school failure. In fact, the most striking observation yielded by our research was the strength of the relationships between family income and parental education with home-based literacy activities, such as having library books in the home, saving children's writing, playing board games with children, and reading to and being read to by children. These findings contrasted with the relatively weak relationship between family literacy events and school outcomes such as reading grades and achievement test scores.

"Handling it Myself" in Adolescence

In extremely dysfunctional families, ambivalence about schooling is reduced to indifference simply because the family's immediate needs are so overwhelming. Susan Murphy, the Cincinnati Public School teacher whose statement about urban Appalachian mothers and their sons began this vignette, observed that the transition from the interdependence of family members that characterizes life in rural Appalachia is not necessarily present in the urban Appalachian context.

Susan described the mothers of her fourth and fifth grade students, boys who were having difficulty in school and who had been assigned to her special education class designed for students with severe behavioral disorders in the following way:

> All of these women, I remember very vividly and exactly what they looked like. They were real open and, like their sons, were easy to get close to, but [they were] overwhelmed. [They were] . . . deeply caring but [they] did not know what to do for the kids. They had no control . . . could not make them come in at night . . . could not make them go to bed . . . could not make them get up and come to school. The sons were more or less running their own show. The mothers had lost control which is a big problem when one of the kids gets in trouble with the law. [The mothers] could parent the younger ones, but once. . .[their sons] grew up, what could . . . [the mothers] do with somebody they considered to be on the same level?

> Up here it's like . . . [the mothers] are alone without their network or else the network is in the same shape . . . there were often a lot of kids which would mean the parenting

network is sort of overwhelmed. Young mothers having babies in the rural areas is not as complicated as all these young mothers having babies in this complicated city.

Susan Murphy's observations on strained family networks and the difficulties facing young mothers in the city underscore the issues that face both the young mother and the child for whom inadequate family resources create an uncertain future. Urban Appalachians constitute the largest group of students (in proportion to their numbers) who leave school in Cincinnati before graduation (Timm & Borman, 1997). For young women, school leaving is most often associated with pregnancy.

Perspectives on the Neighborhood: Gangs and Drugs

Both boys and girls saw life in the neighborhood as dangerous and at the same time boring. The boys talked about gangs of more affluent white youths from Price Hill and elsewhere, who came into the neighborhood, particularly on the weekends. Gangs with colorful names like Miami Vice, C-town, Cincy Boys, and the Mod Squad operate by a "policy" designed to terrify those they encounter. The Youth Program leader, Betsy, a long-term resident of Lower Price Hill and parent of one of the boys, said of the gangs, "Their policy is to find you by yourself and beat the shit out of you. They never fight one-on-one. They keep the odds on their side. They use guns, Mace, you name it, they got it." Gang membership is not seen as attractive by Lower Price Hill youths; nonetheless, two of the boys wearing western style kerchiefs declared, amidst much hooting, that they were the "bandanna bastards." Although gang activity centers around cars (as opposed to motorcycles) and is motivated by claims on girls living in the neighborhood, both of which interest male Youth Program participants, gang membership was shunned primarily for three reasons: (a) "They're always fighting" (Mike), (b) "They want to be black" (Dave), and (c) "You don't need a gang down here to be supported" (Betsy).

The neighborhood as an extension of the family was seen by the youths as supportive and, more negatively, as inhibiting the use of drugs despite their widespread availability. One member of the group, Dave, claimed that parents themselves were the major users and abusers of drugs, particularly marijuana.

K. Borman: What drugs are available on the streets?
Dave: Hardly none at all.
Mike: See, really, it's hard to get anything in this neighborhood because of the parents.
Betsy: Everybody knows everybody's kids. You're not going to give somebody else's kids shit unless you want trouble.
Dave: [That's] . . . A lot of bull—money talks; bullshit walks. The kids are scared their parents will find out and they *will* find out. Most

of the kids are not hooked on pot and drugs—it's the parents. The kids use mostly wine coolers.

Although these youths claim that drug use is virtually non-existent, some spoke quite knowledgeably about the price, quality and sources of marijuana and also spoke of the availability of "pills" and amphetamines in the neighborhood. The availability of "downers" was attributed to the presence of the public health clinic in the neighborhood. Clinic staff were viewed as carelessly dispensing drugs into the community. Nonetheless, drinking is the most widespread abusive activity among these youths. Larry Redden said about the harder stuff: "Crack is virtually no more. It's gone." While still available in African-American neighborhoods, it is rejected by these kids who see it as part of a "black style" they do not find attractive.

Among the girls, being on the streets with the guys is a source of entertainment and fun, although such behavior also exposes them to gang violence, drinking, and drug use. However, these girls spoke of avoiding or being protected from involvement with drugs and alcohol by concerned parents and other adults in the neighborhood, often to their frustration. One of the girls talked about her "experience with drug use" as she called it,

I had an experience with drug use. I mean, it was—I did it last year—well, when I was doing my senior year. I snuck away with some friend of mine up the street. I mean, we'd sit right there in front of the bar and some guy . . . said you don't want to mess up right now—talking to me . . . [that way] since it was my senior year. He said if he saw me doing it again he'd go tell my parents. And then, one of my other friends told me to come down here and talk to Fred and he gave me this long lecture.

As young women, the sense was that they were more severely restricted in their behavior by parents anxious that their daughters avoid early pregnancy. In comparing herself to her brother, Bonnie remarked,

. . . my father is harder on me than on my brother. I mean, I can see why because he doesn't want me to go out there—me being a girl—I mean you see all these girls doing the same thing. Someone's 14 with a baby. He doesn't want me to end up like that. So, I'm living with a man who doesn't want me to mess up.

Parental strategies that aim at sequestering young women are, of course, not limited to urban Appalachian families. Such strategies are prevalent in paternalistic ethnic cultures. While these strategies are, perhaps, effective in the short run, they can deprive young women of opportunities (a) to participate in community life, (b) to have experiences that prepare them for adulthood, and (c) to adopt an active, less passive orientation to life. A striking aspect of my conversation with these young women was the emphasis they placed on their role as companions to boys who initiated fights, drinking bouts, and other street action, while they simply went along for the ride as passive observers.

Drug and alcohol use spill over into school. Kids who smoke marijuana persist in school if they "focus their mind on school" and use pot only occasionally. Pouring beer or whiskey into coke bottles and slipping it into school was reported by the girls. This was an activity undertaken by "a whole bunch of guys" and not by the girls, according to the girls.

LESSONS FROM THE URBAN APPALACHIAN VIGNETTE

These urban Appalachian young people can all too readily be dismissed as lacking in ambition. Clearly, their constrained socioeconomic circumstances are the major contributing factor to their marginalized status. Locally-based agencies must have connections with other neighborhoods facilitated, perhaps by a network or council of such social service delivery centers.

Currently in the United States reformers are stressing the value of creating schools characterized by (a) school site-based management, (2) community participation in decisions both about hiring and firing principals and teachers, and in developing the curriculum, and (c) school site-based staff and community development programs. These strategies are aimed at fostering the active involvement of teachers, parents and students, all of whom have traditionally been least enfranchised to determine the nature of educational structures and experiences in schools. To envision the kind of community-based social service operation that parents describe is to consider a plan that school reformers, social service planners, and the architects of *Goals 2000* support. It is also to recall the model of the settlement house exemplified in Jane Addams' Hull House in late nineteenth century Chicago. Whether plans for such service delivery systems will get the political backing they require for implementation is another question. How these plans might also take into account the reduction the alienation and isolation of urban Appalachian youths from mainstream experiences will also require careful thought. Historically, the invisible minority has not easily gained access to the services it needs and deserves.

This chapter has examined the stories of American Indian and urban Appalachian students whose background experiences are in some respects parallel. Both groups have encountered pressure to "act white" and abandon publicly ridiculed native ways of acting and speaking. Unfortunately, as often alienated and marginalized groups, both young American Indians and Appalachians have taken up lifestyles involving drug use, alcohol and gang activity. Creating enclaved cultures knit together by local ties is a strategy both groups have frequently employed, serving to strengthen the importance of the community as central to each group's economic, social, and educational lives. The social service agency in the neighborhood is a model organization, one we will refer to again at the book's conclusion.

7

Schools and Communities: The African American Experience

The vignettes that follow show something of the diversity of the African American experience. As is also true of the American Indian, it is impossible to utilize a single or even multiple examples to illustrate current conditions experienced by children and young people who claim an African heritage. Nonetheless, as our cases illustrate, certain themes characterize the hopes, aspirations and attainments of African Americans. For one thing, as the following vignette illustrates, it is extremely important that each successive generation build upon the accomplishments of those that have gone before. "Gotta do better" is heard not only in households such as B.J. and Celes' in Florida; it is also a theme in the Boston elementary classroom described later in this section by Michele Foster.

VIGNETTE #10: ACHIEVEMENT ACROSS THE GENERATIONS: NEGOTIATING A BETTER EDUCATION FOR THREE AFRICAN AMERICAN CHILDREN IN ST. PETERSBURG, FLORIDA
by Evelyn Phillips

Growing up in the 1960s

"You gotta do better than we did." "Get a good education and nobody can take that away from you." These two admonitions ring in my ear as loudly and melodiously as Aretha Franklin's lyrics in the song "R-e-s-p-e-c-t" and were drilled into me and my three sisters. If one of us slackened in our quest, our parents, Blanche and Clayton, reminded us of how hard they slaved for us so that we wouldn't have to follow their footsteps. Our mother worked as a maid and sewing machine operator, while our father sawed logs into finished boards at a local sawmill. They got up at 5 o'clock in the morning each day to go work. Yet we knew by the clothes and shoes we wore, the green wood frame house we lived in, and the Ford truck that we owned their pay was insufficient. Our parents' lives during the 1960s in a rural northwest Florida community, known for its conservatism and racism, were a struggle. None of us wished to become trapped in the quagmire of minimum wage jobs that the fate of being born poor and black in the late twenties offered our parents. My sisters and I knew that we had to get an education and do better.

"Getting a good education" was not explicitly defined. However, our parents repeatedly said that school was our job. Unless we were sick, we attended. Yet we learned from their implicit efforts that getting a good education meant more than going to school. It meant reaching for every educational opportunity available. "Getting a good education" is a prerequisite for "doing better." Doing better "is being qualified for the job you want and independent enough so you don't have to take a lot of things," explained our mother. Doing better meant having the freedom to walk away from a demeaning job because one is qualified. Compared to our parents, we all *did* do better. Our mother received her high school General Education Equivalency Degree (GED) in 1981 and acquired a real estate license when she was 60 years old. Our father had only nine years of formal schooling. Despite barriers, they managed to move into a brick home and achieve a semblance of middle-class life. Hence, my sisters and I had to achieve more. We did. Each of us finished high school. The youngest three attended college. One of us achieved a masters and doctorate degree. Yes, my generation did better than our parents'.

However, this vignette is not about my generation's quest for achievement. My family's lore about education and advancement is told to present a context for understanding the underlying assumptions that motivate my younger sister's search for a decent education for her children. Hence, this paper explores how my sister, B.J. Biandudi and her husband, Celes, guarantee their three children, Kinie, Tonda, and Jeremy, the right type of schooling that will expand the family's benchmark of success. I especially examine how they negotiate the issues of busing, magnet schools and neighborhood influence in Pinellas County (St. Petersburg), Florida, to ensure a brighter future for their children. Court-ordered enrollment ratios, changing conditions of neighborhoods, and children's peer relations are integral aspects of their quest to ensure a better future for Jeremy, Tonda, and Kinie. I chart with particular detail how they direct their energies toward Kinie, at 16 their oldest child and only daughter.

Since these children's lives will be measured against their parents' achievements, it is helpful to examine the context in which their futures are developed. B.J. and Celes attended a private liberal arts college in St. Petersburg where they met. B.J.

majored in economics and landed a job as a loan officer in a bank. Celes became a mathematician and a banker also. However, hostile takeovers and savings and loans debacles led them to change careers and become Pinellas County deputy sheriffs. Hence, their children are expected to become more than civil servants with bachelors' degrees.

For Kinie, Tonda, and Jeremy to achieve more than their parents, B.J. and Celes are expected to provide an education that is at least comparable or better than the one they themselves received. Therefore, as we examine how they negotiate schooling for their children, its helpful to understand what B.J.'s and Celes' parents provided them.

Celes and B.J.'s Story

Celes, who was born and raised in Kinshasha, Congo (formerly Zaire), always had private schooling.

> I went to a private state primary school. When you finish, you take a state exam to help you find your strengths. Then I went to college. That is what we call it. You would call it college prep here. The last two years I went to a private high school. You had to pay to go to high school. There was a regular public high school. But this school was run by the Flemish for French, Flemish, and Belgian students. It was for white people. I was bused to a Flemish and French neighborhood. It was sophisticated.

Celes' father's position in the government and his own professional education afforded him one of the best schools Zaire offered. "My daddy had a Master's degree in economics from a university in Illinois and a religion degree from a university in Pennsylvania," he says.

Celes explains that he always wanted to be a doctor and that motivated him to come to the United States to join his brother who taught at Eckerd College in St. Petersburg, Florida. However, Celes, who speaks French, Kiswahili, and Kicongo, found that his command of English was too limited to pursue medicine. Therefore, he decided to major in mathematics because the symbols and formulae were universal.

Unlike Celes, B.J. attended public schools until she entered college. In a rural, racially segregated community, she had no choice. The only school available to her was the all-black elementary school until the eighth grade, when Washington County integrated its schools and turned its black high school into a middle school. For her secondary education, she attended a predominantly white high school in an adjacent town, a 45-minute bus ride from home. There were no alternatives to public education.

Having been given the best primary and secondary education their parents could provide, B.J. and Celes arrived at Eckerd College. The private school was called Florida Presbyterian College until the early 1970s when a financial gift from the Florida-based Eckerd family provided a substantial endowment. Despite class and cultural differences, they bonded, married, settled and established a family in St. Petersburg, the largest city in Pinellas County on the west-central coast of Florida, near some of the world's most beautiful beaches and long a magnet for retirees and vacationers.

St. Petersburg: A Southern City

St. Petersburg is a "southern" racially divided city. Central Avenue in the city's downtown separates the city into Northside and Southside. Northside is a euphemism, disguising the overwhelmingly white population of that area of the city while Southside is shorthand for black enclave. The 1990 census shows that 80 percent of the African Americans residing in the city live in neighborhoods adjacent to downtown. Of the 238,629 residents in St. Petersburg, 46,623 or approximately 20 percent are classified as black according to the 1990 census. As recently as 1970, a city council decree restricted African Americans in St. Petersburg to a residentially segregated zone where most still reside. In October, 1996, the nation watched as residents of Southside, angered by the killing of a black motorist by a police officer, burned and looted residences and businesses in the area.

The division isn't only geographical. The distribution of wealth also indicates a city divided by money. The median income of married-couple families with children under 18 in St. Petersburg is $37,515. However, aggregated figures show the income of an African American family at the median of the income distribution is $16,999. The stark differences in financial resources between blacks and whites in St. Petersburg is seen especially in poverty levels. Of the 11,369 African American families in St. Petersburg, 28 percent (3,195) live below the poverty level. This figure contrasts with comparable data for whites indicating only 5 percent of the 47,601 white families at the poverty level in the city. Thus, "Northside" and "Southside" signify more than race; such nomenclature suggests a quality of life that is divided by race.

Pinellas County (St. Petersburg) Schools

Historically, inequities have persisted in the schools as well. Therefore, in the late sixties, African American parents sought to eliminate such dualities in the public schools to help guarantee a better future for their children. Parents sued the Pinellas County School District. In 1971, 17 years after *Brown v. Board of Education of Topeka, Kansas*, Pinellas County schools were forced to desegregate following a ruling by the Fifth Circuit United States Court of Appeals. With a consensus of the National Association for the Advancement of Colored People Educational Defense Fund, the court disallowed any school in the southern part of Pinellas County to have an enrollment of more than 30 percent African American students. In the northern part of the county, the African American school population can be as small as 4 percent. To place these figures in perspective, without desegregation, only 28 of the 106 regular elementary, middle, and high schools would be naturally integrated.

To accommodate the desegregation order, significant numbers of African American children are bused out of their neighborhoods. In 1990, 88,005 students were enrolled in Pinellas County public schools. African Americans comprise only 15,570 of that number, or 17.6 percent of the public school population. Marlene Mueller, Director of Pupil Assignment for Pinellas County acknowledges that all new schools are built in predominantly white neighborhoods in the northern part of the county. African American students are more likely than white counterparts to be bussed to schools outside of their neighborhood.[2] Hence, they are scattered throughout the county to desegregate the schools. Each year the burden of busing increases for African American children, while white families move to northern Pinellas County to avoid busing and contact with African American students. Twenty-five years after the court ruling, African American children still feel the pain of the legacy of segregation despite desegregation.

School integration poses a dilemma for B.J. and Celes. Both parents acknowledge that integration is necessary. However, they believe that their children should be schooled in their neighborhood so that they may more readily monitor their education. B.J. explains, "Overall, I think integration is best. I want the same equal opportunities for my children . . . I don't want my children bused. I want to get to the school when I need to. Kids not bused do better than the children who are bused. I have first-hand information about this." Hence, B.J. and Celes want an integrated school that offers a great education and that is accessible to their neighborhood.

District officials recognize there are many parents like B.J. and Celes who do not want their children to be bused cross-county to satisfy court-ordered ratios and yet want a first-class education. Therefore, a two-track educational system has been implemented. Parents may either allow the Office of Pupil Assignment to determine the fate of their children or choose the schools they wish their children to attend. If parents are highly selective, have the means to transport their children to school, and have children who meet the intellectual or behavioral criteria, then they may select a magnet school that specializes in such curricula as arts, technology, or international education. Many parents who opt for magnet schools believe it's like choosing to dine at the Ritz-Carlton over McDonald's: magnet schools, like the Ritz, offer a wider selection and attract an exceptional clientele.

Kinie's Experience in a Magnet Elementary School

Celes and B.J. believe that magnet schools better satisfy their aspirations for their children than zoned schools. Each child attends a magnet school. Tonda, 13 years old, and Jeremy, 11 years old, are enrolled in an International Education program. Kinie attends a magnet school that is the site for the International Baccalaureate Education program. Although she is not in the program, she is in advanced classes.

The chosen magnet schools are integrated, close to where B.J. and Celes live, and offer quality education; therefore, they have selected the choicest curricula Pinellas can offer their children.

From the first day of Kinie's schooling, Celes and B.J. opted to become proactive consumers in the Pinellas County school system rather than passive victims of desegregation. They decided to enroll Kinie in Childs Park Fundamental School for kindergarten. Securing that placement was not easy. Although it is a magnet school, it is open to all parents willing to provide transportation for their children. To get Kinie in that school, B.J. arrived at the school at four o'clock one spring morning to register her first-born for the following fall. Yet, she was not the first parent to arrive, but the twentieth. She explains, "Although, I was the first black person in line." Later B.J. learned that, despite her early arrival, Kinie was placed on a waiting list. However by the fall semester, Kinie was awarded a space in kindergarten. Fortuitously, Kinie's entrance in Childs Park also locked in places for Tonda and Jeremy. Enrollment of one child in the school meant that other children in the family were also eligible to attend Childs Park and its companion middle school.

A desire to get Kinie, and later the other children, into a "good program" was the force that led B.J. to stand in line that dawn: "I was reading the paper one morning and I read about Childs Park accepting applications. The program sounded interesting. I mentioned it to another co-worker and she said that the program was excellent. I figured many parents would try to enroll their children. It was on a first come-first served basis. That is why I got there so early. Still I wasn't the first one there." B.J. and Celes consider attending the magnet school as equivalent to a private-public education. Fundamental magnet schools are marketed as strict institutions that focus on the basics—reading, writing, and arithmetic. Although any student may apply, youths who have disciplinary problems are denied. Parent Teacher Association meetings are not optional, but required. Since parents provide transportation for their children to school, there is almost daily feedback from teachers about children's progress. This image attracts many well-educated and influential parents who send their children to Childs Park. Like a private school, Childs Park, until it closed in 1994, was attended by a large number of white children from privileged backgrounds and African American students from families with middle-class aspirations. From 1985 until 1994, African American students comprised 75 of the 309 students. In February 1993, only 57 of the 318 students attending Childs Park were from low-income families.

During 1993, students from Childs Park had the highest test scores in Pinellas County on the Comprehensive Tests of Basic Skills. Third, fourth and fifth grades scored above the 80th percentile in all areas except reading, which was at the 77th percentile. School scores were highest in mathematics—at the 97th percentile. In 1994 Childs Park's students had the highest test results overall among elementary schools in Pinellas County. These scores, among other factors, indicated to B.J. and

Celes that they had made the "right" decision about placing Kinie and her brothers in Childs Park.

In addition to the academic success of students attending the school, B.J. and Celes also valued the personal caring of the school staff, especially the teachers, many of whom respected them and knew the children. B.J. recalled that the day she registered Kinie, she met the school counselor, a former wife of her college mentor. The counselor informed others at the school that B.J.'s brother-in-law had taught at Eckerd College, which she characterized as a prestigious private college in the area. Such statements relieved some of B.J.'s and Celes' anxieties about the treatment their youngsters would receive. Hence, the Biandudi family constructed a foundation on which to build their children's future at Childs Park.

However, their assessment of the school did not mean that their children's relationships with the school were trouble-free. The first major crisis occurred over language when a teacher recommended Jeremy to a special reading group. The teacher was concerned that Jeremy did not enunciate his words "correctly." His pronunciation of "ask," for example, was contested. B.J. met with the teacher to explain that Jeremy's speech was within the expected range of his African American community. Most importantly, she did not want him to be used as a guinea pig and stigmatized to meet a "special student" quota so that the school could receive more money. To place B.J.'s concern in perspective, in the second grade Jeremy had to leave school because of medical problems. Despite his illness, he succeeded in passing the second grade at the top of his class. Reluctantly, B.J. finally agreed to permit Jeremy to enter the special reading group, only after she was assured that he would still be allowed to advance with the rest of his class.

This would not be the last disagreement with teachers. Celes recounts how he was disappointed when a teacher told Jeremy he was doing fine, although he received a "C" in her class. Celes did not confront the teacher, but instead reframed the teacher's perspective for Jeremy. He reminded his son that getting a "C" was *not* doing well. Celes believes that the teacher had lower expectations for Jeremy because he is black. He is concerned that such behavior among teachers "is very dangerous." Celes suggests that the teacher took the easy route rather than motivate Jeremy to perform at a higher level.

While one teacher told Jeremy a "C" is perfectly acceptable, another told Tonda that he read too much. Celes explains that Tonda has always had to study harder than Jeremy and Kinie to get good grades. However, to motivate Tonda, Celes told him that "the person who applies himself will always achieve; they are going to soar like an eagle." Heeding this advice, Tonda discovered reading. He read extensively. In the fourth grade he read the entire autobiography of Frederick Douglass. Also, he stopped watching television. Rather than being rewarded, his teacher scolded Tonda. Of course, the teacher lost this battle. Tonda is continually encouraged to read and not watch television. B.J. and Celes and other family members reward him with money when he reads and does not watch television.

Kinie's Experience in a Magnet Middle School

B.J. and Celes have not only had to intercede on behalf of their sons, they also had to shield Kinie from being wrongfully charged by her teachers. Celes tells about the day in middle school that Kinie was assigned to make sure everyone was out of the locker room. He explains that Kinie left the locker-room thinking that all the students had cleared out. However, a student reported that her purse had been stolen. The teacher gathered all of the African American girls in the gym class and collectively accused them of conspiring and stealing the purse. The principal called the police and the parents to pick up the children because they were expelling them. Since B.J. works evenings and is off during the day, she went immediately to the school after receiving the telephone call. She was appalled at the treatment of the students. B.J. felt that the school principal and the teacher had prejudicially decided that the black girls were responsible for the stolen purse. Therefore, she intervened as the police interrogated Kinie. "I told Kinie, you see this uniform, don't let it scare you. You see them all the time. It is just clothing. I want you to tell the officer what happened." Convinced that Kinie was unaware of the purse being stolen, B.J. challenged the principal's expulsion of her. B.J. told the principal that she was not going to expel Kinie for something that the school failed to do—secure the lockers. The principal backed down and Kinie was not expelled. However, the other girls whose parents were unable to defend them were. Being well educated has helped B.J. and Celes protect their children. "It allows us to bring ideas and mistakes to the teachers. Plus the children can say they have a mama and daddy that know what is going on. The teachers learn that they (Jeremy, Tonda, and Kinie) are not just anybody," Celes posits.

Despite the magnet school offering a more selective education, B.J. and Celes recognize that the climate in which their children are educated did not offer many examples of black achievers. Childs Park only had one African American teacher. Southside Fundamental Middle, the school that Kinie attended, employs four African American instructors.

However, B.J. and Celes caution their children that, while race is not always a deciding factor, educational preparation is. "I grew up in a place where it was only blacks and blacks also want your job. It is the same," offers Celes about his experience in Congo. "I tell them, 'If you study, you will achieve; if you fail to study, you will fail'."

Celes also uses the absence of African American teachers from the school to help his children to understand the consequences of racism and to inspire them. He encourages Kinie, Jeremy, and Tonda to recognize the conditions that lead to so few black teachers:

> I ask the kids sometimes how many black teachers are there. They say two. I say why do you think that there are only two black teachers. I suggest that there are other qualified black teachers but the obstacles were so great that only two were able to get

through while 24 white ones did. I tell them that they have to respect their black teachers. These teachers were not stopped. They also have to find every door and not concentrate on the negative to inspire themselves.

Despite these problems, Celes and B.J. evaluate Childs Park and Southside as "pretty good." However, they realize that these schools are not perfect. Celes argues, "They [schools] have different values clarification. Certain values are taught that we may not agree with. You want to balance those views and help the kids to find out the pros and cons. We teach them to think and find out the source of their values. They are learning to think for themselves." Hence, B.J. and Celes perceive that magnet schools offer their children a decent education, but, as parents, they must monitor and counteract ideas they find disagreeable.

When Kinie reached the ninth grade, the security of the magnet school was no longer automatically available to her. And B.J. and Celes felt that their ability to oversee her activities was eroded. This juncture in her education created a major crisis for B.J. and Celes. Schooling, however, was not the only the thing that concerned them. They also worried about how peer pressure might undermine her future.

Kinie's High School Experiences

To enter a high school magnet program, Kinie had to meet certain academic criteria. She applied to the Computer and Technology (CAT) program, primarily at the insistence of her parents. Kinie did not wish to go to that school but desired to join the neighborhood students at their zone school. Kinie got her wish. Although she was placed on a waiting list for the CAT program, she did not get admitted. B.J. and Celes threatened to enroll her in a private religious school rather than allow her to be bused to her zone school. Kinie continually protested being sentenced to a private school. Finally, B.J. and Celes relented and allowed her to go to Osceola, her zone school. However, they warned that her stay would be evaluated at the end of the year. B.J. and Celes were not pleased with the choices available to them. They perceived that their options for Kinie were significantly reduced.

As the year progressed, B.J. and Celes worried about Kinie's performance. She began to fail her classes. By the end of the school year, she failed English. Her grades starkly contrasted with her middle school performance. B.J. recounts that she felt that she didn't know what was happening with Kinie despite her efforts to contact the school. For Celes and B.J., Kinie's behavior signaled a gloomy forecast.

Concerned about Kinie's lack of motivation and interest in school, B.J. began to regularly call Kinie's teachers. However, teachers often waited four to five days before they returned B.J.'s calls. Dissatisfied with the teachers' lack of response, B.J. increasingly visited the school unannounced. B.J. found that her presence at the school was treated as an intrusion.

The school counselors and teachers were shocked. They were amazed that blacks could come to the school. I did not care if school administrators were astonished to see me or not; it was my duty to be there. I met all of Kinie's teachers because I wanted them to *know* who she is. I wanted them to know that they could not treat Kinie as if she was a nobody.

The teachers' nonchalant attitude reinforced B.J.'s belief that she did not have a handle on Kinie's education. This reality would be confirmed when she later discovered that Kinie was given in-school suspension for one day for not "dressing-out" in physical education class. B.J. explains that she was finally informed that Kinie and some other African American girls had routinely failed to dress appropriately for gym. They usually hung under a tree on the field, B.J. says. "The gym teacher never said anything. She only became alarmed when the students moved their gathering to the school parking lot." Then Kinie and her friends were suspended. "I was not called. Why didn't the school call me?" B.J. answers her question, "The teachers at Osceola are apathetic toward kids being bused in."

Teacher apathy translates into some stark data on student outcomes. In 1994, 153 of the 299 blacks enrolled in Osceola were suspended. During the prior year, 150 of the 301 black students were suspended. Osceola teachers' low expectations for black students and the instructors' failure to develop a collaborative relationship with black parents unmasks institutional racism that undermines black students' outlook and prospects, suggests B.J. Teachers at Osceola do not have high expectations for their African American students, argues B.J.

It seems to me that the teachers do not care. The majority of the black children spend most of their school days working in grocery stores as stock-boys and cashiers. They go to school for only a couple hours. By 11 o'clock they're in the stores. The school calls this preparing them for work. What kind of work? The school does not even consider the students for meaningful jobs.

B.J. further argues that Kinie's performance at the school showed a lack of expectation by the school.

Kinie failed English. She had to go to summer school. There she received an "A." Now, she's in advanced English at St. Pete High. In that school [Osceola] the black children are there just taking up space. No one seems to care about what happens to them. Teachers are used to the black kids not excelling.

By the second semester, B.J. had grown intolerant of the situation at Osceola. "I wanted to get her in a better environment and one closer to home," explained B.J. Although displeased with their relationship with Osceola, B.J. and Celes were not aware how one could move a child from one school to another, because the desegregation ruling seemed etched in stone. A glimmer of hope arose one day. B.J. observed a note attached to Kinie's report card that indicated the deadline for parents seeking special permits for children to attend other schools. Therefore, B.J. began to diligently work to remove Kinie from Osceola.

"I called the School Board to see what I could do to transfer Kinie. I applied to Lakewood and was turned down. I called them again to see why. They told me that Lakewood had met its quota. So I asked about St. Petersburg High. That school had spaces for blacks, so I applied to send her there. I had to go before a committee to explain my reasons. B.J. succeeded in getting a permit to transfer Kinie to St. Petersburg High, a school that is a 20-minute drive from their home. However, this special variance must be renewed annually for Kinie to attend St. Petersburg High. Transferring Kinie into St. Petersburg High is worthwhile despite the hassles. B.J. reflects.

It has the International Baccalaureate Program there. It's a better school. It's serious. The children who go there have college as an aspiration. If I need a teacher at St. Petersburg High, they return my calls immediately. I don't have to wait two to three days as before. They know who Kinie is. Plus, I can easily pop in to check on Kinie. There I feel welcomed.

In contrast to the warm reception she received at St. Petersburg High, B.J. believes that busing to desegregated zoned-schools becomes a major barrier to the achievement of black children at least in part because most black parents work and cannot afford to take the 45-minute drive to the schools like Osceola to see their children's teachers. "I am only able to go to the school because I work at night," she explains. "Black children bear the burden of busing," B.J. insists. "Mine will not be bused out of their neighborhood. I need to know what is going on," she adds. The move sparked a debate between Kinie and her mother. Kinie believes,

Schools are schools . . . Teachers are teachers, it doesn't matter which school you should go to. I don't know why mama gets all worked up about busing. All school is about is working. Schools do not affect your grades.

However, B.J. disagrees.

Not all schools in Pinellas County, Florida are created equally and some schools will better prepare children than others. Environment makes a difference . . . Environment creates the learning environment. If teachers have high expectations for students, parents are involved, and students attend their neighborhood schools, then students do better. Every year a report on the Pinellas County schools shows that students in magnet programs do better, because they have all of these elements.

Data from the Pinellas County Enrollment Office support B.J.'s ideas about differences among schools. For example, at Osceola in 1993, less than 9 percent and only slightly more than 7 percent of the school's 301 black students were enrolled in honors math and science courses respectively. In 1994 only eight (or 5.8%) of all black students were enrolled in honors math classes and 15 (8.3%) were in science honor classes at Osceola. By contrast, in 1993 at St. Petersburg High, 36 (10.6%) of the 379 blacks who attended the school were enrolled in math honors and 48 (16.5%) in science honors classes. By 1994, 59 of the 404 black students who attended St. Petersburg High were enrolled in honors science and 37 were in math honors. Osceola figures also show smaller percentages of African Americans engaged in college prep classes in comparison to St. Petersburg High School.

The issue of school climate or environment for their children is crucial for B.J. and Celes. They are not only worried about teachers' responses to Jeremy, Tonda, and Kinie, but B.J. and Celes also do not want their children's aspirations and future undermined by peers. They are especially concerned about Kinie and Jeremy. Both parents explain that, although Kinie and Jeremy are bright, they seem more susceptible to peer pressure than Tonda. Kinie and Jeremy want to be a part of the crowd; therefore, they underperform despite their abilities, suggest B.J. and Celes. Kinie's mother recalls that removing Kinie from Osceola was necessary because she feared Kinie adopting the values of many of the black students attending Osceola:

> At the beginning of the semester when Kinie caught the bus to Osceola, it was full. Many times students could not find seats. By the end of the year many of the students had dropped out. The girls had gotten pregnant, and the boys simply left school. These kids did not see college in their future. They just want to get out and get a job. Many of these students are already working so many hours they cannot study. I had to get her from around those kids. Even if they did not have classes together, forty-five minutes on the bus together is a long time. I had to do something.

Ironically, Kinie still rides a bus to St. Petersburg High; however, her mother reports that the students are different, holding values and ambitions such as those B.J. and Celes hold for Kinie:

> These students are talking about college, going to college fairs and making plans for the future. I don't mind her being with these kinds of students because they can positively influence Kinie. Just being around these kids, Kinie is now thinking about certain colleges.

Outside School

Just as closely monitored as their lives in school, the three children's lives outside school are similarly scrutinized and regulated by their parents. B.J. and Celes feel that they have to protect Kinie and her brothers from effects of the neighborhood and their friends. Celes explains:

> We are very protective of them. The neighborhood is very important. Ours is not that good. We have to protect them. I ask Kinie about what kinds of friends she has. I want

to know are they the kind that are making good grades and planning to go to college. I tell her, "You look at your friends and their grades and see how they spend their times." We can't stop her from choosing her friends. But we screen her friends, if someone calls who we think is not good for her we ask them not to call back. We don't want her to ruin her life for a few minutes of pleasure.

B.J. adds, "Kinie is very naive. We have sheltered her." B.J. recounts that once Kinie asked to go a party. She decided to allow Kinie to go. When Kinie and her mother arrived, they met a "house full of boys with no adults in sight," claims B.J. "No way was I going to leave her there. I brought Kinie home. She thinks I am too strict and I worry too much." B.J. discounts Kinie's assessment:

I permit her to be involved in extra curricular activities at school. She was in the band at Osceola, and she plays intramural sports at St. Petersburg High. Kinie and the boys can even go to the football game but they must be accompanied by an adult. I let them go with Paul (B.J.'s 30 year-old nephew) or we take them.

While conducting the interviews for this vignette and visiting my sister in June, 1995, I observed first hand B.J. and Celes' attempts to closely monitor Kinie's activities. Kinie informed her mother that students from the county were going to a water amusement park in Tampa. She explained that her friend, Tammy was going to drive. Tammy's mother had rented her a car to drive there. B.J. explained to Kinie that, at the end of each school year, teens are killed from driving too fast and drinking. She also did not trust Tammy's driving abilities. Rather than say no, B.J. allowed Kinie to go only if she could get one of us to take her. In the end, my sister Joann, who was visiting from California, took Kinie to the park. Such attempts to oversee Kinie's and her brothers' activities are the norm.

Outside school, Kinie, Tonda, and Jeremy are often engaged in planned activities. Each summer they participate in a recreational and academic program sponsored by St. Petersburg Junior College. Prior to their entrance in that program, B.J. took them to swimming classes. Tonda and Jeremy often play either soccer or basketball within a league in a middle-class suburban community near B.J.'s and Celes's neighborhood. Jeremy is also involved in a YMCA program that offers after-school academic tutoring and recreational activities until he finishes high school. Also, Celes, as pastor of his church, organized a youth program and invites guest speakers who are professionals. B.J. and Celes seek to control the environment of their children in all respects.

The issue of surroundings is highlighted against the neighborhood that they live in. As Celes stated earlier, "It's not a good neighborhood." The Biandudi's live in the predominantly African American neighborhood south of Central Avenue. They moved to that community in the early eighties shortly after Kinie was born. When they settled, the community was comprised mostly of working-class and professional people and considered a respectable neighborhood. The homes were modest two- and three-bedroom Florida bungalows painted pastel colors and framed by streets lined with sabal palms. Their neighbors included a pharmacist, nurse, retired cook, retired maid, and one Quaker-raised white woman who refused to flee as African Americans moved in. In those early days, their children played freely outside. The only theft they worried about was grapefruits being stolen from their backyard trees every winter. However, by the end of the eighties, their home was routinely burglarized. Many nights they heard police chasing drug dealers through their yard. Even the fence they built did not deter drug traffickers from invading the family's privacy. Their car was destroyed by a white drug consumer trying to flee a bad drug deal. By the time they eventually moved in 1993, their children were captives in their own home.

Although the Bianduduis moved, they relocated only one street over six blocks away. Celes was appointed pastor of a Mennonite church in that neighborhood. The church provided a parsonage in a large compound on Lake Maggorie, the largest fresh water lake in St. Petersburg. Because waterfront property is valued, a large number of professional people live in this area. On one side their neighbors are a retired couple and on the other, a physician. Their home has not been burglarized. Celestin, B.J., and their children experience less harassment.

B.J. and Celes believe their actions directly affect Kinie's attitudes and behaviors. Kinie is projecting college as a part of her immediate future. Her grades as well as her companions have improved according to her parents' desires. She admits that she has adjusted to St. Petersburg High. Tonda has proven to be a child prodigy with the saxophone and has won citations for his abilities. Jeremy and Tonda both have been making the honor roll, and each has amassed a little nest egg because they have both refrained from watching television. Of course, the final results of B.J. and Celes' work will not be known until the children are grown.

It is their belief that the exigencies of the current era require that they vigilantly monitor their children and the schools each attends to ensure that they accomplish more than their forebearers. Such tasks are mediated in a climate of court-ordered desegregated schools, a neighborhood devastated by drugs, and their children's peers who, as children and adolescents, have a limited view of the future. In this terrain they move their children from school to school as pieces in a chess game and supervise virtually their every move to ensure their success. Celes reminds me, "I don't want our children to see their parents and think that is all there is. There is more. I say your auntie and uncle have doctorates. You got to do better. Each generation has to do better."

"Get a good education and no one can take that away from you," is a mantra my parents and many other African American parents repeat over and over. Education for African Americans is seen as a shield against the adversities of racism. Acquiring this protection has never been straightforward for people of African descent in the United States. A litany of court decisions —*Brown v. Board Education of Topeka, Sweatt v. Painter*, and *Bakke v. University of California*—show that historically securing schooling has been an arduous and enduring task for African Americans.

Procuring a good education for African American children may be as problematic currently as it was previously.

LESSONS FROM THE ST. PETERSBURG VIGNETTE

Kinie and her siblings carry the full weight of their parents' and family's hopes for the next generation. They are reminded of their family's history in the context of the broader social, political and economic experience of all African Americans by their parents, uncle and their aunt (who is also the author of this vignette). What might seem an unduly confining and authoritarian context to some, whose histories do not include the rise from slavery and myriad economic, social, and educational sanctions, makes perfect sense to Kinie's parents who know first hand what less than a strict regimen could mean in outcomes for their children.

One of the continuing dilemmas for many African American families, including the Biandudis, is the question of desegregated schooling for their children. Many, like Celes, believe that busing in and of itself accomplishes very little and that children do better universally in neighborhood schools because their parents can closely monitor their children's day to day activities, maintain contact with children's teachers and be on hand for any emergencies that might arise during the school day. Both parents place considerable weight upon students' performance on school-wide achievement tests as a primary indicator of school quality. Yet, many social scientists, who have built careers studying the effects of desegregation, argue that test scores are but one measure of how well a particular school is doing. Robert Crain and his colleagues point out that children who attend racially and economically isolated schools do not gain the benefits of opportunities and networks that lead to economic mobility. These are the sorts of social ties that create peer groups such as the one at St. Petersburg High School valued by B.J and Celes because it emphasized the importance of selecting and attending a good college. It is very important to be mindful of the intersection of ethnicity and social class because of the powerful impact of social class in determining access to a lifestyle valued by many parents whose family goals and values accentuate the importance of achieving more in terms of material and social success than prior generations as is true for the parents of Kinie and her brothers.

We have seen in this vignette how one family both monitors and provides opportunities for their children in a southern city not always hospitable to them. We turn next to cases from Michele Foster's work in Boston, an early site of the Abolitionist Movement in pre-Civil War days. Because of its history, one might suppose that Boston, and the Northeast in general, would be a more supportive context for the educational development of African American students. However, during the 1970s, Boston was the scene of ugly racial tension and opposition from white working class ethnics, particularly the Irish, to desegregation decrees. Unlike other vignettes included in this volume, Foster's focuses on students' responses to teachers whom they value and consider among the best. These African American community college and elementary school students alike view teachers who are strict, demanding and fun-loving and also knowledgeable about their black heritage as among the most powerful and important teachers they have ever had.

VIGNETTE #11: GOOD TEACHING MAKES A DIFFERENCE: AFRICAN AMERICAN STUDENTS AT REGENTS COMMUNITY COLLEGE AND IN AN ELEMENTARY SCHOOL IN BOSTON
by Michele Foster

The following case studies are taken from my fieldwork in one urban Northeast city. The first case draws on my research in a predominantly black urban community college that is part of the state community college system. The second comes from my research in an elementary school serving a predominantly black student body, where I have been studying the practice of one exemplary African American teacher.

Regents Community College

Founded in 1973, Regents Community College was the fifteenth community college chartered by the Massachusetts State Board of Education. Although not a historically black institution, because of its location in the heart of the black community, it would become the predominantly black institution envisioned by one of its founders. When Regents opened in 1973, the city in which it was located was less than 20 percent black. And while a predominantly black community college might seem like an anomaly in a city with such a small black population, the black community that spawned it was marked by an activism common in the 1960s and early 1970s, especially in the Northeast and West.

My affiliation with the college spanned ten years. From 1976–1980, I worked as a part-time English instructor in the Division of Continuing Education; between 1980–1984 as a full-time English instructor; and between 1984–1986 as a researcher. Although always an acute observer of life at Regents, both my full time status and concurrent graduate study enabled me to see daily life with new eyes and from a new perspective. When my role shifted from insider participant observer to outside observer in 1984–1986, my insider's knowledge, familiarity and proficiency in the norms of Regents, as well as with community norms from which most of the students came and in which I also resided, made my presence as an outsider less intrusive.

When I began teaching in 1976, the College was housed in a condemned building that had once been a Catholic nursing home in the heart of the black community. Its recent incarnation was as Regents' second temporary site, the first having been a converted automobile showroom in the same general vicinity. Six years after I began working at Regents, the College moved to a third temporary site, a former university campus, the first site specifically designed to function as a college.

The student body grew over the years. During the first academic year, the enrollment was only 375 students. In 1977, the student body had grown to 654. By the time of my involvement with Regents had ended, the enrollment approximated 1800 students with 225 students graduating in 1985 and again in 1986.

The class I studied intensively while at Regents was a management class taught by Miss Morris, a teacher students had identified as one of the College's best. Although only 22 students completed the class, initially it was composed of 38 students. Of these, 24 were black, seven were from Anglo or Franchophone Caribbean countries, six were Latinos—all from Puerto Rico, two were Ethiopian, and one was white. Two-thirds of the students were high school graduates; the remainder had earned GED certificates. Their ages ranged from 20–40 with 85 percent of them in their twenties. Like most students attending Regents, their achievement as measured by standardized tests was low. Reading achievement scores were not available for students in this class; however, a college-wide placement test administered to 486 entering students in Fall 1983 placed 54 percent in Development Writing I or II classes. The mean reading achievement of these students—34 percent of all the students placed in Developmental Writing II—was 8.8. The mean reading achievement level of the 117 students placed in Developmental Writing I was 8.2. These scores indicate that both groups were reading at less than ninth grade proficiency.

Statistics do not adequately portray the students, however. Therefore, what follows next are five student profiles designed to give flesh to the bones of the data I have just presented. The sketches are based on interviews and observations and are chosen more for their diversity than their representativeness.

Louise, Khalilah, James, Millie, and Stephen—Miss Morris' Students

Louise Borden is a 36 year old woman who had returned to Regents for a second degree in Business Management. She was graduated in 1980 with an Associate of Arts Degree with a focus in pre-nursing. Born in Americus, Georgia, she moved to the city when she was two years old. She attended segregated elementary school in the city before the desegregation order and graduated from a single sex majority black high school where the majority of teachers were white. A divorced mother of three, she hoped to start her own business one day. This was her first class with Miss Morris, although she was also taking another class with the same teacher at the time she was interviewed. At first, Louise did not do well in Miss Morris' class. Her attendance was erratic and, at midterm, she was failing. By her own admission, she "didn't expect to learn anything in this class" when she first found out that Miss Morris was black, so she spent the first months trying to figure her out instead of doing the assignments. "I couldn't see where she was coming from and because

Miss Morris was so heavy into Black History, this threw me off, downplayed my expectations and I felt I didn't have to study."

The week before mid-term, Louise contemplated dropping the class, but before dropping out she went to speak with Miss Morris who gave her the confidence that if "I stayed and did what I was supposed to I could pass." Right after the conference, Louise began attending class more regularly, asking questions and participating in class discussions. The conference had only a momentary effect, and unfortunately the improvement lasted less than a month; the week before Thanksgiving, Louise stopped attending regularly and finally stopped attending altogether. Nonetheless, Louise felt that Miss Morris was a good teacher and especially liked the way "she draws from our real experiences to explain the textbook." She also felt that, because Miss Morris had overcome tough experiences in her own life, she could learn from her.

> I can learn from her presentation, manners and ways. I don't learn from books. When I see where she is and I am not, there is something she's done to get there that I haven't . . . I want to tap on the knowledge she has.

The same age, Miss Chevonne Morris (the teacher) and Louise Borden graduated from the city's schools in the same year. Louise did not pass this class, but still maintained that it was valuable. "I don't pass the work in but even if I fail, I still have learned something."

Khalilah Azizah is 44 years old and in her first semester at Regents. She is a management major, specializing in hotel management. Eventually she plans to buy property in the Bahamas where she hopes to build and operate guest houses, a bar and a restaurant. She grew up in Harlem with both parents. Her mother had moved there from St. Augustine, Florida. Her father, who named her, was a Muslim from Mocha, Yemen, who first immigrated with his family to Georgia and later moved to New York. Khalilah attended a predominantly white single sex high school on 16th Street in downtown Manhattan. "I can't remember having a black teacher in high school, although I did attend a mostly black junior high school and elementary schools which had mostly black teachers in Harlem." After graduating from high school, Khalilah worked as a secretary at Harlem Hospital. Never considering herself a good student, Khalilah just wanted "to get out of high school." Nonetheless, in Miss Morris' class, she is one of the better students. Khalilah finds herself "spending more time on work for Miss Morris' class than for any other class because she (Miss Morris) expects a certain amount from me and I always try to please her."

This is her first class with Miss Morris, whom Khalilah believes is the best teacher she's ever had. "If I had instructors like her in the past, I would have come out a much brighter person." In spite of the fact that she believes she didn't acquire good basic skills at the elementary and secondary levels, Khalilah was determined to do well in college and in this course. Her determination paid off and final grade was an "A".

James O'Banyon, age 26, was born and raised in Boston. He has strong roots in the South, however. Both his parents were born and raised in South Carolina where they lived until their early twenties. As a child, James returned every summer to visit relatives in the South.

He didn't attend high school, but earned his GED in 1980. He describes himself as having been a "naive" student when he was attending the Malcolm X Junior High School. James attended a junior high school that had an all black student body and a predominantly white teaching staff. He describes the teaching-learning relationship as one of mutual disinterest. "The teachers didn't give a shit about teaching, and I didn't give a shit about learning." James is in his third semester at Regents, majoring in Business Management. After graduating, he hopes to pursue a career in management and "become an entrepreneur in the business world." He also plans to attend school part-time to work on his bachelor's degree once he begins full time work.

James has a work study job at Regents. Because he spends most of his time at the College, more than many of the other students, he believes he has a good feel for the faculty there. He maintains that Miss Morris is an excellent teacher, "one of the best if not the best, she's a good, a damn good teacher." According to James, "she gets to the point of the conversation, is direct and aggressive," qualities he believes show signs of leadership. It is because of these qualities, he says, that he takes her seriously. Jim is generous with his praise of Miss Morris' teaching, not only commenting to me privately, but letting her know how he feels as well. One day as he was leaving class, he shouted out to her, "the truth is we need more teachers like you."

This is his first course with Miss Morris, but he had heard from other students that she was "very aggressive and gave you an overload of work." He took the course because "I'm a person who loves a challenge and wanted to find out about myself." Jim rates his performance in this class as "good" and maintains that, if other teachers at Regents were as aggressive as this teacher, he would apply himself as much in their classes.

In spite of the high marks he gives Miss Morris for her teaching, his own marks as a student are mediocre. Early in the semester, he was frequently absent, failed to complete assignments or turn them in on time. He also argues with Miss Morris over the reasons he failed to do his work. He "flunked" the mid-term and several other quizzes. Nonetheless, he participated eagerly in classroom discussions, and by mid-November his grades, like those of many other students in this class, had improved. Just before Thanksgiving, he reported that he was "really working and doing much better." The day he made this claim was the very first time in the semester that he had turned in an assignment when it was due, a fact he was pleased to boast about. Jim finished the course with a "D", but he claims that this grade does not adequately reflect all that he learned in the class.

Millie Grant is 24 years old and a native of Jamaica. She attended high school there until 1979, when she moved to the city to complete her last year in high school.

Compared to school in Jamaica, she found her classes in a majority white high school much easier. She was an honor roll student, earned "excellent SAT scores," and attended a summer science institute for promising minority students that was held at a prestigious boarding school. In addition, she was accepted by one of the "Seven Sister" colleges in New England.

She was not as successful in Jamaica. Although she was the highest achieving student in her school, she did not do well enough on the common entrance examinations at age 12 to go to an advanced secondary school. She decided against attending the women's college because it was "too far from home." She chose, instead, to attend a large urban private university in the city. She received "almost all D's there, felt inferior and dropped out." She feels that although the school "has a big name and sounds good, it wasn't so good at teaching; they just threw the work at you and I knew it wasn't for me. I need teachers who can explain."

This is her third semester at Regents, where she is majoring in Business Administration. Eventually, she hopes to attend one of the well-known business schools in the East and earn an MBA. This is her second course with Miss Morris, whom she considers one of the best teachers she has ever had. So good in fact, that "I wish I could clone her for my children." According to Millie, good teachers like Miss Morris are "tough, demanding and insist on quality work. When you are soft with students, they don't understand." When Millie took her first class with Miss Morris, she complained about her "hardness and toughness." She struck me as "someone you couldn't fool around with."

In her first course Millie did not live up to Miss Morris' expectations or listen to her warning and got an "F" at midterm. That was in the beginning. Gradually, she realized that, although Miss Morris is "tough and communicates it; she really cares." Millie still complains about Miss Morris' "big book list"; however, she appreciates her sociability, sense of humor and enjoys the jokes that she makes about the students. Millie maintains that it is probably lack of sociability that distinguished the "merely competent teacher from the truly great teacher." This semester Millie was one of Miss Morris' best students, always turning in her assignments on time, doing exceptionally well on quizzes and exams and partici-pating actively in all class discussions. This time "I was prepared for Miss Morris," and she earned an "A" for the course.

Stephen Sims, 20, grew up in New Jersey. Both of his parents grew up in the South, however, his father in Mississippi and his mother in St. Petersburg, Florida. They both moved to New Jersey in their early twenties. At first, his father, a graduate of an all black college, moved the family to a largely black community in New Jersey where Stephen completed elementary school, all of the ninth and half of the tenth grades. These schools had a mostly black student body but equal numbers of black and white teachers. In the middle of tenth grade, the family moved to a town farther away from the city, "out in the woods and with better schools." Better schools, notwithstanding, Stephen dropped out of school in the eleventh grade and earned his GED in 1984.

By his own admission, Stephen has disappointed his family by not doing as well academically as his sister, who graduated from Wellesley College, earned an MBA at Yale and is currently a manager at a local computer company. Stephen feels that he currently is doing something about his previously poor academic achievement. In his second semester at the College, he is majoring in mathematics and hopes to transfer to the state university to earn a bachelor's degree in math and then to attend a private institute of technology to get a master's degree in civil engineering. He wants to start his own construction company eventually.

This was Stephen's first course with Miss Morris, but he had heard that "she was pretty strict from other students" who have been around the College for a while. He maintains that Miss Morris is a great teacher and, compared to other teachers at the College, is the best. "She seems to be organized, knows her subject, explains the lesson clearly, answers questions clearly and completely, expects students to do the work and teaches well enough for both beginners all the way to advanced." On a scale of one to five, he gives her a five.

Stephen believes that he can call "from the first day" if a teacher is going to be good. According to him, "good teachers have a helpful attitude which he can discern by the way they answer questions completely before moving on. He contends that many professors deliberately try to confuse students, especially those they "believe aren't as smart. The more you know the more they teach and the less you know, the less they teach." Stephen maintains that not teaching black students is part of a conspiracy, and that white teachers are guilty of this most often. Stephen's attendance and performance in this class were erratic. Like Jim and Louise, he was frequently absent, failed to do his homework, rarely studied for or passed tests, frequently turning in blank exams. Yet, Stephen maintains that he was personally benefitting from the class, "learning how to deal in the real world, how to make it in the corporate environment." He believes that a test "can't tell all that a student has learned, or that 'failing a test' doesn't mean a person hasn't learned anything." He contends that in Miss Morris' classes, even students who fail will have learned something. In the end, Stephen was counted among them.

A "Good" Community College Teacher

When they describe good teachers, students at Regents often link two seemingly contradictory terms. Terms like old-fashioned, mean or strict are often paired with terms like fun or interesting. The following excerpt comes from a conversation I overhead between two Regents students discussing a particular teacher whose identity was unknown to me:

> We had fun in her class, but she was mean. I can remember she used to say, "Tell me what's in the story, Wayne." She pushed and she used to get on me and push to know. She made us learn. We had to get in the books. There was this tall guy and he tried to take her on, but she was in charge of that class and she didn't let anyone run her. I

still have this book we used in her class. It's a bunch of stories in it. I just read one on Coca-Cola again the other day.

Miss Morris employed two different speaking styles that expressed each of the characteristics used to describe her. She generally used standard English to convey her expectations for success. When she wished to admonish students, sanction them for failing to apply themselves to their studies, she employed a very different style of speaking than she used to convey intellectual and cognitive information, Miss Morris used a speaking and an interactional style that are common in the black community, one that can be found in the preaching style in black churches, the verbal patterning heard in children's play songs, adolescents raps and adult male verbal interchanges.

Not only did Miss Morris' speaking and interactional style vary, according to her intention, but students in turn responded accordingly. When Miss Morris used more standard, mainstream language, students spoke very little, often answering with very few utterances. In these instances, it was not uncommon for Miss Morris to speak 20 to 25 times more than students. On the other hand, when Miss Morris shifted to a style of speaking that was more black, students often interjected comments into the ongoing discussion, participation was lively and students were actively engaged. These familiar interactions also had a positive effect of student achievement. Students were much more likely to remember, recall and be able to apply information that the teacher had encoded in familiar interactional and speaking styles.

What is notable about these interactions is that the teacher used standard material from the textbooks and required that student adhere to a rigorous regimen of class work, homework and reading, but she supplemented this material with information that presented a black perspective on the issues, frequently asked students to draw on their own experiences of family or community members, and used familiar ways to speaking in classroom interactions.

Haley Elementary School

Less than three miles from Regents Community College is the Haley School, a two story brick urban elementary school of 1920s vintage, where Mrs. Jane Vander teaches first grade. She has been teaching elementary school in Boston since 1955. At the time of our first interview in 1988 she had been teaching in the same district for 33 years. When she began teaching in the mid-fifties, all of the black teachers were assigned to one section of the city. Between 1955 and 1974, Mrs. Vander was a primary grade teacher in two majority black elementary schools. In 1974, when the schools were desegregated, she was reassigned to a largely white middle class school, where she taught Title I Reading for several years.

By the early 1980s, she was back in the classroom as a first grade teacher at the Haley, one of the schools in which she had previously taught between 1961 and

1974. When she first began teaching at Haley, it had an all black student body. Desegregated by the 1974 court order, within eight years it was once again a majority black school. Many of her current pupils are the children of the students she taught in the 60s and 70s.

It was February when I first visited. The 26 first graders, all of them black except two, who I later learned are bused in from an Irish working class neighborhood, seem familiar with the classroom routines; they move about the classroom from activity to activity with no discernible direction from Mrs. Vander. Oral recitations are a conspicuous feature of literacy events. Several times throughout the day, before and after lunch, after recess and before school begins and is dismissed, Mrs. Vander reads her students a poem, a tradebook, or chapter from a continuing story. Also during the day, students perform several choral readings of Langston Hughes' *I Am the Darker Brother*. On subsequent visits, the prominence of oral performances becomes apparent. Students regularly recite poems they have memorized, act out plays they have learned by heart or dramatize stories they have heard.

Various adults are in and out of the classroom. A young woman with an infant comes to the door, and Mrs. Vander asks her into the classroom. Some of the cafeteria workers drop by to chat with the children. Another woman comes to the classroom and, after a brief discussion with Mrs. Vander, the woman sits down to hear a pupil read aloud.

During our interviews, Mrs. Vander interprets what I have witnessed. The teacher tells me that her class is getting ready to participate in a Black History Month celebration. Mrs. Vander comments on the African American community's propensity for, and the value it places on, verbal proficiency and notes that she deliberately incorporates oral performances into daily classroom lessons. She explains how oral performances are manifest in her own teaching and are folded into individual student and whole class activities.

> Now reading aloud to them a lot, that's one thing I do because I think reading is very important to building vocabulary. Also, they are becoming familiar with the cadence of reading when I read to them. So when we are reading, I say, "You've got to read the way I do when I read to you." That's how I interpret the necessity of literature. The black community is known for its verbal artistry. But most classrooms don't take advantage of black kids' strengths. Teachers don't draw on this strength or their other strengths. I'm building on my kids' strengths, and so you will see oral activities stressed and reinforced over and over in this class.

I inquire about all the adults that come and go. Adults, including parents, are an important part of the extended support network that Mrs. Vander makes available to her pupils. Every adult in the school is enlisted to provide support, discipline, and attention for the children. Before school begins, parents receive phone calls, which extend an open invitation to visit the classroom at any time. These calls, which continue throughout the year, are supplemented by weekly reports to parents which review student's problem areas and achievements. When phone calls and reports don't get a response, Mrs. Vander follows up with a home visit.

> I keep on calling. I call them any place. Right? If I don't get you in the morning I may get you at night. I'm going to get somebody. I call until I get 'em. I really do, or I go visit. Yeah, I go in people's homes. In fact, I have taken kids home. We just get on the bus. I take them home.

Probed for the source of pedagogy, Mrs. Vander praises the teacher training she received at the local teachers college. But she names the black church as an important institutional context for the kind of social support and learning that works best with her students.

> In the traditional black church everybody is involved, everyone participates, everyone is responsible for everyone else, especially the children. The preacher plays an important role in motivating the congregation, but he alone isn't responsible. You can be called by the preacher to read from the text, to interpret a passage, and you better be ready. There's always a lot of encouragement from the congregation. All of the children are cherished and included. The adults want them to learn, want them to grow to become the best people they can become, because any of them could grow up and become their neighbors. So in the church all of the children are expected to participate in church plays. You know everyone has a part to play and even the youngest children are expected to learn several stanzas to recite in a Christmas, Easter, or Children's Day service.

UNDERSTANDING THE BOSTON VIGNETTES

Although Miss Morris and Mrs. Vander teach students who are very different in age—community college students in the first case and elementary students in the second case—it is clear from these vignettes that these two highly valued and effective teachers use similar approaches to teaching their students by incorporating black dialect, humor, caring and a highly demanding academic agenda into their work with students. Because of her interest in language issues, Michele Foster, the author of this vignette, pays particularly close attention to patterns of interaction in the classrooms of both teachers. Each teacher uses language in a purposeful way, invoking students' own experiences in black institutions such as the church and in black street culture. However, each is aware that to be successful in U.S society, it is imperative for students to be able appropriately to use what Basil Bernstein and others have termed "Marketplace English," referring to the syntax, grammatical constructions and cadences of the English dialect spoken in business offices, banks and in most work places.

Miss Morris faces the challenge in teaching at Regents of working with a highly diverse set of students. These students come from a wide variety of educational and cultural backgrounds; although many are African American, they do not constitute a "homogeneous" group. Her students also have different criteria by which to judge success, some crediting their efforts as successful despite failing the course or receiving a grade of "D." How, I wonder, would the Biandudi family from the St. Petersburg vignette react to such an evaluation of one of their children's performance under these circumstances?

Mrs. Vander, a teacher in the same school system for over 30 years, realizes the value of the involvement of community members on a day-to-day basis in her classroom. Maintaining close connections with her students' parents is critical to her students' achievement in school, and she is quick to make a home visit when messages are not given a timely response. Many successful teachers similarly visit their students' homes before the academic year gets underway to establish a working partnership with parents in advance of any problems or issues that might come up during the course of the school year. In this way, the relationship between parents and teacher begins on a cordial, mutually supportive note.

These vignettes demonstrate the importance of cultural congruity between teachers and their students. While most would not argue that teachers must claim the same cultural heritage as the majority of their students—an almost impossible criterion in most settings as the Regents Community College vignette demonstrates—it is extremely important for teachers to be aware of and to incorporate into their lessons components of students' cultural experience that will allow students to learn in a meaningful way.

8

Ethnicity, Education, the Community and Children's Learning

This volume has encompassed issues related to learning in school, community, and the context of children's families. In this concluding chapter we bring together what we have learned from the preceding vignettes and earlier analyses of the background histories of each of the groups we have considered here to focus on curricular strategies that build upon children's strengths.

Children learn important lessons about their own identities and probable futures from their ethnic community's history, folkways, and contemporary experiences in addition to learning the limitations and possibilities that the larger society imposes (Ogbu, 1993b). In constructing their collective identities, ethnic groups build on their unique strengths. We conceptualize these strengths along dimensions of *local and lateral cultural ties*. *Local cultural ties* bind groups closely to the institutions and practices of ecological spaces they inhabit. *Lateral cultural ties* extend beyond borders and oceans to ancestral places. These dimensions of children's experience must be taken into account in designing (a) all phases of the curriculum, (b) the pedagogical strategies for teaching the curriculum, and (c) the social organizational arrangements in schools to organize teaching and learning activities, topics we discuss in this concluding chapter.

Before we examine specific approaches to guiding student learning, it might be helpful to describe what we are *not* attempting to do here. First, we are not calling for a curriculum that accommodates "learning styles" along ethnic or racial lines. We agree with those who contend, in the case of the Navajo, that characterizing students along continua such as "holistic/analytical" and "verbal/nonverbal" can perpetuate deficit models of student learning, reinforce patterns of learned dependence that extend beyond the classroom, and justify remedial, nonacademic and unchallenging curricula.

Second, we are not arguing that the interrelationships among students' family, peer and school worlds are invariate across or within a particular racial or ethnic group. Rather, we agree with those who state that how peer, family, and school worlds combine to affect students' lives in and outside school is little understood (Phelan, Davidson, & Cao, 1991), and that this situation should be remedied. Extending Bronfenbrenner's view of overlapping spheres, we see students' multiple worlds as intersecting and disconnecting in important ways during particular periods in children's lives, such as adolescence, when critical life decisions must be made. Phelan and her colleagues offer a conceptualization of high school students' multiple worlds and their "boundary crossing behavior" to understand how students may successfully navigate diverse and/or harmonious sociocultural spheres that constitute their life spaces. Students' worlds and the ways they negotiate boundaries among these overlapping structures present a picture of students' multiple worlds and boundary crossing behaviors as illustrated in Figure 8.1.

Students may perceive boundaries among spheres and the strategies for crossing them differently. Distinctive patterns characterizing perceptions and responses of students from various racial and ethnic backgrounds including high and low achieving Vietnamese, African American, Chinese, Latino, and white students in California lead Phelan and her colleagues to conclude that race and ethnicity by itself is insufficient in explaining variations in student behavior. Socioeconomic status (SES) is also of critical importance, as is gender.

As an illustration, research on Asian Americans shows that Asians as a group do not constitute a homogeneous "model minority." SES, not surprisingly, is a "marker of difference," functioning to allow elitist Korean-identified students in Lee's study to maintain an air of superiority vis à vis other Asian students. Further, differentiation along class lines was more likely to occur among female Korean students specifically and was manifest in their clothing, shopping preferences and the like. In summary, unless SES, gender, family experiences in migration and settlement and other important structural factors are taken into account, students will continue to encounter problems of stereotyping and generalizing on the basis of race and ethnicity while schools reserve academic curriculum and access to other resources to a favored few.

Finally, the approaches presented in this chapter must be framed mindful of the political context in which schools and society are located. A politics of difference

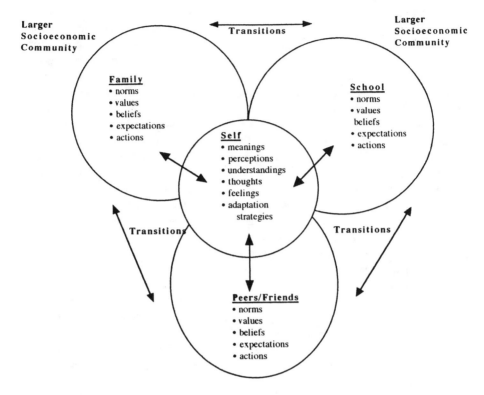

FIGURE 8.1. A model of the interrelationship between students' family, peer, and school worlds.
Source: Anthropology and Education Quarterly (Phelan, Davidson, & Cao, 1991).

that is emancipatory rather than oppressive must guide the creation of the curriculum. Henry Giroux's introduction to Mitchell and Weiler's edited volume *Rewriting Literacy* (1991) reminds the reader that an ideological regime was developed and popularized by authors such as Alan Bloom in the 1980s under two conservative presidents, Reagan and Bush, whose policies enhanced the status of the wealthy while undermining that of the poor and disenfranchised. Bloom and others whose rhetoric reflected their horror at expressions of popular culture, cultural difference and poor grammar promoted a "concept of difference . . . seen as a threat to what is labeled as Western culture" (Giroux, 1991, p. xi). Instead, it is our conviction that an emancipatory literacy should "move away from traditional approaches which emphasize the acquisition of mechanical skills while divorcing reading from its ideological and historical context" (Giroux, 1991, p. xi) to one consonant with Freirean notions of literacy as a vehicle for participation in the transformation of society.

Following an initial discussion of the creation and maintenance of local and lateral cultural ties and ethnic group identities, the chapter moves to a discussion of programs and projects that constitute promising strategies for promoting the success of diverse students. These strategies are promising because they assume (a) an actively engaged, cognitively complex individual whose life chances are enhanced by long term and continuous engagement with academically challenging and rich curricula; (b) an individual whose multiple worlds must be negotiated daily to minimize the effects of cultural dissonance; and (c) an orientation among educators that Hall (1997) calls "equity pedagogy," involving a rejection of tracking and ability grouping and the substitution of high expectations, a common academic core curriculum, critical thinking skills, knowledge of student backgrounds and interests, and a multicultural context.[3] Throughout the chapter, we will draw upon the material presented in preceding chapters to illustrate issues necessary for those who work with diverse student populations and their families to take into account.

What can we learn from the vignettes and background analyses of the diverse student populations we have considered in this book? First, it is useful to point out what anyone working with diverse students knows: Each student is unique, bringing her or his own special talents, background experiences, hopes and dreams to the situation. Nonetheless, as I hope this book has underscored, ethnic group affiliation (along with SES and gender) is of central importance to a consideration of who each of us is and what possibilities and constraints lie before us. Ethnicity encompasses, as we have seen, shared history, values, and religious preferences as well as choices in food, predispositions to excel in particular activities and tasks. It also embraces a set of social structural and sociohistorical arrangements that may create barriers to children's achievement in U.S. schools. What is important is that, while each of us is unique, we share in a particular collective history that contributes to a definition of the self. Thus, one lesson to be learned from the vignettes is that racial and ethnic culture matters, although how it matters may vary by group and locale as we have seen. A major determinant of how ethnic heritage plays a central role in shaping values, attitudes and behavior is how an individual relates to either a local or lateral ethnic culture.

LOCAL VERSUS LATERAL CULTURES

For some students and their families, cultural identity is firmly rooted in the local community context. Lateral cultural ties to the country of origin and ancestral folkways may be more tenuous, perhaps because families have been located in a particular community, apart from direct contact with their native culture for a number of generations. For others, the reverse may be true as a result of shorter residency in a new locale, political and/or spiritual ties to an indigenous past or for other reasons. And for still others, affiliations with both the local ethnic culture and the lateral cultural scene may be either equally powerful or equally weak. The degree of cultural dissonance between institutions such as the family and school will likewise vary along these lines.

Even when students hold only tenuous ties to their cultural heritage, once connections to those roots have been personalized for such students, the ethnic identity evoked in the process is extremely powerful in subsequent growth, development, and learning. Groups we have focused upon in this volume have been considered in connection with their cultural orientations, not to stereotype but rather to provide an understanding of relationships with their ethnic communities.

Strong Local and Lateral Ties

Of the groups we have considered in this volume, three in particular possess *both* strong local and lateral ties—African Americans and American Indians as well as Asian groups who migrated to the United States prior to World War II.[4] This dual orientation—to the construction of social identities and ties at the local level and to the maintenance of symbolic and/or real connections to the country of origin—is deeply linked to the political and economic histories of these groups in the United States. The result may be alienation and the creation of oppositional cultures and identities.

These three groups, as people of color, have had their heritages exploited or ignored and have suffered false incarceration and genocide. In considering these and other forms of exploitation, the perspective on ethnic and racial group history provided by Ogbu is useful in understanding how developing both local and lateral ties materially affects each group's economic and social position over time. Ogbu's perspective, however, is not so helpful in understanding dimensions of the cultural development of these groups whose collective histories have also provided inspiration and vision. These are, significantly, the very groups who have developed both local and lateral connections but whom Ogbu characterizes as "oppressed." A major limitation of Ogbu's classification system is that it focuses on social, political and economic conditions adversely affecting various groups rather than upon their strengths and resiliency as reflected in the formation of local and lateral ties and related strategies. In fact, the very adverse conditions that made their lives so difficult ultimately compelled the resilient and highly adaptive responses of these groups.

In the case of African Americans, from at least the time of W.E.B. DuBois onward, a strong local orientation coupled with an attachment to a national movement have figured in the political and economic success of those involved in such catalyzing efforts as the Civil Rights and Black Power movements. These movements have also inspired others, including those affiliated with both Asian and Puerto Rican empowerment efforts. In addition, African Americans' strong and committed orientation to community, close neighbors and kin has also served as a model for other groups involved in subsequent similar movements, whose objectives include empowerment for movement members. As Carol Stack (1974) pointed out long ago, low income African American communities maintained solidarity and cohesiveness through informal economies of exchange and support that enhance the overall welfare of the community in addition to creating strong emotional bonds among community members.

Lateral connections back to an African past have also been evident in such movements as Marcus Garvey's "Back to Africa" efforts in the 1920s. The Universal Negro Improvement Association and its related enterprises emphasized a need to "look to Africa" for the solution to the social problems African Americans were facing. More recently, Afrocentric curricula and schools such as Marva Collins' popular and successful academies in Chicago and elsewhere emphasizing high achievement for all students serve as compelling models for enhancing educational outcomes for African American students. To argue that strong lateral ties back to the African continent exist in actuality for many American blacks makes little sense given a lack of specific knowledge of tribal origins that, unfortunately, is the case for most. In addition, the enormous complexity of the culture and social organization of nations on the African continent makes a direct link problematic. On the western coast of the continent alone more than 4,000 dialects are spoken, making the very definition of "African culture" difficult indeed. Nonetheless, there is no denying the strength of the symbolic attachment to a continent that, although perhaps never seen, exerts an enormous pull on the soul and imagination of many African Americans.

The interpretation of an African culture in contemporary times provides powerful icons. "Becoming a man" is an overriding concern for many young black men. Arguably, this somewhat ambiguous objective is clarified by an interpretation that takes into account an African past—one that values taking responsibility for one's self and family despite the difficulties of doing so in pre-Civil War times in the United States. Indelibly marking the African American experience of material success and failure is this nation's unrelenting racism. In her analysis of Newark, New Jersey's public schools, Anyon (1997) finds clear documentation of policies that promoted black children from elementary school who had still not learned basic skills in math and reading; lower than average class sizes in schools with low black student enrollments; systematic denial of permanent positions to highly qualified black teachers; and other injustices.

The unresolved nature of the continued struggle to reach educational parity with whites points up an increasingly important and ongoing issue in the black community—community-based education—an issue ignored in the *Brown* decision which de-emphasized community control in favor of desegregation policies. Given the failure of such policies, sizable numbers in black communities have periodically pressed for control over their children's' educations. From the Reconstruction period to the Black Power era into the present, blacks have sought to assert their own agenda in the education of their young. Of late we see this recurrent sentiment expressed concretely in efforts to establish black male schools, Afrocentric curriculums, charter schools, and in efforts to ensure the survival of historically black colleges and universities.

Control over their children's experiences in school is a more powerful and important goal than desegregation for many African American communities. Busing, the creation of magnet schools and other strategies to integrate school have failed. As a result, African Americans are likely to continue to strengthen local ties to communities while shaping and influencing national trends, such as the charter school movement, to enhance their overall stature as a distinct group. We can readily see this strategy in connection with the Million Man March in 1995, and subsequent events in the year following it, as participants in the march went home and worked to strengthen their local institutions.

Among American Indians, the strong spiritual link to tribal elders is a defining dimension of Native people's identity as a nation. Intellectual leaders such as the Wisdom Keepers advocate an understanding of current lifeways and values of Indian peoples with respect to an honored heritage that includes an emphasis on economic self sufficiency and stewardship. Valuing spirituality and the ceremonial past, the Wisdom Keepers perpetuate a living heritage which is incorporated into all aspects of Native peoples' contemporary lives. In Chapter 5, in the vignette authored by Margaret LeCompte and Abbie Willetto, we saw how native language attrition diminishes connections to tribal practices sustaining all aspects of being. In creating the curriculum and practicing it in Native American classrooms, the case examples, particularly the case of Wilson, the only Navajo child and only non-Anglo in his elementary school, reminds us of how important it is for Native children to be connected to their heritage as they are acquiring skills in speaking and using English.

The implementation of a curriculum based on a clear understanding of the importance and meaning of Native cultural practices is illuminated by the work done at the Rough Rock Navaho reservation by a research-practitioner team including Lynn Vogt, Cathie Jordan, and others from the Kamehameha Early Education Program (KEEP) in Hawaii. That experience demonstrates the power of local connections for Navaho children who did not readily respond initially to curriculum developed for Hawaiian Native students. Because the talk-story is a commonly used narrative strategy in Hawaii, it became an important dimension for constructing aspects of literacy learning in the original KEEP curriculum. It was not, however, useful in illustrating and reinforcing narrative practices among the Navaho whose cultural ways characteristically do not draw attention to the speaker as is the case in the talk-story. Rather, cooperative story telling and mutually affirming literacy learning strategies were far more effective in the Navaho case (Vogt, 1987). *The critical dimension in each instance is utilizing curricular practices that build upon and reflect talents and strengths students bring to their learning.*

Strong Local Ties

Students and their families in Carpinteria, California, as you will recall from Delgado-Gaitan's vignette, were very strongly attached to the local community where many families had lived and worked for four or five generations or more. While these Mexican American families still spoke Spanish in the home and in other contexts involving friends and neighbors, the practice of customs and rituals tied to a Spanish heritage was unknown in the community.[5] Instead, families used strategies in working with institutions, including the school, that are characteristically "American." For example, Delgado-Gaitan describes how individuals return to the community as teachers of successive generations of children.

The practice of service to one's own community, after one has gained a good education and the necessary credentials, is at the heart of volunteerism in this country in addition to being a fundamentally useful approach to empowering future generations of, in this case, Mexican American students. On the down side, Anglos have reinterpreted and commodifed Mexican American music, food and other folkways, creating what might be regarded as a pseudo- or "plastic" Mexican American culture associated with drive-in food service and bland, commercialized salsa. Detrimental to institution-building in the Mexican American community are the economic limitations imposed by the job status of many workers, who remain employed in low skill jobs paying low wages. Similar to Appalachians and Asians, who also create and maintain strong localized ties, Latinos, especially Mexican Americans, are likely to be among the most isolated and segregated groups in the United States. According to recent analyses of resegregation patterns in U.S. schools, Latinos are, in fact, the most segregated ethnic group in schools (*New York Times*, April 8, 1997).

Similarly, third and fourth generation Appalachian migrants to the cities have constructed community-based institutional structures that serve children and their families in ways congruent with practices followed by their city-dwelling neighbors, but that also retain aspects of their mountain heritage. They have done this in the face of such damaging stereotypes as the naive hillbilly of the "Li'l Abner" comic strip, *The Beverly Hillbillies* television series and other negative portrayals of mountain life.

The construction of a positive cultural identity has been accomplished in large part through a community-based organization staffed by city-dwelling Appalachians. The Urban Appalachian Council (UAC) in Cincinnati operates as an organization similar to the Urban League, providing both a strong positive cultural identity and political clout in the form of advocacy in the city of Cincinnati, the state of Ohio and the region, especially in other locales where Appalachians have settled. It is also the sponsor of neighborhood-based GED programs that carry out tutoring, job placement services and child care as needed by those attending tutoring and counseling sessions. These services are offered in the context of churches and settlement houses furnished with brightly colored quilts and other artifacts that make clients feel welcomed and comfortable.

By lobbying for improved health care delivery and other services, including school curriculum more sensitive to the needs of urban Appalachian students, the Urban Appalachian Council has been an effective culture broker for children and their families for almost 30 years, reinforcing strong lateral ties among those who are city-dwelling and yet retain a strong Appalachian identity. Annual neighborhood and city-wide festivals celebrate the Appalachian heritage, bringing crafts persons, musicians and others together at these well attended events. In the public schools of Cincinnati, all students observe Appalachian Heritage Month in May, and each school library has a copy of the "Idea Book" put together by teachers and others through the Urban Appalachian Council and designed to provide teachers with materials to use in teaching virtually any subject matter curriculum at any grade level. The UAC serves as an important, *exportable* model linking the concerns of ethnic groups with social action and advocacy, research and social change.

By virtue of their long term residence in locales where several generations of family members have developed strong social, economic and other meaningful linkages, both Mexican Americans in southern California (and elsewhere) and Appalachians who have settled in large Midwestern urban centers possess exceedingly strong local ties. Far from giving up their values and distinctive tastes (and more), these groups nonetheless maintain an attachment to an honored heritage. This is not to say that culturally-based practices and the values upon which they are founded are not altered over time but rather to say that important personal, political, and other aspects of their lives remain grounded in indigenous ways.

Similarly, Asian immigrants and refugees and their children who have come to the United States following the passage of the Immigration Law of 1965, and especially after 1975, have very quickly found local economic niches. They have settled in places such as the Los Angeles area where family members and others from Asian nations have historically resided, as well as places such as Garden City, Kansas, where jobs in the meat packing industry lured a number of Chinese immigrants, and Minneapolis and St. Paul where approximately 40 percent of Hmong refugees have settled.

Because U.S. immigration legislation in 1965 and 1975 was designed, among other things, to advance American policy as a nation defending humanitarian concerns in the world, it provided for the reunification of families through unrestricted access by spouses, parents, and unmarried minor children of U.S. citizens, a policy that was particularly effective in promoting a local orientation on the part of those arriving under these provisions. Likewise, in the case of refugees, most poignantly captured by the plight of the Vietnamese boat people fleeing their ravaged nation in the wake of the Vietnam War in the late 1970s and early 1980s, the bleak prospect of returning to their native lands compelled a strong local orientation to U.S. institutions and customs once refugees were settled in their adopted country. We saw, for example, in the Dan and Mei vignette how readily

Mei as an adolescent took on the patterns of dress and speech of her thoroughly Americanized adolescent peers.

One of the important developments within this group of Asian American immigrants and refugees is the creation of a powerful and unifying Pan Asian Movement focused on issues of justice, political empowerment and educational opportunity (Wei, 1995). William Wei's (1995) analysis of the origins and development of the Asian American Movement from the 1960s onward describes focused social action to create an "inter-Asian coalition that embraces the entire spectrum of Asian ethnic groups, acknowledging their common experiences in American society and calling for a higher level of solidarity among the groups" (Wei, 1995). Contributing to the power of the movement is the creation of the concept "Asian American," that "implies that there can be a communal consciousness and a unique culture that is neither Asian nor American, but Asian American." The origins of this movement were decidedly middle class and stemmed from a concern for representation in the postsecondary curriculum through programs in Asian Studies. Largely invisible, according to Wei, the Movement also took up other educational issues including the historic *Lau v. Nichols* case in 1974, mandating bilingual-bicultural education in the United States. Although political activism has been concentrated in the areas where most Asian Americans live, primarily the large cities on the West Coast, New York and Chicago, the outcomes and repercussions of this coalition have clear and obvious implications for educational policy and practice nationally. Such is the strength of local ties when activity is focused on the larger issues.

Strong Lateral Ties

By celebrating the *Qunceañera* in honor of their daughter's birthday, the Martinez family is demonstrating the strength of their lateral ties to a Cuban heritage that remains a centerpiece of their lives. In the United States there is currently no other ethnic group with stronger lateral political ties than Cuban Americans. Ironically, some might argue that many Cuban Americans have almost as passionately embraced aspects of their adopted American culture; it has been reported that the largest American flags in Miami fly over car dealerships owned by members of the Cuban American community. Nonetheless, Cuban-Americans remain strongly attached to their heritage through the observation of rituals such as the "Quinse" and through their language, politics and religion. Children attend Catholic parochial schools from an early age much as their parents and grandparents had done while living in Cuba.

Political fervor is very close to the surface in many Cuban American communities, especially the highly politicized Cuban community in Miami. In the spring of 1996, the United States became aware of the depth of that community's political passion when members of Brothers to the Rescue, an organization of individuals dedicated to the cause of restoring government structures in Cuba from the pre-Castro era, were shot down over international waters close to Cuba. José Basulto, the founder of the volunteer pilots' group, had formed Brothers to the Rescue in 1991 in response to the death of a teenager who had drowned while attempting to flee Cuba on a homemade raft. According to the *New York Times* (February 28, 1996, p. 1):

> The change in tactics . . . is part of a broader movement among some anti-Castro exiles . . . from the crude military actions of the past to nonviolent but aggressive methods of protest. Invoking the legacy of Gandhi and Martin Luther King . . . [Brothers to the Rescue] are using militant methods of civil disobedience to promote democratic change within Cuba and harsher measures against Mr. Castro by the United States. Indeed, the financial support of Brothers to the Rescue flows from a broad base of Cuban exiles and corporations, including American Airlines. Interestingly, members of Brothers to the Rescue describe their pledge to nonviolence as the outcome of a process that has turned members of the group away from military tactics and toward the tenets of such figures as Ghandi and Martin Luther King, Jr.

By virtue of the strong presence in local politics discussed in Chapter 3, in addition to their success as entrepreneurs, many Cuban Americans have demonstrated a remarkable capacity to create and utilize extremely beneficial local ties. Some argue that this is in large part attributable to the extraordinarily privileged status accorded Cuban immigrants and refugees by U.S. policy. Nonetheless, the strength of Cuban American reverence for, and commitment to, their island nation is sufficient in most individual cases to portray them as a group with exceedingly strong lateral ties.

The discussion in this section of the chapter has focused on the communities that ethnic groups construct as they build on the strengths of local, lateral or both local and lateral ties with other members of their ethnic group. Local ties tend to be created by groups that have less opportunity for either geographic or economic mobility. For example, Appalachians resided in remote mountainous enclaves for centuries by choice and in part due to a lack of material resources. By contrast, strong lateral ties are maintained by many Cubans who, despite their relatively comfortable lives in the United States, consider themselves exiles. *Whatever the orientation or tendency, all groups, in the face of racism and other forms of hostility, build on strengths to create strong positive group identities.*

EDUCATIONAL REFORM AS ASSIMILATION

Educational reform from the mid-1960s into the 1980s focused on the education of culturally diverse children; however, it was characterized by approaches emphasizing remediation undergirded by a philosophy of paternalism. Ethnic children, their families, and communities were seen as less than standard and as needing assistance to rise to the levels of "mainstream" society. This position ultimately generated a response by social scientists, particularly anthropologists of education who challenged the deficiency model (see Leacock, 1971). These researchers convincingly claimed that the notion of a poverty culture appealed to powerful people who had developed it for their own purposes to justify a series of policies which were bound to fail to alter the status quo. This perspective, they argued, resulted in a number of outcomes including: research demonstrating that particular students were destined to occupy subordinate statuses; data contributing to a distorted view of students' cultural realities; and ultimately the denigration of individual differences among students. The need to change the social organization of schools was deferred by moving the focus to individuals as the ultimate source of unequal school outcomes. The goal of mainstream educational reformers was to understand what was "wrong" with a particular ethnic group, how this affected their educational outcomes, and what particular "remedy" would alleviate the problem. The reformers strove for assimilation to mainstream standards, explaining failure in terms of individual incompetence or a disinclination to take advantage of opportunities. They blamed the victim and did not question the structure and practices of schooling (deMarrais & LeCompte, 1995).

Not all, however, embraced this deficiency perspective. Some sought explanations of both differential school performance and productive ways of teaching urban, poor, or ethnic minority students. This effort was multidisciplinary; it drew psychologists, anthropologists, educators, and sociologists into the pool of individuals who saw the causes of academic problems as greater than individual or ethnic characteristics. Many used the theories of educational anthropologists as a foundation for their work; they started either from the premise that cultural and/or communicative discontinuity hampered students' efforts to achieve or from a broader systemic explanation such as the importance and value of cultural ties that simultaneously created opportunities for group members but that also might put them at odds with the larger society.

Several models were developed from the basic research and subsequent classroom applications: *unequal resources and treatment* (Jencks, 1972; Rist, 1970), *cultural background* (Au & Mason, 1981; D'Amato, 1988; Labov, 1972), and *the labor market* (Fordham & Ogbu, 1986; Ogbu, 1987). These conceptions offered alternatives to the genetic, culture of poverty, and status achievement explanations that had dominated earlier discussions of the education of minority children. Other scholars have examined school success from the viewpoint that accommodation (Gibson, 1988) and resistance to school authority are ways in which culturally diverse youths establish their own cultural identities and reject the ideologies posited by the educational institution (Deyhle, 1986; MacLeod, 1987; Willis, 1977). We turn next to the implications of these perspectives for changing educational practice.

ALTERNATIVE APPROACHES TO EDUCATIONAL REFORM: CURRICULUM AND PEDAGOGICAL STRATEGIES THAT BUILD ON STRENGTHS

In response to cultural deprivation theories and related compensatory programs for minority children, researchers looked for differences between school and home cultures that explained differential school performance. Identifying unequal resources and treatments across schools and school districts within each state constitutes an important first step in institutionalizing educational reform. This means providing high level academic courses, eliminating tracking arrangements, and eliminating inequities among wealthy and poor districts. As a nation, we have barely begun to take on this agenda (see, e.g., Anyon, 1997).

Curriculum and tasks related to a plan for learning at any stage of children's development must be based on a strengths-oriented learning agenda and the conviction that the community is where children acquire important knowledge. This approach has a basis in a highly respected tradition, that of Paulo Freire's "pedagogy of hope" (Freire, 1993). Additionally, it emphasizes the importance of students' own understanding of their ethnic identity as a base upon which to build literacy skills and as a source of political empowerment. Henry Trueba and his collaborators, most recently Yali Zou in 1995, have forcefully made this point in a series of studies of Hmong (or Miao) students in the United States.

As Bronfenbrenner's ecological model for understanding the development of children's skills and abilities argues, it is also necessary to take into account social, political and economic structures to adequately address issues of diversity as manifest in family, school and community settings. Earlier in this chapter we offered an analysis of these settings in our discussion of how ethnic communities construct and maintain local and lateral ties. Such an account will ultimately lead to a reconceptualization of power relationships including the notion of who owns the schools. The development of charter schools, and the rising interest in home schooling, for-profit schools and school choice have all placed public education on notice: Current practices that lead to the alienation and failure of too many children and adolescents must be eliminated. The educational research community has now assembled sufficient information on strategies that support the academic growth of all students, and that also are remarkably consistent on what works to ensure favorable outcomes. What constitutes promising practices, particularly for culturally diverse students? When in students' careers are they most effective? What are the roles to be taken on by teachers, parents and others? And, finally, what factors inhibit or block the implementation of programs and practices that, though beneficial, draw political flack or are simply too narrowly focused or in other ways flawed?

At the present moment, educational researchers whose interests encompass the education of culturally diverse children are converging upon a similar set of ideas regarding how best to provide instruction in literacy learning to encourage children's success throughout their school careers. These promising practices also move our thinking away from the sorting and labeling practices that have traditionally dominated educational pedagogy to a *talent development model* that works toward favorable outcomes for *all* students (Boykin, 1996; Slavin, 1996). These practices target student academic skill-building and, while using culturally relevant curricular strategies (Ladson-Billings, 1994), go beyond them by promoting mastery of difficult concepts. As long as universities persist in requiring high scores on standardized tests, such as the SAT, for admission, skill-building in all youth is critical. In addition, as discussed in Chapter 1, cognitive skills are linked to occupations and income in adulthood. Further, they also create structures that build a framework to promote resilience by having students and teachers take on supportive roles to enhance all students' academic progress, particularly during the tough middle school years.

We turn next to a discussion of a set of key approaches or general strategies in delivering the core technology of teaching and learning to *all* children. These approaches, it should be underscored, must be implemented in settings that have taken patterns of cultural ties discussed earlier in this chapter into account. We have organized these approaches under the following headers: *Acquiring Literacy Skills in the Elementary School Years; Providing High Option, High Quality Instruction: The Program for Complex Instruction; Building Strong Academic Skills in Middle School and High School, Utilizing Comprehensive Developmental Instructional Strategies in Secondary Schools and Creating a Climate Promoting Student Learning at the Secondary Level.* While this order suggests an age-graded continuum of strategies, we argue for a continuous progress approach, coupled with a school organization emphasizing a continuity of caring that allows students to remain in the same multi-age arrangement as long as possible.

Acquiring Literacy Skills in the Elementary School Years

An outstanding source of research and best practices using a talent development model is the ongoing work at the Center for Research on the Education of Students Placed at Risk (CRESPAR) located at Johns Hopkins University and Howard University. Incorporating lessons learned from the effective schools research[6] in combination with their own work in schools with highly diverse student populations, the researchers assume that every child can and must succeed in school and that the role of the school and supporting community agencies is to create opportunities for students to overcome challenges along the way. These notions stand in stark contrast to the old label and sort ideology that regards so-called "homogeneous grouping" as the only way lessons can be accomplished.

Slavin (1996) describes several "key hurdles" that children encounter in their school careers. These include important transitions such as children's initial school entry, the movement from elementary to middle school, from middle to high school, and from high school to postsecondary schooling. Throughout each student's experience in school, the successful passage over each hurdle requires students to have appropriate "language skills, school skills, background knowledge and other skills needed for success."

An important hurdle in the primary grades is the acquisition of literacy competence in the first grade: "Children who fail to read adequately in first grade are often retained, assigned to special education, or relegated to long-term remedial services such as Title I." (Slavin, 1996, p. 43) Early on, children who do not acquire literacy and the other academic skills which build upon competence in reading and writing face a host of unfavorable outcomes including the propensity to leave school before completion, an outcome that virtually ensures reduced job-related and personal life opportunities. Among those students most at-risk for these outcomes are students whose first language is not English. Recall the difficulties faced by Mei, the young girl whose family fled China and who struggled without adequate support to acquire English literacy skills, eventually becoming alienated from her family and more interested in her adolescent peers than in academic life in school.

What seems to work well for *most* students (not just culturally diverse students) in acquiring literacy skills in the early grades are pedagogical strategies emphasizing the active engagement of children. Such approaches are enhanced by children's involvement in learning tasks that also allow thinking, creativity, and flexible problem solving, according to Slavin and other experts. Two strategies in particular, cooperative learning and whole group mastery learning, have shown encouraging results.

In the case of bilingual education or when children have difficulty acquiring literacy skills for any set of reasons, as we argued in Chapter 1, it is critical for educators to assess each child's skills, capabilities and weaknesses on an individual level. The Success for All (Slavin, 1996) model and others similar to it such as Reading One-One (Farkas, 1993) and Reading Recovery employ either or both cooperative and whole group mastery approaches. They can be cost effective and beneficial across the board to students, teacher interns and others if the plan is worked out with the cooperation of college or university-based-programs in teacher education, as proposed by the Reading One-One strategy.

Originally developed in New Zealand, the Reading Recovery and Reading One-One approaches focus on intensive assistance in beginning reading for children who experience serious problems learning to read. The hallmark of these programs is one-on-one tutoring in intensive sessions with tutors who generally work 12 to 20 weeks for approximately 30 minutes each day with a first grade student. Instruction in this manner may extend to second and third grade, depending on the student's progress. Learning to read is facilitated through writing and oral expression, diagnoses and correction of individual learning problems, and detailed recording of student behavior and performance when producing language independently. Initial results of evaluations of student performance indicate that gains in student achievement persist beyond the fourth grade. The widespread success of this approach under any of its guises as Reading Recovery, Reading One-One and the like argue for its widespread adoption with culturally diverse students.

Success for All is probably the most comprehensive, consistently effective and demonstrably successful intervention developed in recent years to improve the performance of economically disadvantaged students. The program provides intensive preschool and kindergarten instruction stressing language development and learning-to-learn skills followed by individualized assistance in primary grade reading and mathematics delivered to small classes and groups of students. It emphasizes cooperative learning, mastery-oriented instruction and development of thinking skills.

Technical support and staff development is provided by coordinators and resource persons assigned to each participating school, and—much as in the Reading Recovery and Reading One-One models—tutoring for students who need individual help in learning to read and function successfully in the classroom is also available. Success For All has resulted in impressive gains in reading and mathematics achievement and reduces retention in grade and special education placements, with largest gains often among students in the lowest performance percentiles.

The emphasis in all of these formulations is on *prevention and early intervention* rather than upon remediating children's deficits, retaining students in grade or stigmatizing children by placing them in groups that negatively label group members who are viewed as lacking competence. Instead,

> prevention includes the provision of high-quality preschool and/or full-day kindergarten programs; research-based curriculum and instructional methods in all grades, preschool to five; reduced class size and nongraded organization in reading; building positive relationships and involvement with parents; and other elements. Early intervention includes one-to-one tutoring in reading from certified teachers for students who are beginning to fall behind in first grade, family support programs to solve any problems of truancy, behavior, or emotional difficulties, and health or social service problems. (Slavin, 1996, p. 12)

These strategies assume a faculty ready to use a variety of methods and to work flexibly with resources including members of the community, parents and other family members. We saw in Chapter 1 that the last-mentioned point *alone* presents an enormous obstacle to children's success in school. As recent research (Lareau & Shumar, 1996) demonstrates, although parents and teachers may use the same words when discussing children's school experiences, they often talk past each other, since each has a different set of operative assumptions behind their terminology. Approaches that promote student success also require a flexible school organization with a complement of high quality school-linked services and a willingness to depart from such procedures as the use of classroom aides, special education placements, and retention in grade. These practices should be replaced with the systematic involvement of parent and community volunteers who know and can build on children's strengths; high option and high quality instruction for all; and ungraded, continuous progress school organization.

In the case of second language learners, the most promising approach for teaching elementary students is what Virginia Collier (1992) and her colleagues term "two way bilingual education," particularly at the elementary school level with program effects sustained at the secondary school level. Such sustained progress does not characterize the experience of students in programs providing reduced amounts of academic support in the home language. In sum, Collier's research suggests that programs include the following components: (a) learning and teaching with groups of both English and non-native speakers with students engaged in academic learning in the represented languages; (b) providing instruction that all perceive as "gifted and talented" and that involves the active engagement of parents bringing their skills and abilities to enrich classroom learning; (c) promoting equal status of the languages—English and Spanish (Chinese, etc.); and (d) utilizing continuous support for staff development that emphasizes "whole language approaches, natural language acquisition through all content areas, cooperative learning interactive and discovery learning and cognitive complexity of the curriculum for all proficiency levels" (Collier, 1992).

Providing High Option, High Quality Instruction: The Program for Complex Instruction

Once a teaching staff has made a school-wide commitment to reinvent itself through the adoption of Reading One-One, Success for All, two-way bilingual education (as appropriate), and a continuous progress model, several questions still remain: How can teachers teach at a high intellectual level in classrooms with students of diverse academic, linguistic, racial, and ethnic backgrounds? How can teachers of such classrooms prevent some students from dominating and others from withdrawing from participation? How can teachers produce equal status interaction in small groups of students working on a collective task when some of these students are just learning English or read well below grade level? According to Elizabeth Cohen and Rachel Lotan (1995), if we are to meet the educational needs of a diverse student population, we need to address these important technical, classroom-level challenges.

If teachers respond to academic, linguistic and ethnic/racial diversity by "dumbing down" the curriculum, then many students will lack access to instruction that develops higher-order thinking skills. If, in contrast, teachers respond to diversity by teaching to the more advanced students and ignore the needs of those who are not yet proficient in English or score well below grade level in reading and mathematics, many students will be doomed to failure. To maintain a high level of curriculum and to address the needs of a diverse population, teachers need to learn how to organize instruction so that students (and their parents and other volunteers) can serve as resources to one another as they work on intellectually demanding learning tasks.

The Program for Complex Instruction emphasizes *access* and *equal-status interaction to create high option, high quality instruction.* Building on 16 years of research, development and dissemination, Elizabeth Cohen and Rachel Lotan (1995) have developed a knowledge base supporting:

- the widespread use of interventions designed to produce *equal-status interaction* among diverse students;
- the capacity of teachers to adapt curricula to the needs of a diverse student population so that all students have *access* to a high level curriculum;
- the capacity of teachers to assess student work in classrooms utilizing small group learning;
- the capacity of colleges of teacher education to prepare students who can work successfully with interventions designed to treat status problems and curricula designed to provide access.

To produce equity in classrooms, the Program has developed two major strategies: (a) multiple ability curricula and (b) special interventions designed to produce equal status behavior. In the service of these strategies, the Program has also developed practical methods of classroom organization and management that permit teachers to delegate authority to groups of students while maintaining individual and group accountability. Students use each other as resources as they work together on open-ended, problem-solving, multiple ability group tasks that allow different students to make different intellectual contributions. The effectiveness of these status treatments has been evaluated and documented at the elementary level. However, we do not yet know if the use of these status treatments at the middle school is equally compelling in producing equal status behavior.

Prototypes of multiple ability curricula that are organized around central concepts in human biology, mathematics, social studies, and language arts have been created and implemented in the middle school. Program staff have documented achievement gains on content-referenced tests for each of these curricula, implemented with a complex instruction format. At the elementary level, students in complex instruction show strong gains in standardized achievement tests as a result of a bilingual curriculum (*Finding Out/Descubrimiento*) designed to develop thinking skills in mathematics and science.

Many classrooms with diverse student populations are implementing the set of strategies known as complex instruction (California, Arizona, Oregon, Washington, Delaware, Massachusetts, and in Israel, the Netherlands, and Sweden). In addition, at nine campuses of the California State University system, several professors are currently incorporating strategies of complex instruction in the teaching of pre-service candidates.

Building Strong Academic Skills in Middle School and High School

Just as it is important in the early grades to provide students with challenging academic tasks in an interactive, problem solving mode, it is equally important in the middle grades to provide a challenging, motivating and supportive learning environment, one particularly suited to the young adolescent's developmental tasks related to seeking autonomy and establishing close peer relationships. In order for middle school students to develop confidence in their ability to tackle increasingly difficult academic tasks, researchers at CRESPAR have devised strategies for keeping motivation to learn high, creating cooperative student work groups, and utilizing intellectually stimulating materials.

The Student Team Reading Program (Stevens, 1993) utilizes outstanding literature, including award-winning short stories, poems and novels that hold students' interest. As described by MacIver and Plank (1996, pp. 5–6) the curriculum is implemented in the following manner:

> The teacher prepares the students to read the book by introducing the author and the genre, discussing relevant background information, and introducing the new vocabulary words. Then, for each section . . . , students engage in a series of cooperative learning activities which the teacher monitors. The teacher leads the students through a discussion of the daily activities as the students complete them. The activities include partner reading, treasure hunts, word mastery, story-retelling, story-related writing, extension activities, tests and explicit instruction in comprehensive strategies.

Each of these approaches is designed to reinforce skill learning through highly interactive, cooperative activities that build a learning climate of peer support, teacher encouragement (using a model of teacher as coach), and skill building. For example, the treasure hunt strategy involves students working with questions about the material they are reading that demand highly analytical problem solving and comparative techniques. To illustrate, in thinking about the importance to the plot of key characters in a novel, students are "asked to explain the significance of the main characters and setting in relation to the story, draw conclusions about any special relationship between characters, make predictions regarding what will happen next based on solid textual evidence that they have already read, and develop interesting, unusual or thought-provoking ideas related to the book's theme" (MacIver & Plank, 1996, p. 6).

Higher order analytic skills are developed in this exercise while other activities, such as story-retelling or story-related writing, teach other highly generalizable skills including summarizing and abstracting ideas from text and elaborating material under current consideration and relating it to other material. These strategies are not unlike those practiced by the "good" teachers at Regents Community College and Halley Elementary School in the Boston vignette by Michelle Foster.

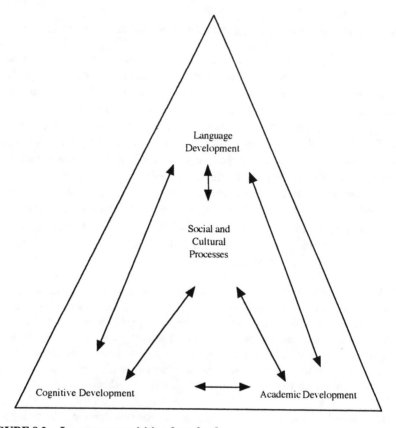

FIGURE 8.2.   Language acquisition for school.
Source: Directions in language and education (Collier, 1995).

For culturally diverse secondary school students as well as for students from "traditional" backgrounds, what seems to work best to heighten students' academic achievements is a model put forward by Collier (1992) and displayed in Figure 8.2. What Collier terms "language development" and what might better be termed the development of "communicative competence" in addition to academic and cognitive development, more generally requires uninterrupted support from social and cultural processes.

Utilizing Comprehensive-Developmental Instructional Strategies in Secondary School

A virtual revolution has resulted in successfully developing comprehension and thinking skills of students whose performance is unsatisfactory in reading, history, math, science, and other subjects. Recall our discussion in Chapter 1 of the Gamoran and associates' research in English literature classes. We know that *both* tying subject matter to readings and discussing pertinent readings before giving students a writing assignment contribute to students' comprehension of material and lead to higher levels of academic performance in class. Instructional strategies stressing comprehension and thinking along with active rather than passive learning activities can also improve student achievement generally. This was the overall conclusion to a research project reported by Knapp, Shields, and Turnbull (1992) conducted by these researchers in 140 classrooms with high percentages of culturally diverse students from low income homes. These and similar findings are very important in emphasizing the point made at the outset of this chapter, namely that challenging academic curricula should be provided to all students, not just an elite group (See also Stringfield, Ross, & Smith, 1996).

Creating a Climate Promoting Student Learning at the Secondary Level

Several factors contribute to creating a school atmosphere that engenders student learning. Among the most important is a movement away from the shopping mall high school curriculum that is largely an outcome of a response to perceived "student needs." Rather than adding more courses tailored to students' idiosyncratic interests, schools with a constrained curriculum that is academic in nature have a powerful effect on their students in both individual student learning and in equitable distribution of learning opportunities across the curriculum.

The second is the creation and maintenance of a communal culture, one that draws students and faculty alike into a small (or at least middle-sized) school-based society framed on a belief system held in common by all members. Catholic schools have been particularly successful on this dimension (Bryk et al., 1993). However, it is possible to envision a communal culture that derives from an ideology, not necessarily religious in nature, held in common by members of the school community including students, their parents, teachers and school administrative staff.

Currently, the Annenberg Foundation supports 46 small schools in New York City. These are experimental schools implementing curricular change and offering their programs as choices to students and parents. One of these schools is documented in the book, *The Power of their Ideas: Lessons for America from a Small School in Harlem* by Deborah Meier (1995), principal of Central Park East in Harlem, the subject of this case study. Central Park East grew from one school to four during its development in the years since 1974 when the first school was started, adding a secondary school in 1984 at the urging of Ted Sizer whose account of a high school teacher named Horace showed how his contact with 150 students a day compromised standards not so much out of malice or stupidity as from necessity. The communal culture at Central Park East is predicated upon the adoption of five habits that are at the heart of each subject matter curriculum and also serve as the basis for evaluating student performance: "They are the question of evidence or "How do we know what we know?"; the question of viewpoint in all its multiplicity or "Who's speaking?"; the search for connections and patterns or "What causes what?"; supposition or "How might things have been different"; and finally "Why it matters?"

A factor working *against* student learning is the commitment of most public high schools in the United States to the comprehensive ideal. Smaller schools can provide a more academically challenging and supportive environment for all students, including culturally diverse students, when there is an emphasis on academic course work (despite the distaste that some students hold for such a curriculum). This emphasis leads to a level of high expectations for *all* students, not just an elite few, and a school-wide commitment to academic instruction informed by comprehensive-developmental instructional strategies as described earlier in this chapter. The community, however, is critical to the success of school-based teaching and learning. We turn next to strategies that explicitly rely upon the strengths of the community.

THE COMMUNITY AND CHILDREN'S EDUCATION

The role of the community in the educational achievement and later economic successes of low income minority students is complex and varies over the course of the child's development. By community we refer to the institutions, organizations, and value structures operating in a locale. These include, but are not limited to, families, businesses, community-based organizations, government and quasi-government agencies, peer groups, non-school based education and training programs, individuals (as in the "I have a Dream" programs) and local collaborative bodies. These community organizations offer programs and direct services to young people and their families, work with education systems, and provide the cultural context, attitudes and values that shape and influence educational outcomes for children.

The potential importance of linkages between schools and the community has been recognized by foundations, federal and state government, and local communities themselves. Within the past 15 years, collaborative programs have emerged related to dropouts, teenage pregnancy, school-to-work transition, counseling, teacher recruitment, and literacy (Seely, 1982; Levine & Trachtman, 1988; McLaughlin, Irby, & Langman, 1995). We believe that such community-school linkages are vital for two principal reasons. First, it is our conviction that teachers and other school personnel know far too little about the communities in which their students live, and that their existing perceptions are distorted by stereotypes that underestimate the abilities of children to learn and the willingness of parents to provide meaningful support to that process. Second, there is little understanding of the social and cultural resources that exist in local communities where residents are poor and/or members of ethnic minority groups. Research and action projects in communities should be designed to fill these gaps and lay the groundwork for productive partnerships between schools and communities and the creation of brokering agencies such as the UAC described earlier in this chapter.

Parents and community activists have a large role to play in school reform and a large stake in the outcomes of such efforts. These actors are too often overlooked in educational research and their contributions and capacities are similarly misunderstood and not properly appreciated. Too much attention is given to problematic aspects of parent influence on student achievement and too little is focused on the constructive roles that parents can, and often do, play in making the difference between success and failure. A major emphasis of the work between communities and schools should be to identify the strengths of families and communities and to reframe concepts of parent and community involvement in schools. Educators can then design better strategies for bi-lateral relationships that capitalize effectively on common goals that parents have for the success of their children within more culturally appropriate and structurally conducive approaches to building partnerships.

Community Values

Coleman and Hoffer (1987) speculate that the critical differences between students attending private or parochial schools and their public school counterparts lies in the relationship of schools to the communities they serve. In their analysis of data from the High School and Beyond Survey they found higher achievement levels and lower dropout rates among students in Catholic schools than among those in public schools. Coleman (1987) suggests that these differences are due to different relations between schools and communities. He terms these relationships "social capital"—"the norms, social networks, and relationships between adults and children that are of value for the child's growing up" (Coleman, 1987, p. 36). Social capital is produced, not only in the family as we have seen in our discussion of Lareau's work earlier in this volume and in this chapter, but in the community as well. It is this community social capital that aids the educational process for students in Catholic schools.

What values do community organizations hold for schooling and education? What are the other community organizations and institutions that provide positive social capital? How can community organizations induce the kinds of attitudes, norms, motivations, and values that children need to succeed in school? These are the critical questions we must address in creating school-community partnerships.

Diversity of Community Organizations

While community values are important for charting the educational directions of students, our understanding of the different organizations and institutions that directly or indirectly influence the educational process of ethnically diverse students is critical. From direct services to partnerships with schools, community organizations powerfully affect student outcomes. Anecdotal information abounds on the impact of school-business partnerships, and "second chance" programs on students who have not been successful in traditional school arrangements.

Communities have a range of options for establishing localized services. Walk-in community centers offer free literacy services and open enrollment (Obermiller et al., 1987). Community institutions such as churches, neighborhood associations, self-help groups, and community development agencies can be utilized for recruitment and program delivery (Bastian et al., 1986). For example, community-based literacy programs delivered through community-based services organizations have attracted growing national interest. "Right to read" programs in Chicago and Philadelphia, sponsored by municipal governments and civic groups, and approximately 6,000 literacy programs operated nationwide have been established. Of these, 185 have been identified as independent, community-based programs, and their records indicate widespread success (Kamer, 1983). Second chance programs for youth who are out of school and out of work represent useful strategies for increasing basic skills and strengthening economic outcomes.

The impact of community organizations on the educational attainments of students is bound up with how these organizations, independently or in concert with schools, affect student values, goals, and performance. These issues and relationships vary for different groups of students. For some groups the community plays a far more vital role in the learning process than does the school. We have seen, for example, how the lore, traditions and values of many American Indian tribal people are preserved and transmitted in the context of tight and highly valued community contexts. For many individuals in other groups the community's support of school programs is central, and for still others the role of community organizations may be negligible, although it would be difficult to imagine any group specifically for whom that is the case. Even among Haitian immigrants and refugees, transnational organizations that figure so prominently in their experience take institutional and organizational forms.

Lipsitz (1980) suggests that schools are relatively tangential to the process of identity formation among many ethnically diverse youth. This may be due to damaging experiences in the early grades in schools insensitive to cultural difference. Many Latinos, for example, do not trust schools because schools threaten family solidarity and structure emphasized in their communities (Lipsitz, 1980). As was true in the years before the formation of the community-based action group in Carpenteria, in many Latino communities the school is isolated from the community of which it is a part. Notices go home from the school not in the home language; there is no liaison with social services; and there is still all too infrequent use of Latino consultants, although in some major cities this situation is changing (Lipsitz, 1980). There are signs that schools are becoming increasingly sensitive to these issues. At a recent (June, 1996) TESOL conference, a commercial vendor offered for purchase a relatively inexpensive service to school districts wishing to communicate to families in their native tongue. The firm routinely assists districts in writing communiques in languages including Urdu and Haitian Creole in addition to Spanish, Polish, and other languages.

Other examples of the critical *independent* role played by community organizations in the education process of diverse students can be found in the counseling and development programs offered through Y's, urban 4-H, Scouts and Explorers, and neighborhood-based organizations emphasizing the heritage of the particular culture in question (Muller & Frisco, 1997). In Cincinnati, as we saw in Chapter 5, the Urban Appalachian Council provides a host of services that encourage the healthy development of a strong ethnic identity, essential for personal growth. These organizations provide opportunities for adolescents to explore themselves and the world around them. They also help combat drug use and early sexual activity.

Collaboration between schools and community organizations has been shown to stimulate changes in both school-based and community-based programs that benefit students. When schools collaborate with community organizations, worn out structures are typically discarded in favor of more innovative programs (Levine & Trachtman, 1988). In an era when our identity as a nation is challenged by our substantial transformation into a more diverse population, there is no more profound and more pressing issue than to balance students' cultural identities with academic achievement and participation in community life.

NEW LEARNING MODELS FOR A NEW WORLD

This book has considered several important concepts around the topic of how the family, community and school nexus create a context for all kinds of learning and particularly for literacy learning. Literacy learning, after all, is worthy of our consideration because skills in reading, writing, and reasoning to decipher linguistic, mathematical and other codes are arguably the foundation to the acquisition of all subsequent skills. Currently, educators are moving towards a model of "literacy as reasoning within multiple discourses," characterized by the integration of ways of thinking, talking, interacting, and valuing as well as reading and writing within a particular social setting. This conception of literacy centers around the idea that each child learns culturally appropriate ways of using language and constructing meaning from texts in their early years at home (Gee, 1990). To build on home literacy practices, researchers and teachers are developing social networks that connect classrooms to community resources (Moll & Diaz, 1997). "Culturally relevant teaching" centers on valuing students' linguistic and cultural diversity and highlights the knowledge that students bring with them from their communities (Ladson-Billings, 1994).

Teachers need opportunities to learn about students' home lives and the communities in which they live in order to capitalize on family strengths, not to reinforce prejudices about family weaknesses and failure. Through professional development and teacher-conducted ethnographic research, teachers can learn to better serve their students, inviting greater participation and hence better understanding. However, in order to generate knowledge and understanding of the community, teachers need to be co-researchers of the community, to learn the research methods to conduct research, and to be accorded the time amidst their other professional responsibilities (Cochran-Smith & Lytle, 1993). When given such professional support, they are able to make significant changes in how they perceive their students and the ways they teach (Heath, 1983).

Historically, programs for the gifted and talented have enrolled insufficient numbers of children from nondominant ethnic groups. This situation derives from the kinds of decisions made by school district personnel about what evidence is required of actual or potential giftedness (Barakan & Bernal, 1991). For immigrant and refugee children, it is frequently the case that their cultural differences lead to their classification by school personnel only in terms of perceived disabilities. Even when giftedness and talent are recognized among these children, educational alternatives and opportunities may be perceived by their parents as ephemeral, in conflict with indigenous sex role expectations, or threatening in other ways to family stability.

Further, traditionally under-represented gifted minority children and their families are less likely to take advantage of special programs for the gifted after children have been identified and referred (Scott, Perou, Urbano, Hogan, & Gold, 1992). The best method to combat the problem of under-representation of gifted minority students may be to develop an identification procedure which incorporates both culture-based and culture-free rationales. Since referring a child for evaluation is the first step in the placement process, under-representation of African American and Latino children in programs for the gifted may, in part, relate to the differential role their parents currently play in the referral process. Awareness of superior abilities appears to be a necessary, but not sufficient, condition for an active parent role in the referral process. Even better, the strategy of creating "gifted" educational programs to challenge virtually all children, utilizing the skills and talents of their parents in implementing the curriculum, is a strategy now practiced in Chicago and Miami public elementary schools. Middle class Anglo parents vie for places in these programs, recognizing the importance to their children as citizens of the twenty-first century in acquiring literacy skills in more than one language.

SCHOOLS AND CULTURALLY DIVERSE COMMUNITIES

It is our collective hope in writing this book that the fathomless gulf that separates diverse cultural communities from the schools will be bridged in the very short term. We see encouraging signs that this is occurring. But, we are also aware, as this book has shown, that some groups establish ties to local institutions including the schools more readily than others do. Schools cannot be the passive recipients of the students who arrive on the doorstep. Ties to parents and community agencies including universities, workplaces and agencies of all kinds are far too important in all aspects of children's education.

The discontinuity between schools and culturally diverse communities has been highlighted by Delpit (1995), Erickson (1987), Heath (1983) and many others. The unresponsiveness of urban school systems has also been widely documented (Hess, 1991 & 1995; Rogers, 1968; Rogers & Chung, 1983; Fine, 1994). Hess (1993) characterized urban schools as outposts of a colonial enterprise, administered by persons both geographically and culturally distant from the local service distribution unit. In major cities in the United States it is unusual for schools to see themselves as community institutions. Yet, there are exciting instances where such has happened. In New York, staff at *El Puente*, an Hispanic community organization in Brooklyn, have begun a small high school which is part of the New York City Public Schools, but is closely integrated into community building efforts that include economic development, health, housing, and welfare (Gonzalez, 1995). In Chicago, the John A. Spry Community School concentrated its school improvement efforts on building close and intense relationships with block clubs, stores and restaurants in the area, and the local Girls and Boys Club to align the school with community and parent interests (Chicago Panel, 1994).

In these and other similar efforts, such as the School for Immigrants in New York City, school personnel view their communities as resources in the educational enterprise and see themselves as community institutions. Not surprisingly, such schools also see their students possessing strengths on which school-based instruction and learning education can be built, rather than seeing students having major deficits that must be remediated (Swadener & Lubeck, 1995). What is not well known is whether such efforts can be replicated in culturally diverse settings across a city or in cities with very different social contexts in a manner that will enhance the engagement and achievement of all children. This must be our agenda as we move into the 21st century.

Notes

[1] Originally, we hoped to choose Latino children from one national origin, assuming that we could find a "homogeneous cultural group," if all were Mexican or Mexican-American, for example. Not only was this impossible in the specific context, but we later critiqued our own assumptions on the quest for homogeneity.

[2] This pattern of busing African American students was initiated in the early elementary grades. While allowing whites to attend their neighborhood schools, such policies mandates the attendance of often-remote schools by African American children. Furthermore, these practices were not limited to the South. One of the earliest districts to desegregate, Berkeley Unified Schools (CA) employed the same practices in the late 1960s.

[3] By "multicultural context" we have in mind a learning environment shaped by what Christine Sleeter (1996, p. 9) and others see as "a form of resistance to oppression" that is comprehensive of class, race and ethnicity, and gender oppression in its pedagogical strategies.

[4] Because those Asians who came as immigrants to the United States in the post-World Warr II period, particularly after the passage of the 1965 Immigration Act, came either to be reunited with family members, as workers with special skills, or as refugees, we consider them a primarily locally oriented, eager to become Americans.

[5] The absence of celebrations such as the Quinceañera could be explained by a number of aspects of the cultural development of the Mexican American community in southern California including the strong influence of indigenous Indian tribal practices, the distance in time from Spanish influences, and so forth.

[6] This approach, brought to the current school reform movement by Ron Edmunds and his collaborators, identifies characteristics of schools that are successful in bringing about high levels of academic success for students from diverse backgrounds.

References

Ada, A. F. (1986). Creative education for bilingual teachers. *Harvard Educational Review, 56*, 386–394.

Anyon, J. (1997). *Ghetto schooling: A political economy of urban educational reform.* New York: Teachers College Press.

Aronowitz, S., & Giroux, H. (1985). *Education under siege: The conservative, liberal and radical debate over schooling.* South Hadley, MA: Bergin & Garvey.

Au, K., & Mason, J. (1981). Social organizational factors in learning to read. The balance of rights hypothesis. *Reading Research Quarterly, 17*(1), 115–152.

Baca, L., & Cervantes, H. (1989). *The bilingual special education interface.* Columbus, OH: Merrill.

Baker, C. (1993). *Foundations of bilingual education and bilingualism.* Clevedon, England: Multilingual Matters Ltd.

Barakan, J., & Bernal, E. (1991). Gifted education for bilingual and limited English proficient students. *Gifted Child Quarterly, 35*(3), 144–147.

Barr, R., & Parrett, W. (1995). *Hope at last for at-risk youth.* Boston: Allyn & Bacon.

Bauer, F. (1989, January 27). Minorities rank joblessness as chief problem, survey says. *The Milwaukee Journal.*

Bean, F., & Tienda, M. (1987). *The Hispanic population of the United States.* New York: Russell Sage Foundation.

Bloom, A. (1987). *The closing of the American mind.* New York: Simon & Schuster.

Borman, K. M., Cookson, P., Sadovnik, A., & Spade, J. (1996). *Implementing educational reform: Sociological perspectives on educational policy.* Norwood, NJ: Ablex.

Borman, K. M., & Pink, W. T. (1994). Community involvement in staff development in school improvement. In K. M. Borman & N. Greenman (Eds.), *Changing American education: Recapturing the past or inventing the future?* (pp. 195–220). Albany, NY: State University of New York Press.

Borman, K., Dubeck, P., Carreon, S., & Cassedy, A. (Eds.) (1997). *Women and work.* Rutgers, NJ: Rutgers University Press.

Borman, K. M., & Spring, J. (1984). *Schools in central cities: Structure and process.* New York: Longman.

Borman, K. M., Mueninghoff, E., & Piazza, S. (1988). Urban Appalachian girls and women: Bowing to no one. In L. Weis (Ed.), *Class, race, and gender in U.S. Education.* Buffalo: SUNY Press.

Bowles, S., & Gintis, H. (1976). *Schooling in capitalist America: Educational reform and the contradictions of economic life.* New York: Basic.

Boykin, K. (1996). *One more river to cross.* New York: Anchor.

Braddock, J. H., II. (1990). Tracking the middle grades: National patterns of grouping for instruction. *Phi Delta Kappan, 71,* 445–449.

Braddock, J. H., & Williams, M. M. (1996). Equality of educational opportunity and the Goals 2000 Educate America Act. In K. Borman, P. Cookson, A. Sadovnik, & J. Spade, (Eds.) *Implementing educational reform: Sociological perspectives on educational policy.* (pp. 89–109). Norwood, NJ: Ablex.

Bronfenbrenner, U. (1979). *The ecology of human development.* Cambridge, MA: Harvard University Press.

Bronfenbrenner, U. (1986). Ecology of family as a context for human development: Research perspectives. *Developmental Psychology, 22,* 723–742.

Bronfenbrenner, U. (1989). Ecological systems theory. In R. Vasta (Ed.), *Annals of child development* (Vol. 6, pp. 187–249). Greenwich, CT: JAI.

Bryk, A. S., Lee, V. E., & Holland, P. B. (1993). *Catholic schools and the common good.* Cambridge, MA: Harvard University Press.

Campbell, K., & Lee, B. (1992). Sources of personal neighbor networks: social integration, need or time? *Social Forces, 70,* 1077–1100.

Centers for Disease Control & Prevention (1996). Statistical Rolodex. African American Health Facts. Monthly Vital Statistics Report. (4661, Supplement).

Chicago Panel on School Policy. (1994). Reporting reform: Spry school connects reform to family, community needs. *Reform Report, IV*(5), 7–11.

Childe, I. (1943). *Italian or American? The second generation in conflict.* New Haven, CT: Yale University Press.

Children's Defense Fund. (1991). *The state of America's children.* Washington, DC: Children's Defense Fund.

Clark, K. (1965). *Dark ghetto: dilemmas of social power.* New York: Harper & Row.

Clark, R. (1992). Critical factors in why disadvantaged students succeed or fail in school. In H. J. Johnston & K. M. Borman (Eds.), *Effective schooling for economically disadvantaged students* (pp. 67–81). Norwood, NJ: Ablex.

Clark, R. (1983). *Family life and school achievement.* Chicago, IL: University of Chicago Press.

Cochran-Smith, S. M., & Lytle, S. L. (1992). Teacher research as a way of knowing. *Harvard Educational Review, 6*(4), 447–474.

Cohen, E. (1996). An animal guide to opportunity-to-learn standards: Response and rejoinder. In K. Borman, P. Cookson, A. Sadovnik, & J. Spade, (Eds.), *Implementing educational reform: Sociological perspectives on educational policy.* (pp. 111–126). Norwood, NJ: Ablex.

Cohen, E. (1995). Producing equal-status interaction in heterogeneous classrooms. *American Education Research Journal, 32*(1), 99–120.

Cohen, E., & Lotan, R. A. (1995). Producing equal-status interaction in the heterogeneous classroom. *American Educational Research Journal, 32,* 99–120.

Coleman, J. S. (1987). Families and schools. *Educational Researcher, 16,* 32–38.

Coleman, J. S., & Hoffer, T. (1987). *Public and private high schools: The impact of communities.* New York: Basic.

Collier, V. P. (1992). A synthesis of studies examining long-term language minority student data on academic achievement. *Bilingual Research Journal, 16,* 187–212.

Collier, V. P. (1995). Acquiring a second language for school. In *Directions in language and education, 1,* (4, Fall).

Comer, J. P. (1988). Educating poor minority children. *Scientific American, 259,* 42–48.

Connors, L. J., & Epstein, J. L. (1994). *Taking stock: The views of teachers, parents, and students on school, family, and community partnerships in high schools.* (Center Report 25). Baltimore, MD: Center on Families, Communities, Schools and Children's Learning, Johns Hopkins University.

Crane, J. (1991). Effects of neighborhoods on dropping out of school and teenage childbearing. In C. Jencks & P. E. Peterson (Eds.), *The urban underclass.* Washington, DC: The Brookings Institution.

Cummins, J. (1981). The role of primary language development in promoting educational success for language minority students. In *Schooling & language minority students: A theoretical framework* (pp. 3–49). Los Angeles: Evaluation, Dissemination & Assessment Center–California State University.

Dahl, K. (1988). Writers teaching writers: What children learn in peer conferences. *English Quarterly, 21*(3), 164–173.

D'Amato, J. (1988, May). "Acting": Hawaiian children's resistance to teachers. *Elementary School Journal, 88*(5), 529–544.

Delgado-Gaitan, C. (1988). The value of conformity: Learning to stay in school. *Anthropology & Education Quarterly, 19,* 354–381.

Delgado-Gaitan, C. (1990). *Literacy for empowerment.* New York: Falmer.

Delgado-Gaitan, C. (1991). Involving parents in the schools: A process of empowerment. *American Journal of Education,* 20–47.

Delpit, L. (1995). *Other people's children: Cultural conflict in the classroom.* New York: The New Press.

DeMarrais, K. B., & LeCompte, M. (1995). *The way schools work: A sociological analysis of education* (2nd Ed.). New York: Longman.

Deyhle, D. (1986). Break dancing and breaking out: Anglos, Utes, and Navajos in a border reservation high school. *Anthropology & Education Quarterly, 17*(2), 111–127.

Deyhle, D. (1989, August). The styles of learning are different, but the teaching is just the same: Suggestions for teachers of American Indian youth. *Journal of American Indian Education,* 1–14.

Deyhle, D. (1991). Empowerment and cultural conflict: Navajo parents and the schooling of their children. *International Journal of Qualitative Studies in Education, 4*(4), 277–297.

Deyhle, D. (1992, January). Constructing failure and maintaining cultural identity: Navajo and Ute school leavers. *Journal of American Indian Education,* 24–47.

Deyhle, D., & LeCompte, M. Cultural difference in child development. *Theory into practice, 33*(3), 66–156.

DiPrete, T. A. (1981). *Discipline, order and student behavior in American high schools.* Contractor Report NCES 82-202. Washington, DC: National Center for Education Statistics.

Eames, E., & Goode, J. (1973). *Urban poverty in a cross-cultural context.* New York: Free Press.

Eckstrom, R. B., Goertz, M. E., & Rock, D. E. (1989). *Education & American youth.* London: Falmer.

Education Studies Group. (1991, August). *Resources and Actions: Parents, their children and schools*. A report to the National Science Foundation & National Center for Educational Strategies. Ogburn-Stouffer Center, NORC/University of Chicago.

English, F. W. (1988, May). The utility of the camera in qualitative inquiry. *Educational Researcher, 17*, 8–15.

Erickson, F. (1987). Transformation and school success: The politics and culture of educational achievement. *Anthropology & Education Quarterly, 18*(4), 335–356.

Estrada, L. E. F., Garcia, C., Nacias, R. F., & Maldonado, L. (1988). Chicanos in the United States: A history of exploitation and residence. In C. Garcia (Ed.), *Latinos and the Political System* (pp. 28–64). Notre Dame, IN: Notre Dame Press.

Farkas, S. (1993). *Divided within, besieged without: The politics of education in four American school districts*. New York: The Public Agenda Foundation.

Feenstra, H. J. (1969). Parent and teacher attitudes: Their role in second-language acquisition. *Canadian Modern Language Review, 26*, 5–13.

Fernandez, R., & Velez, W. (1985). Race, color and language in changing public schools. In L. Maldonado & J. Moore (Eds.), *Urban ethnicity in the United States* (pp. 123–144). Beverly Hills, CA: Sage.

Fine, M. (Ed.) (1994). *Chartering urban school reform: Reflections on public high schools in the midst of change*. New York: Teachers College Press.

Firmat, G. (1994). *Life in the hyphen: The Cuban-American way*. Austin: University of Texas Press.

Flaxman, E., & Inger, M. (1992, November). Parents and schooling in the 1990s. *Principal, 72*(2), 16–18.

Foley, D. (1990). *Learning capitalist culture*. Philadelphia: University of Pennsylvania Press.

Fordham, S. (1991). Peer-proofing academic competition among black adolescents: "Acting white" black American style. In C. Sleeter (Ed.), *Empowerment through multicultural education*. Albany: State University of New York Press.

Fordham, S., & Ogbu, J. (1986). Black students' school success: Coping with the "burden of 'acting' white." *Urban Review, 18*(3), 176–206.

Foucault, M. (1980). *Power/knowledge*. New York: Pantheon.

Freire, P. (1987). *Literacy, reading the word and the world*. South Hadley, MA: Bergin & Garvey.

Freire, P. (1993). *Pedagogy of the oppressed*. New York: Continuum.

Frey, W. (1995). The new geography of population shifts. In R. Farley (Ed.), *State of the union: America in the 1990s, Volume Two: Social trends* (pp. 271–336). New York: Russell Sage Foundation.

Gamoran, A. (1995). *Differentiation and opportunity in restructured schools*. Washington D.C.: U.S. Department of Education.

Gamoran. A., Nystrand, M., Berends, M., & Lepore, P. (1995). An organizational analysis of the effects of ability grouping. *American Educational Research Journal, 32*(4), 687–715.

Garcia, E., McLaughlin, B. with Spoder, B., & Saracho, O. (1995). *Meeting the challenge of linguistic and cultural diversity in early childhood education*. New York: Teachers College Press.

Gardner, R. C. (1968). Attitudes and motivation: Their role in second-language acquisition. *TESOL Quarterly, 2*, 141–150.

Gardner, R. C., & Lambert, W. (1972). *Attitudes and motivation in second language learning.* Rowley, MA: Newbury House.

Gee, J. P. (1989). Literacy, discourse, and linguistics: Introduction. *Journal of Education, 171,* 5–17.

Genesee, F. (1978). *Second language learning and language attitudes: Working papers on bilingualism,* No. 16. ERIC document # ED165475.

Gibson, M. A. (1988). Punjabi orchard farmers: An immigrant enclave in rural California. *International Migration Review, 22*(1), 28–50.

Gibson, M. A. (1993). The school performance of immigrant minorities: A complicative view. In E. Jacob & C. Jordan (Eds.), *Minority education: Anthropological perspectives* (pp. 113–128). Norwood, NJ: Ablex.

Gill, W. (1991). *Issues in African American education.* Nashville TN: One Horn Press.

Giroux, H. (1991). Border Crossing. In C. Mitchell & K. Weiler (Eds.), *Rewriting literacy* (pp. ix–xvi). New York: Bergin and Garvey.

Gold, S. J. (1992). *Refugee communities: A comparative field study.* Newbury Park, CA: Sage.

Gonzalez, N. (1995). Funds of knowledge for teaching in Latino households. *Urban education, 29*(4), 443–470.

Graue, M. E., Weinstein, T., & Walberg, H. J. (1983). School-based home instruction and learning: A quantitative synthesis. *Journal of Educational Research, 76,* 351–360.

Gray, S. T. (1984). How to create a successful school-community partnership. *Phi Delta Kappan, 65,* 405–409.

Greenwald, R., Hedges, L. V., & Laine, R. D. (1996). Interpreting research on school resources and student achievement: A rejoinder to Hanushek. *Review of Educational Research, 66,* 411–416.

Hakuta, K. (1986). *Bilingualism and cognitive development.* Los Angeles: Center for language education and research, University of California.

Hale-Benson, J. E. (1982). *Black children.* Baltimore, MD: Johns Hopkins University Press.

Hall, P. M. (1997). *Race, ethnicity and multiculturalism.* New York: Garland.

Halpern, G. (1976). An evaluation of French learning alternatives. *Canadian Modern Language Review, 22,* 162–172.

Hare, N., & Hare, J. (1991). *The Hare plan to overhaul the pubic schools and educate every black man, woman, and child.* San Francisco: The Black Think Tank.

Harrison, B., & Bluestone, B. (1988). *The great U-turn: Corporate restructuring and the polarizing of America.* New York: Basic.

Harrison, R., & Bennett, C. E. (1995). Race and ethnic diversity. In R. Farley (Ed.), *State of the union: America in the 1990s. Vol 2: Social trends.* New York: Russell Sage Foundation.

Harry, B. (1992). *Cultural diversity, families, and the special education system.* New York: Teachers College Press.

Harry, B., Allen, N., & McLaughlin, M. W. (1995). Communication vs. compliance: African-American parents' involvement in special education. *Exceptional Children, 61*(4), 364–377.

Harste, J., Woodward, V., & Burke, C. (1984). *Language stories and literacy lessons.* Portmouth, NH: Heinemann.

Heath, S. B. (1983). *Ways with words: Language, life and work in communities and classrooms*. Cambridge, England: Cambridge University Press.

Heath, S. B., & McLaughlin, M. W. (Eds.) (1993). *Identity and inner city youth: Beyond ethnicity and gender*. New York: Teachers College Press.

Henderson, P. (1987). Effects of planned parental involvement in affective education. *The School Counselor, 35*, 22–27.

Hess, G. A. (1991). *School restructuring, Chicago style*. Newbury, CA: Corwin.

Hess, G. A. (1993). Decentralization and community control. In S. L. Jacobsen & R. Berne (Eds.), *Reforming education: The emerging systemic approach*. Newbury Park, CA: Corwin.

Hess, G. A. (1995). *Restructuring urban schools: A Chicago perspective*. New York: Teachers College Press.

Hill-Collins, P. (1991). *Black feminist thought: Knowledge, consciousness, and the politics of empowerment*. New York: Routledge.

Hispanic Development Project. (1984). *"Make something happen:" Hispanics and urban high school reform* (2 Volumes). New York: Hispanic Policy Development.

Institute of Medicine, Commission on Behavioral and Social Sciences and Education, Board on Children and Families. (1995). Immigrant children and their families: Issues for research and policy. *Critical issues for children & youths, 5*, 72–89.

Izzo, S. (1980). *Second language learning: A review of related studies*. Rosslyn, VA: National Clearinghouse for Bilingual Education.

Jarvis, S. (1992). Historical overview: African Americans and the evaluation of voting rights. In R. C. Gomez & L. F. Williams (Eds.), *From exclusion to inclusion: The long struggle for African American political power* (pp. 17–24). New York: Greenwood.

Jencks, C. (1972). *Inequality: A reassessment of the effect of family and schooling in America*. New York: Basic.

Johnson, V. R. (1994). *Parent centers in urban schools: Four case studies*. (Center Report 23). Baltimore, MD: Center on Families, Communities, Schools and Children's Learning, Johns Hopkins University.

Knapp, M. S., Shields, P. M., & Turnbull, B. J. (1992). *Academic challenge for the children of poverty*. Washington, DC: U. S. Department of Education, Office of Policy and Planning.

Kozol, J. (1991). *Savage inequalities: Children in America's schools*. New York: Crown.

Labov, W. (1972). *Language in the city: Studies in black English vernacular*. Philadelphia: University of Pennsylvania Press.

Ladson-Billings, G. (1994). *The dreamkeepers: Successful teachers of African American children*. San Francisco: Jossey-Bass.

Lamphere, L. (1992). *Structuring diversity: Ethnographic perspectives on the new immigration*. Chicago: University of Chicago Press.

Lareau, A. (1989). *Home advantage: Social class and parental intervention in elementary education*. London: Falmer.

Lareau, A., & Shumar, W. (1996). The problems of individualism in family-school policies. *Sociology of Education*, Extra issue, 24–39.

Leacock, E. B. (1971). *The culture of poverty: A critique*. New York: Simon & Schuster.

LeCompte, M. D., & Dworkin, A. G. (1991). *Giving up on school: Student dropouts and teacher burnouts*. Newbury Park, CA: Corwin.

Lee, V. (1994). *High school restructuring and student achievement.* Washington DC: Department of Education.

Lee, V. E., Dedrick, R. F., & Smith, J. B. (1991). The effect of the social organization of schools on teachers' self-efficacy and satisfaction. *Sociology of Education, 64,* 190–208.

Levine, M., & Trachtman, R. (1988). *American business and the public schools: Case studies of corporate involvements in public education.* New York, NY: CED.

Lewis, H. (1967). The changing Negro family. In J. Roberts (Ed.), *School children in the urban slum.* New York: The Free Press.

Loeb, P., Friedman, D., & Lord, M. C. (1993). To make a nation: How immigrants are changing America for better and worse. *U.S. News and World Report,* October 4, 47.

Lightfoot, S. L. (1978). *Worlds apart: Relationships between families and schools.* New York: Basic.

Lipsitz, J. S. (1980, March). Public policy and early adolescent research. *High School Journal, 63*(6), 250–256.

Littlebear, D. (1994). Getting teachers and parents to work together. In J. Reyhner (Ed.), *Teaching American Indian students* (pp. 104–114). Norman, OK: University of Oklahoma Press.

MacIver, D. J., & Plank, S. B. (1996). *Creating a motivational climate conducive to talent development in middle schools: Implementation and effects of student team reading.* (Unpublished manuscript.)

MacLeod, J. (1987). *Ain't no makin' it.* Boulder, CO: Westview.

Maloney, M., & Borman, K. M. (1987). Effects of schools and schooling upon Appalachian children in Cincinnati. In P. Obermiller & W. Philliber (Eds.), *Too few tomorrows: Urban Appalachians in the 1980s* (pp. 89–98). Boone, NC: Appalachian Consortium Press.

Matute-Bianchi, M.E. (1986, November). Ethnic identities and patterns of school success and failure among Mexican-descent and Japanese-American students in a California high school: An ethnographic analysis. *American Journal of Education, 95*(1), 233–255.

McCarty, T. L., & Schaffer, R. (1994). Language and literacy development. In J. Reyhner (Ed.), *Teaching American Indian students* (pp. 115–131). Norman, OK: University of Oklahoma Press.

McLaughlin, M. W., & Talbert, J. E. (1993). How the world of students and teachers challenges policy coherence. In S. H. Fuhrman (Ed.), *Designing coherent education policy: Improving the system.* San Francisco: Jossey-Bass.

McLaughlin, M., Irby, M., & Langman, J. (1995). *Urban sanctuaries.* San Francisco: Jossey-Bass.

Meier, D. (1995). How our schools could be. *Phi Delta Kappan, 76*(5), 369–373.

Meier, K., & Stewart, J. (1991). *The politics of Hispanic education.* Albany, NY: SUNY Press.

Menchaca, M., & Valencia, R. (1990). Anglo-Saxon ideology in the 1920s–1930s. *Anthropology & Education Quarterly, 21*(3), 222–249.

Mitchell, C., & Weiler, K. (1991). *Rewriting literacy.* New York: Bergin and Garvey.

Moll, L., & Diaz, S. (1993). Change as the goal of educational research. In E. Jacob & C. Jordan (Eds.), *Minority education: Anthropological perspectives* (pp. 67–82). New Jersey: Ablex.

Moses, W. J. (1990). *The wings of Ethiopia*. Ames, IA: Iowa State University Press.

Muller, C., & Frisco, M. (1997). Social institutions serving adolescents. In K. Borman & B. Schneider (Eds.), *Adolescent experience and development: Social influences and educational challenges*. Chicago: National Society for the Study of Education.

National Adult Literacy Survey. (1992). Princeton, NJ: Education Testing Service.

National Research Council, Gonzalez, N. (1994). Lessons from research with language—minority children. *Journal of reading behavior*, 26(4), 439–456.

Natriello, G., McDill, E., & Pallas, A. (1990). *Schooling disadvantaged children: Racing against catastrophe*. New York: Teachers College Press.

Navarro, M. (1996). Nonviolence of Castro's foes still wears a very tough face. *New York Times*, February 28, A1.

Nobles, W. (1981). African-American family life: An instrument of culture. In H. McAdoo (Ed.), *Black families* (pp. 77–86). Beverly Hills, CA: Sage.

Oakes, J. (1985). *Keeping track: How schools structure inequality*. New Haven, CT: Yale University Press.

Obermiller, P. J., & Philliber, W. W. (1987). *Too few tomorrows: Urban Appalachians in the 1980s*. Boone, NC: Appalachian Consortium.

Obermiller, P., & Philliber, W. (1994). *Appalachia in an international context*. Westport, CT: Praeger.

Ogbu, J. (1974). *The next generation*. New York: Teachers College Press.

Ogbu, J. (1982). Cultural discontinuities and schooling. *Anthropology & Education Quarterly*, 13(4), 290–307.

Ogbu, J. (1987). Opportunity structure, cultural boundaries and literacy. In J. Langer (Ed.), *Language, literacy and culture: Issues of society & schooling* (pp. 149–177). Norwood, NJ: Ablex.

Ogbu, J. (1991). *Minority status and schooling*. New York: Garland.

Ogbu, J. (1993a). Differences in cultural frame of reference. *International Journal of Behavioral Development*, 16(3), 483–506.

Ogbu, J. (1993b). Variability in minority school performance: A problem in search of an explanation. In E. Jacob & C. Jordan (Eds.), *Minority education: Anthropological perspectives* (pp. 83–112). Norwood, NJ: Ablex.

Okagi, L., & Sternberg, R. (1993). Parental beliefs and children's school performance: A multi-ethnic perspective. *Child Development*, 64, 36–57.

Ovando, C., & Collier, J. (1985). *Bilingual ESL and classrooms: Teaching in multicultural contexts*. New York: McGraw-Hill.

Pear, R. (1997). Clinton and Congress at odds on aid to legal immigrants. *New York Times*, April 8, A1.

Perez, L. (1980). Cubans. In S. Thernston (Ed.), *Harvard Encyclopedia of American ethnic groups* (pp. 256–261). Cambridge, MA: Harvard University Press.

Perkins, D. F., Ferrari, T. M., Covey, M. A., & Keith, J. G. (1994). Getting dinosaurs to dance: Community collaborations as applications of ecological theory. *Home Economics Forum*, 7, 39–47.

Perlmann, J. (1988). *Ethnic differences: Schooling and social structure among the Irish, Italians, Jews and Blacks in an American city, 1880–1935.* New York: Cambridge University Press.

Phelan, P., Davidson, A., & Cao, H. (1991). *The flow of ethnicity.* Washington DC: U.S. Department of Education.

Portes, A. (1994). *The economic sociology of immigration.* New York: Russell Sage Foundation.

Portes, A., & Bach, R. L. (1985). *Latin journey: Cuban and Mexican immigrants in the United States.* Berkeley: University of California Press.

Portes, A., & Schauffler, R. (1994). Language and the second generation. In R. G. Rumbaut & S. Pedraza (Eds.), *Origins and destinies: Migration, race, and ethnicity in America.* Belmont, CA: Wadsworth.

Portes, A., & Zhou, M. (1993). The new second generation: segmented assimilation and its variants among post-1965 immigrant youth. *The Annals of the American Academy of Political & Social Sciences, 530,* 74–96.

Purdy, M., & Newman, M. (1996). Lessons unlearned. *New York Times,* May 14, 15, A1.

Rado, D. (1996). Session little help to schools. *St. Petersburg Times,* May 2, 1B.

Ramirez, J. (1992). Executive summary. *Bilingual Research Journal, 16,* 1–62.

Rangel, J. C., & Acola, C. M. (1972, March). Project report: The sure segregation of Chicanos in Texas schools. *Harvard Civil Rights Liberties Law Review,* 387–392.

Raudenbush, S. W., & Kasim, R. M. (1998). Cognitive skill and economic inequality: Findings from the National Adult Literacy Survey. *Harvard Educational Review, 68*(1), 33–79.

Reyhner, J. A. (1994). American Indian/Alaskan Native education. *Phi Delta Kappa Fastbacks, 367,* 7–41.

Rist, R. C. (1970). Student social class and teacher expectations: The self-fulfilling prophecy in ghetto education. *Harvard Educational Review.*

Rogers, D. (1968). *110 Livingston Street: Politics and bureaucracy in the New York City schools.* New York: Bantam.

Rogers, D., & Chung, N. H. (1983). *110 Livingston Street revisited: Decentralization in action.* New York: New York University Press.

Rumbaut, R. G. (1994, February). *Immigrant America: A contemporary portrait.* Paper presented at the meetings of the American Association for the Advancement of Science. San Francisco.

Sassen, S. (1991). *The global city.* Princeton, NJ: Princeton University Press.

Schneider, B., & Lee, V. (1990). A model for academic success. *Anthropology & Education Quarterly, 21*(4), 356–377.

Schumann, J. H. (1976, June). Social distance as a factor in second language acquisition. *Language Learning, 26*(1), 135–141.

Scott, M., Perou, R., Urbano, R., Hogan, A., & Gold, S. (1992). Identification of giftedness: A comparison of white, Hispanic, and black families. *Gifted Child Quarterly, 36*(3), (Summer), 131–138.

Seeley, D. S. (1982). Education through leadership. *Educational Leadership, 40*(2), 42–43.

Slavin, R. (1996). *Education for all.* Exton, PA: Swets and Zeitlinger.

Sleeter, C. (1996). *Multicultural education as social activism.* Albany: SUNY Press.

Sleeter, C., & Grant, C. (1996). *After the school bell rings.* Washington DC: Falmer.

Sontag, D. (1993). New immigrants test nation's heartland. *New York Times*, October 18, A1.

Spergel, I. A., & Curry, G. D. (1988). Gang homicide, delinquency, and community. *Criminology, 26*(3), 381–405.

Spring, J. (1994). *The American school 1642–1993*. (3rd ed.).

Stack, C. (1974). *All our kin: Strategies for survival in a Black community.* New York: Harper & Row.

Stevens, F. I. (1993). Opportunity to learn and other social contextual issues: Addressing the low academic achievement of African American students. *Journal of Negro Education, 62*, 227–231.

Stevenson, D. (1996). Standards and assessments in Goals 2000. In K. M. Borman, P. W. Cookson, A. R. Sadovnik, & J. Z. Spade (Eds.), *Implementing educational reform: Sociological perspectives on educational policy* (pp. 43–64). Norwood, NJ: Ablex.

Stier, H., & Tienda, M. (1992). Family, work and women: The labor supply of Hispanic immigrant wives. *International Migration Review, 26*(4), 1291–1313.

Stringfield, S., Ross, S., & Smith, S. (1996). *Bold plans for school restructuring: The new American schools designs*. Mahwah, NJ: Erlbaum.

Suarez-Orozco, M. M. (1987). "Becoming somebody": Central-American immigrants in U.S. inner-city schools. *Anthropology & Education Quarterly, 18*, 287–300.

Suarez-Orozco, M. M. (1989). *Central American refugees and U.S. high schools: A psychosocial study of motivation and achievement*. Stanford, CA: Stanford University Press.

Suarez-Orozco, M. (1995). *Transformations*. Stanford, CA: Stanford University Press.

Suro, R. (1992). Mexicans come to work, but find dead ends. *New York Times*, January 19, A1.

Swadener, B. B., & Lubeck, S. (1995). *Children and families at promise: Deconstructing the discourse of risk*. Albany, NY: SUNY Press.

Takaki, R. (1993). *A different mirror: A history of multicultural America*. Boston, MA: Little, Brown.

Takaki, R. (1989). *Strangers from a different shore: A history of Asian-Americans*. Boston, MA: Little, Brown.

Teale, W. H. (1982). Toward a theory of how children learn to read and write naturally. *Language & Arts, 59*(6), 555–570.

Teale, W. (1986). Home background and young children's literacy development. In W. Teale & E. Sulzby (Eds.), *Emergent literacy: Writing and reading*. Norwood, NJ: Ablex.

Thornton, J. (1995). "An Interview with Rosa Parks." US News Online. (http://www.womenshistory.miningco.com). April 18, 1998.

Thornton, R. (1987). *American Indian Holocaust and survival: A population history since 1492*. Norman, OK: University of Oklahoma Press.

Timm, P., & Borman, K. (1997). The soup pot don't stretch that far no more. In L. Weis (Ed.), *Beyond black and white voices*. Albany: SUNY Press.

Tobin, J., Wu, D., & Davidson, D. (1989). *Preschool in three cultures*. New Haven, CT: Yale University Press.

Topping, K. J. (1986). *Parents as educators*. Cambridge, MA: Brookline.

Trueba, H. T. (1988). Peer socialization among minority students: A high school dropout prevention program. In H. T. Trueba & C. Delgado-Gaitan (Eds.), *School and society: Learning content through culture* (pp. 201–128). New York: Praeger.

Tucker, G. R. (1977). The linguistic perspective. In L. L. Parker (Ed.), *Linguistics, bilingual education: Current perspectives* (pp. 1–40). Arlington VA: Center for Applied Linguistics.

U. S. Department of Commerce, Bureau of the Census. (1984). *Statistical Abstract of the United States: 1984* (104th ed.). Washington, DC: U.S. Government Printing Office.

U. S. Department of Commerce, Bureau of the Census. (1990). *Statistical Abstract of the United States: 1990* (110th ed.). Washington, DC: U.S. Government Printing Office.

U. S. Department of Commerce, Bureau of the Census. (1991). *Statistical Abstract of the United States: 1991* (111th ed.). Washington, DC: U.S. Government Printing Office.

U. S. Department of Commerce, Bureau of the Census. (1992). *Poverty in the United States, 1992.* Current Population Reports, Series P-60, No. 185. Washington, DC: U.S. Government Printing Office.

U. S. Department of Commerce, Bureau of the Census. (1993). *Statistical Abstract of the United States: 1993* (113th ed.). Washington, DC: U.S. Government Printing Office.

U. S. Department of the Interior. (1991).

Vogt, L. *(1987). Explaining school failure, producing school success. Anthropology & Education Quarterly, 18*(4), 276–286.

Waggoner, D. (1994). Language-minority school-age population now totals 9.9 million. *NABE News, 18*(1j), 1, 24–26.

Walberg, H. J. (1984a). Families as partners in educational productivity. *Phi Delta Kappan, 65,* 397–400.

Walberg, H. J. (1984b). Improving the productivity of America's schools. *Educational Leadership, 41,* 19–27.

Wallerstein, J. (1983). Children of divorce: The psychological tasks of the child. *American Journal of Orthopsychiatry, 53,* 230–243.

Walsh, C. E. (1991). *Pedagogy and the struggle for voice, issues of language, power and schooling for Puerto Ricans.* New York: Bergin & Garvey.

Wehlage, G. (1987). A program model for at-risk high school students. *Educational Leadership, 44*(6), 7–73.

Wei, W. (1995). *The Asian American movement.* Philadelphia: Temple University Press.

Willis, P. (1977). *Learning to labor: How working class kids get working class jobs.* New York: Columbia University Press.

Wong, K. (1972). *An investigation of the reasons for changing political mood in San Francisco Chinatown.* Unpublished manuscript, Berkeley, CA: Department of Anthropology, University of California.

Wozniak, L. (1996). Farm laborer's advocates take on child-care crisis. *St. Petersburg Times,* May 9, 1E.

About the Authors

Kathryn M. Borman

Received her Ph.D. from the University of Minnesota in 1976. Before 1994, when she joined the University of South Florida's Department of Anthropology and the David C. Anchin Center where she serves as the Associate Director of the David C. Anchin Center, she was Professor of Sociology and Education and Associate Dean of Research and Development in the College of Education at the University of Cincinnati. A well-known scholar in the field of Sociology of Education and immediate past president of the Sociology of Education section of the American Sociological Association, Dr. Borman has an extensive background in research across diverse cultural groups. She has extensive experience in community-based research, serving for five years as president of the Urban Appalachian Council, a neighborhood-based agency with an agenda of applied research that influences practitioners and policy makers in regional issues related to Appalachians.

M. Yvette Baber

Is a doctoral candidate in Applied Anthropology/Education at the University of South Florida in Tampa. Her research interests are school-community linkages, the impact of race/ethnicity, class, and gender on these linkages, and community development. She has worked for over 20 years with urban children and their families on issues related to education and equality of opportunity, most recently in St. Petersburg, Florida.

Richard Alvarez

Collaborated with King and Barksdale-Ladd on the vignette about Cuban-Americans in Tampa. He lives and works in Tampa, Florida. He is currently researching ethnic cuisine.

Mary Alice Barksdale-Ladd

Is an Associate Professor of Reading in the Department of Childhood, Language Arts, and Reading at the University of South Florida in Tampa. She earned her doctorate in Curriculum and Instruction in 1988 at Virginia Tech. Her current research focuses on teacher improvement, case methodology, and on a study of children in fourth and fifth grades who read well below their grade level.

Marianne Bloch

Is a Professor in the Department of Curriculum and Instruction at the University of Wisconsin-Madison. She received her Ph.D. from the School of Education at Stanford University in 1977, and completed a Post-Doctoral fellowship at Harvard University in Comparative Human Development. She has done anthropological research in West Africa on gender and child care and education. She is also interested in cross-national policies concerning women, child care and education in Eastern and Central Europe. The research reflected in her chapter for this volume reflects her long-term interest in examining relationships between home, community, and school cultural contexts within the United States and elsewhere.

Li-Rong Lilly Cheng

Is a professor of Communicative Disorders at San Diego State University. She received her Ph.D. in a joint doctoral program of the Claremont Graduate University and San Diego University in 1983. Her current research and teaching interests include bilingualism, speech and language pathology among bilingual/multilingual populations, and cross-cultural communication.

Julia (Jay) Hammond Cradle

Is a doctoral candidate in the Department of Curriculum and Instruction at the University of Wisconsin-Madison, where she is completing her dissertation on issues related to cultural diversity, representation and identity.

Carolyn Dean

Recently completed her Ph.D. in the Department of Continuing and Vocational Education at the University of Wisconsin-Madison in 1996. She is currently working in Thailand.

Concha Delgado-Gaitan

Is an Associate Professor of Education at the University of California, Davis. She is the author of many books and articles about education and the role of culture in the education of Spanish-speaking children. Her research interests include human development, change and empowerment in culturally diverse communities, and conceptions of self.

Miryam Espinosa-Dulanto

Is a doctoral candidate in the Department of Curriculum and Instruction at the University of Wisconsin-Madison, where she is completing her dissertation on issues related to cultural diversity, representation and identity.

Michele Foster

Is a Professor in the Center for Educational Studies at The Claremont Graduate School. Author of *Growing Up African American in Catholic School* (1996) and *Black Teachers on Teaching* (1997), she has received prestigious funding, numerous awards, and fellowships. Her current research involves a staff development program in the San Francisco Unified School District. The study exposes teachers to cultural information and seeks to understand how teachers utilize this information in the classroom, as well as how the students might be affected.

Jim King

Is a Professor in Childhood/Language Arts/Reading at the University of South Florida. He received his Ph.D. in Reading, Language and Linguistics from West Virginia State University. His current research investigates classroom teachers' construction of error and accuracy in reading and writing pedagogy.

Margaret D. LeCompte

Received her M.A. and Ph.D. from the University of Chicago, Department of Education and the Social Order, in sociology and comparative and international education. She is currently Associate Professor of Education at the University of Colorado-Boulder, where she teaches courses in qualitative and ethnographic research methods and in the sociology of education. She has just concluded two long-term studies of dropout prevention and school reform projects in American Indian reservations and with urban American Indian children in a major metropolitan area in the Southwest. Her current research explores the impact of an intensive program in the visual, literary, musical, and theater arts on public middle school children.

Evelyn Phillips

Received her Ph.D. in Applied Anthropology in 1994 from the University of South Florida in Tampa. She is currently an Assistant Professor at Central Connecticut State University where she holds a joint appointment in the Departments of Anthropology and Social Work. She is an activist scholar, investigating issues of political economy and their intersection with oppression and discrimination. Her current research projects are in Florida, where she is researching the intersection of tourism and African American life in St. Petersburg, and in Connecticut, where she is analyzing HUD policies on reconfiguring neighborhoods in the Hartford area.

Pamela Quiroz

Is an Assistant Professor at the University of Massachusetts at Amherst in the Department of Sociology. She holds a Ph.D. in Sociology from the University of Chicago. She teaches courses on sociology of education, gender and education, and Latinas in the United States. Her current research considers how high school extracurriculum participation is structurally constrained by the social organization of the school and how it varies by race, ethnicity, and gender in multiethnic high schools. She is also studying the increasing use of technology to establish intimate relationships without the support of traditional institutions (e.g., family, church).

B. Robert Tabachnick

Is an Emeritus Professor in the Departments of Curriculum and Instruction and Educational Policy Studies at the University of Wisconsin-Madison. He is former Associate Dean of Teacher Education and International Education. He received his Ph.D. from Stanford University. He has published numerous volumes on topics related to teacher education in the United States and elsewhere.

Abbie Willetto

Is a doctoral student at the University of Colorado, Boulder in the Multicultural and Bilingual Foundations of Education program of the School of Education. A certified science teacher and former staff developer in public schools on the Navajo Reservation, she is now employed as an educational researcher. Her interests are in exploring the educational careers of academically successful Native American college students.

Author Index

Subject Index

A

Abolitionist Movement, 173
Accommodation, 15
Acculturation, 15
Achievement, family influences on, 22
Advocacy, 192
Advocates, 88, 114, 148–149
AFL-CIO, 69
Alienation , xiv, 150–151, 154, 157. *See also*
    Immigrants, isolation of
American Indian Movement (AIM), 139
Asian American Movement, 194
Assimilation, 25, 46–47, 56, 147–148, 195–196

B

Bilingual education, 1–2, 115, 199
Bilingual Education Act (1968), 115
Bilingual program, in Carpenteria, 81
Bilingualism, 12–13
Black Power Movement, 66, 69–70, 189–190
Bronfenbrenner's sociological-ecological
    model, 13–18, *fig* 14, 197
    exosystem, 17
    macrosystem, 14–17, 30
    mesosystem, 14
    microsystem, 17–18
Brown v. Board of Education of Topeka,
    Kansas, 70, 162, 172
Building bridges, 31. *See also* Schools and
    communities, collaboration between
Busing. *See* School, busing

C

Castro, Fidel, 54
Center for Research on the Education of
    Students Placed at Risk (CRESPAR), 198,
    202
Charter schools, 190–191

Chicago School Reform Act, 89
Civil Rights Movement, 66, 69–70, 189
Comite de Padres Latinos (COPLA), 84,
    86–87
Communities
    demographic shifts in, 29–49
    and schools. *See* Schools and communities
Community
    organizations, 208
    and school-based teaching and learning,
        205–209
Crime, 90. *See also* Drug use; Gang activity
Cultural capital, 20
Cultural dissonance, xiv, 28, 189
Cultural Revolution (China), 125
Cultural ties
    lateral, 185, 189–195
    local, 185, 188–194
Curricular tracking, 8–9

D

Dawes Act (1887), 138
Demographic patterns, 1–2, 36–44
Desegregation, 162–163, 168, 173–175,
    180–181, 190
Development, children's, ecology of, 78. *See
    also*, Bronfenbrenner's sociological-
    ecological model
Discontinuities,
    between families and schools, 20
    cultural, 20
    structural, 20–21
Discrimination, 9, 56. *See also*
    Disenfranchisement; Alienation
Disenfranchisement, 51, 65–66, 187
Dropout. *See* School leaving
Drug use (including alcohol), 98, 155–157